THE ART OF DYING

ABOUT THE AUTHOR

Yvonne Williams is a former Child Life Specialist and a retired educator and clinical practitioner (Certified Grief Counselor, Registered Play Therapist Supervisor, and Certified Marriage & Family Therapist). She has 31 years' experience divided among pediatric and psychiatric settings, private counseling practice, and clinical teaching and supervision.

Ms. Williams has contributed to professional journals and programs throughout the U.S. and Canada. In 1996, she received the Award of Merit for Innovative Service to the Profession of Play Therapy given by the Indiana Association for Play Therapy. This annual award has been renamed the Yvonne Williams Award of Merit.

Ms. Williams is a member of the Association for Death Education and Counseling. She was an adjunct member of the clinical faculty, Indiana University, and was a clinical supervisor for the Counseling Center, Christian Theological Seminary, Indianapolis. Since 1988, she has been a contributing editor for *Bereavement* magazine. Ms. Williams became a hospice volunteer after retirement from her clinical career in 1996.

THE ART OF DYING
A Jungian View of Patients' Drawings

By

YVONNE BARNTHOUSE WILLIAMS, M.S.

Contributing Editor, Bereavement Magazine

Former
Certified Play Therapist Supervisor
Certified Grief Counselor, and Clinical Member
American Association for Marriage & Family Therapy,
Wellspring Counseling & Consulting Resources
and
Clinical Supervisor
Christian Theological Seminary Counseling Center,
Indianapolis, Indiana

CHARLES C THOMAS • PUBLISHER, LTD.
Springfield • Illinois • U.S.A.

Published and Distributed Throughout the World by

CHARLES C THOMAS • PUBLISHER, LTD.
2600 South First Street
Springfield, Illinois 62794-9265

© *1999 by* CHARLES C THOMAS • PUBLISHER, LTD.
ISBN 0-398-06932-8

Library of Congress Catalog Card Number: 98-44796

With THOMAS BOOKS *careful attention is given to all details of manufacturing
and design. It is the Publisher's desire to present books that are satisfactory as to their
physical qualities and artistic possibilities and appropriate for their particular use.*
THOMAS BOOKS *will be true to those laws of quality that assure a good name
and good will.*

Printed in the United States of America
CR-R-3

Library of Congress Cataloging in Publication Data
Williams, Yvonne Barnthouse.
    The art of dying : a jungian view of patients' drawings / by
Yvonne Barnthouse Williams.
        p.   cm.
    Includes bibliographical references and index.
    ISBN 0-398-06932-8 (cloth)
    1. Terminally ill--Psychological aspects. 2. Drawing--Psychological
aspects. 3. Children's drawings--Psychological aspects. 4. Death-
-Psychological aspects. 5. Jungian psychology. 6. Cystic fibrosis-
-Psychological aspects. I. Title.
R726.8.W545 1999
155.9'37--dc21   98-44796
                                                                               CIP

In memory of
William Monroe Barnthouse
(1896-1981)

INTRODUCTION

This book is about living and dying. Particularly, it is about dealing with the life-threatening, genetic illness of cystic fibrosis (CF). *The Art of Dying* examines patients' drawings that express reality beyond words, conscious thought, and present time. My attitudes about life and death were shaped by drawings that taught me how to relate to dying patients. I offer this book to all therapists and caregivers to patients with life-threatening conditions in hope that it will help them to give patient care that honors spirit and soul.

In patients' drawings we find examples of the apparent need to reconcile life and death and the transcendent experience this tension generates. We examine how drawings might reflect a near-death experience and how one's reproduction of images related to that brief loss of life might give one courage in critical times. We also examine in drawings the reflections of both somatic and psychic content. (I use the term psyche to mean all that is encompassed in mind and soul, and the term soma to indicate all that is involved with the physical, organic body.) I use amplification, as C. G. Jung applied it to dreams, to enlarge upon psychic and somatic processes noted. (Amplification is discussed in Chapter 1.) Finally, I examine what is meant by Spirit (animus) and Soul (anima) energies, and relate these to one's orientation to dying and death. My hypothesis concerning the closure of life contains a spiritual dimension involving the archetypes of spirit and soul. I trust the material presented here will show that the drawings of seriously ill patients can benefit these patients therapeutically and can reveal diagnostic or prognostic clues.

In critical or life-threatening situations, the tension between life and death compels the bonded psyche and soma to follow a soul-searching journey. Commonly, individuals can relate only to the life side of this journey at first, for the natural desire to recognize and honor life, order, or beneficence seems invariably to negate death, disorder, or pain. In time, especially when one's condition is terminal, the forces of life and death are reconciled by the aid of an archetype, which the individual can experience in the appearance of a symbol. This image awakens a new attitude that transcends the original, limited view of life and death. Then the two paths (life and death) are united and transformed. Jung (1972) called this process the transcendent function.

For the sake of readers who are not familiar with the psychological teachings of C. G. Jung, I have tried to provide easy-to-grasp explanations for the Jungian concepts I have applied. Although these explanations are unnecessary for my Jungian colleagues, it is appropriate to include them for others for whom this book is also intended. The word "Self" is capitalized when it refers to the holistic, regulating Self that consists of both conscious and unconscious psyche. When it refers to the conscious ego self, the word is not capitalized.

Throughout this book, the term "drawing" designates either a drawing or painting. Most of the art works in my study were rendered on white paper with either plain graphite or colored drawing pencils; a few were painted in tempera, and fewer were done with crayons. (A standard set of colors was available in each medium.) Patients engaged in the art activity "just for fun" or as a relaxation technique, with no concern for artistic skill or lack of it.

It is customary to change the subjects' names in the publication of case studies. Many children put their first name on their drawings; some include their surname. I regard this as an integral part of their pictorial expression. For this reason, I use the child's authentic first name (with permission from their family, or with direct permission from patients of legal age). I have blacked out surnames here for obvious reasons.

Owing to my training and experience as a therapist, I sometimes refer to a "therapist's" mode of caring for a patient. Readers who are not therapists, but who are involved in patient care, may simply read the word "therapist" as "caregiver."

This book is written partly from my perspective as a private practitioner (certified marriage and family therapist, registered play therapist-supervisor, and certified grief counselor) in adolescent and child therapy (from 1985 to 1996). It also comes from the perspective of the clinical position I held in 1976 to 1985, when I worked with a population of CF patients. I was a Child Life Specialist, in charge of the Adolescent and Child Life Development services at Methodist

Hospital of Indiana and I served on the multidisciplinary, CF treatment team. I share with the reader what the CF patients taught me through their drawings. What these patients reveal in their drawings, I trust, will engage the analysis of mental health clinicians, art therapists, and Jungian analysts and therapists. Further, I expect that medical personnel, hospital chaplains, seminary faculty, and their students will find that they have some common interest in the thesis of this book; it offers more than clinical case studies or theories. *The Art of Dying* takes an archetypal view of the process of dying and finds that this process is the ultimate stage of inner growth and learning.

By the 1960s, I had become intensely interested in patients' drawings. Working as a play therapist in the pediatric unit of a university teaching hospital, I often gazed spellbound into the drawings of seriously ill, hospitalized children. At those times, I felt I was standing on some mysterious threshold, witnessing something of great meaning, but knowing no way to discover what it was. I wondered whether these drawings might be a reflection of the patients' physical condition and their emotional response to it.

My curiosity and enthusiasm in this area led me to examine all the books I could find on "projective techniques" – the standardized, diagnostic use of drawings in assessing mental and emotional states. I studied also several books and articles on art therapy. Reading such material helped me; I could begin to see what I thought were expressions in patients' drawings of psychological conditions – anxiety, depression, anger, a feeling of powerlessness – to name the more common ones. But was there more to learn?

Might the things that I saw possibly pertain to patients' preconscious knowledge of a physical condition and prognosis? I was convinced that these pictures expressed more than what the patient felt, and more than what the patient's ego knew about the body's condition. However, I sadly lacked the expertise and courage that were required to pursue such a conviction. Not until a 1974 pediatric conference, where I heard Elisabeth Kubler-Ross lecture about the symbolic language of terminally-ill children, was my faith emboldened concerning the validity of pictorial expressions of psychological and physical states.

Kubler-Ross elaborated on the pioneering work of Susan Bach (died 1995), a Jungian analyst in London who dealt with understanding pictorial expressions of organic and psychological aspects of one's condition. She claimed that this analyst probably understood better than anyone the symbolic language of drawings. A strange feeling came over me that I cannot completely describe. I believed strongly that I would study with this London analyst, but I could not imagine how or when this would ever be possible and did not consciously strive to make it happen.

The unconscious will is a powerful force; it can move us where we need to be seemingly with no conscious effort. It appears that our unconscious functioning influences even the attitudes of others such that they help us to realize deep yearnings. Through remarkable consequences of this kind, I had my first meeting with Mrs. Bach in London in the summer of 1976. Here at last, I found the missing piece that I had been seeking — the somatic dimension. The wondrous alliance of psyche and soma was revealed through Bach's empirical findings she shared with me, and through the pictures by my own patients she used to teach me how to analyze.

I returned to London to study with Bach in 1978, and again in 1981. I came to understand what that marvelous, meaningful essence was that I saw in patients' drawings; it was a reflection of their soul.

ACKNOWLEDGMENTS

I wish to thank the C.E. Warren Fund and the Department of Medical Research, Methodist Hospital of Indiana, and The Omega Foundation, London, England. Without the generous support from these funds and the kind encouragement from the administrators representing them, this book would not be.

I am grateful to Dr. Gabriel Rosenberg, the Cystic Fibrosis Treatment Team, the Pediatric Nursing staff, Chaplaincy, and the Adolescent and Child Life Development staff, Methodist Hospital of Indiana. From 1976 to 1985, these people gave their interest, support, and assistance to the collection of drawings from the patients referred to in this book.

I am deeply indebted to Great Ormond Street Hospital For Sick Children, London, England—specifically, May Bywater, Social Worker; Dr. Robert Dinwiddie and his Pulmonary Medical Staff at G. O. S.; and the staff at G. O. S. Hospital's former country branch, Tadworth, Surrey, for their remarkable help and hospitality during my brief affiliation with them. I am, of course, grateful to the late Susan R. Bach, London, for teaching me how to evaluate patients' drawings and for supervising my work in England.

I am indebted to the parents and patients in the U.S. and England who agreed to participate in my CF study.

I give thanks to Dean Frantz and Sister Olga Wittakind, Jungian analysts, as well as to Susan Bettis and Sandy Hurt for reading and critiquing portions of the manuscript. I am grateful to Sheldon Shalley and Susan Hicks for helpful observations in our evaluations of the drawings.

I thank Fritz Dolak, Digital Services and Copyright Librarian, Bracken Library, and Stacey Nance, Health Science Library Assistant, Ball State University for their research assistance; Donna Minnick, Clarion Health (formerly Methodist Hospital of Indiana) for internet assistance in relocating a "lost parent" of a patient in this book; Gregg

Furth for introducing me to the Omega Foundation; and Harold Caldwell for software advice and technical help in preparing the manuscript.

Finally, a very special thanks to my husband, Nyal Williams, for editing the manuscript when he would much rather have been flying gliders and building his airplane.

CONTENTS

LIST OF FIGURES

THE ART OF DYING

Part 1

THE SYMBOLIC LANGUAGE OF DRAWINGS

We live in a world that gorges on rationalism, science, and technology. But these cannot satisfy our hunger for experiences that nourish the soul nor can they answer haunting questions about the mystery and meaning of life and death. Materialism and sophistication separate us from spirituality and instincts; we are hooked by a collective devaluation of the inner life. C.G. Jung believed that both personal and global peace depend on our balancing inner experiences with the outer world. He recognized that dreams and art work offer a bridge between inner and outer realities.

Chapters 1-9 examine a way of crossing that bridge by giving honor to images spawned in the depths of the unconscious. The first three chapters describe some Jungian concepts and the pioneering work of Susan Bach, who detected expressions of both psyche and soma in drawings made by seriously-ill patients. They contain highlights of a 9-year study of a cystic fibrosis (CF) population (ages 5-30). Prognostic revelations in these patients' drawings agree with Bach's study (lasting more than three decades) of drawings made by cancer patients.

These three chapters also contain practical recommendations for relating to patients and to the images their drawings present. Chapters 4-9 describe the therapeutic quality of a relationship that helps move a patient to prepare for and reconcile with death.

Chapter 1

ENCOUNTERING IMAGES

W hat can we learn from drawings made by patients who have a life-threatening illness? Do their drawings contain a symbolic language? Can we "read" the images in their pictures as a map of psyche and soma? What psychodynamic impact do these images have on the patient?

To answer these questions, we need first to accept that there is no dictionary for translating symbolic expressions. We can never fully grasp all that an image has to convey, even though we use every available resource to illuminate their messages concerning the human experience. Owing to the metaphorical potential of an image, and the fact that the image is merely a representation of a process still in progress, our access to an image's meaning is limited.

I am repeatedly impressed by the power of images to bring spiritual healing to critically-ill people. As we track images through a series of drawings, we often find that they symbolize a patient's encounters with soul and spirit as reflections of common, human experiences. (I perceive soul and spirit to be the eternal, transcendent aspects of the psyche.) One's journey of life meets its last destination when images and fantasies join the individual to the transcendent psyche. By this process, ego-consciousness (self) is abandoned in favor of a deeper level of being, where there is a sense of oneness or harmony with God.

I believe we are born knowing what we need to do to live and how to die; that knowledge resides in the primordial Self.[1] Various factors may hinder our instinctual expression of life, but when death beckons, an urgency to redeem or redefine the Self (as contrasted with mere ego) envelops the psyche. Invariably, it causes a change in our conscious attitude. Apparently, this is when we come face to face with our God.

Those who are close to an individual's dying at this stage are infectiously drawn to the metaphysical-spiritual milieu generated by the dying person's struggle to connect with what really matters. A centering occurs that transcends all fears and earthly commitments. This phenomenon may answer the question often raised by those outside the occupations that minister to seriously ill persons: "How can one work with such patients without becoming depressed?"

As physical death draws near, the dying individual experiences an inner transformation. Dying begets a new attitude. This is particularly so when physical and emotional needs are acknowledged by someone else. I believe this transformation and new attitude are experienced vicariously by those close to the dying person.

The rebirth that death evokes is not confined to one's own physical death; rebirth may occur when old attitudes or biases die, when a valued material possession is lost, when one loses an important status, position, or responsibility, when there is a mid-life crisis, or when a loved one dies. Such losses prompt an adjustment to the change; we can experience a rebirth, provided we adapt to our losses.

The first step in adaptation is to acknowledge the grief and all the feelings it stirs. This step involves a deep penetration to our inner reality. Going deep within awakens a new energy that entices one to embrace life anew. It ultimately leads to emergence from that "dark night of the soul" into a new status that is rebirth.

Those who engage in creative activities (e.g., gardening, painting, journaling, potting, weaving, making music, or meditation) usually make the transition faster, I believe, than those who do not. Creative activities provide a vehicle to carry the psyche's image-making that is vital to growth and change; it is therefore not surprising that such activities encourage a rebirth experience.

Creative activities also channel this renewal of energy so that it is not projected onto someone else, or seized by the ego to support an inflated attitude. By being creatively engaged we remain grounded to the Self. Painting, cultivating a garden bed, reading or writing a poem, or strumming a guitar may nurture a certain attitude that the self/Self needs to adopt. This nurture may be experienced as liberating and healing. The awakening of the Self that our images inspire near death is a profoundly metaphysical, spiritual experience.

Some examples will show that archetypal content can be found in drawings; they will illustrate the healing role that image-borne archetypes can play. These examples come from patients who experienced a life-threatening illness. They all had cystic fibrosis (CF). They were the focus of a 9-year study I conducted to discover whether my findings would replicate, or in any way agree with, those of Susan Bach's studies. When I began my investigation in 1976, Bach had already spent over two decades examining drawings by cancer patients and defining a symbolic language of cancer.

My study consisted of 47 subjects with CF. It included relatively healthy and seriously ill inpatients and outpatients, ranging from ages 5 to 30. During the 9-year course of the study, 14 of the patients died. An 8-week affiliation with London's Great Ormond Street Hospital For Sick Children gave me the opportunity to collect drawings from their CF patients as a sampling for cross-cultural comparison. The London study consisted of 21 patients who produced 30 drawings, whereas the U.S. group produced 292 drawings. Of the 322 drawings collectively obtained from both studies (initially consisting of a total of 68 patients, reduced by death to 54) 147 drawings were produced shortly before, during, or just after an acute episode in their illness.

These drawings were evaluated *before* reviewing the patients' current medical records. (This practice prevents the investigator from concentrating on what is already known and possibly overlooking what is yet unknown or that has not yet been clinically detected.) My study comprised a small sample compared to populations of similar size, and to studies of the same or similar duration, in the field of art therapy. However, the studies in art therapy are very often done with psychiatric patients or with patients who are not severely weakened or restricted by medical apparatus.

Three factors limited my ability to collect drawings. (1) My time with the patients was not primarily to have them draw pictures; I also concentrated on many other therapeutic activities. (2) I found that the acute symptoms of hospitalized patients (e.g., paroxysmal coughing), along with treatment procedures and restrictions such as IV arm boards, frequently interfered with either their ability or desire to draw. (3) In the outpatient clinic, I had to "sandwich" drawing time in the brief waiting periods before and after physical examinations or clinical tests.

I obtained most of the drawings by inviting the patients to draw whatever they wished; I label these "invited." Gregg Furth, in *The Secret World of Drawings* (1988), uses the term, "impromptu" (p. xix).

Some drawings were unsolicited ones that the patients drew just because they wanted to draw, and these were voluntarily presented to me. The latter drawings I label "spontaneous." Why differentiate between invited and spontaneous drawings? I believe that the content expressed in spontaneous drawing is closer to consciousness and will be integrated sooner than the content expressed in invited drawings.

Examination of drawings from the U.S. study shows that 12 patients produced 17 drawings in which particular features corresponded with specific physiological developments; these were problems such as headaches, collapsed lung, gastric ulcer exacerbation, and significant fluid accumulation either as peripheral edema, sinusitis, or pulmonary congestion.

In some instances the drawings preceded by 2 to 17 days the medical confirmation of the physiological change. Eight of the 14 patients who died made 17 drawings that suggested the approach of death. Viewed retrospectively, 12 of the drawings contained elements that indicated how much time the patient had to live, just as has been found in similar studies by Bach (1990) and Kiepenheuer (1980). As Susan Bach (1969) has taught us, "drawings contain strong indications that the patients know deep within themselves not only whether they will recover, but also when their life will end" (p. 64).

Twenty-three patients produced 34 drawings containing features that suggest specific psychological components we later confirmed. Twelve patients accurately reflected in 35 drawings an increase or decrease of a healthy condition. These data support the body of research that demonstrates that humans have an unconscious awareness about the condition and prognosis of the psyche and of the body and its life span.

My findings support those of Bach and Kiepenheuer with respect to finding in patients' drawings clues that forecast the ending of life. These clues include the characteristic use of colors, motifs, and especially the number of repetitions of objects or figures that appear. This does not mean, of course, that the unconscious has revealed the amount of time left to live every time someone draws a quantity of flowers or birds. However, a number that is repeated, especially in more than one way, might refer to a date, age, or an amount of something that is particularly significant at the time of the drawing.

C. G. Jung (1970) gives an example of the significance of numbers in his discussion of a dream. He tells of a man who dreamed of a large number on a ticket. The man examined the numbers individually and in various groupings and shared with Jung his associations with different numbers or number combinations. Then, by the manipulation of birth dates and ages for himself, members of his family, and his mistress, a sum was found to match the number on the ticket in his dream. This is an example of what Jung referred to as searching for the unconscious roots of number symbolism. This man's play with numbers represents a ritual that enables individuals to be receptive to what their unconscious strives to make conscious. It should be noted that the numbers do not make the meaning; the unconscious makes meaning from the numbers.

Numbers in dreams or drawings do not always have an unconscious, symbolical connection to strictly personal issues and relationships. Numbers can be considered from a collective symbology stemming from ancient beliefs, rituals, or religion. Jung maintained that we are related to all past, present, and future generations through a collective unconscious or objective psyche that contains an inherited imprint of human history and feelings.

Thus, when no personal associations can be found between the numbers and the dreamer or artist, the symbolic meaning of these numbers in myths, anthropology, religion, and other similar sources can amplify or enlarge the meaning of the dream or drawing. We then see that our personal life is resounding with some event or experience in human history.

Our rational, Western culture finds it difficult to accept that humans sense unconsciously the precise rhythm or time required for significant events to unfold in their lives. Yet it is confirmed that all root vegetables, blooming bulbs, algae, earthworms, and other forms of life respond to the relative position of the moon and synchronize their life's energy with the moon's rhythm in order to thrive. Further, birds know when the time is right to fly north or south. Is it not possible that the human organism might respond like our planet's flora or fauna?

I do not regard numbers that coincide with the time remaining in one's life to be the most important element in drawings by seriously ill people. Numbers derived by counting the repetition of objects cannot be linked accurately with a precise unit of time involved until after the fact. One might make an educated guess by basing it upon all the knowledge gained from the drawing and the case history. However, the only way to verify this guess is to compare it with the actual amount of time that occurs between the drawing of the picture and the individual's death. This does not imply that drawing analysis as a prognostic tool is useless; it does mean, though, that its use is limited.

Because of this limitation, some people dismiss this form of drawing analysis as incapable of reliably showing anything of significance. Nonetheless, I believe it is significant to find that a completion of life can be reflected and detected in drawings, whether or not there is any reference to how much lifetime remains. Even if recurring numbers are interpreted incorrectly in relation to one's life span, it remains that the signs suggesting that *life is ending* have proved to be reliable; it is to these signs that I attach the most importance.

One drawing that did appear to forecast the patient's death came from a woman who made the drawing around the time of her 30th birthday (Fig. 1). She drew a scene that she described as "a park with a brick walk . . . and a hill to the left that goes up into some woods over here [pointing to the far right side of the paper]." She did not fill in the far right side of the paper; she left a margin approximately two and one-half mm wide all the way down.

Psychologically considered, the woods might represent unconscious issues that she is not yet ready to confront – she does not show her path actually entering the woods. Because the woods appears on the far right of her paper, it might also be associated with her future, about which she cannot yet be conscious. We might also consider whether her life will end before she can become conscious of the future.

Her park contains a playground with a swing set, a seesaw, and a carrousel. There are 4 blue birds in flight in the upper right sky plus 1 flying on the far left side, totaling 5; a butterfly also flies just over 1 of 7 flowers blooming along the brick path. Her picture contains a pale blue sky with 1 colorless cloud and pale green grass having a section on the lower left side shaded over with blue; she explained that this shading is the shadow from the hill. She placed her initials, in blue, near the lower right edge of the paper.

Birds and butterflies are sometimes viewed as symbols for the soul; in Scandinavian lore, the bird may also symbolize the spirit freed from the body. Birds are common symbols for transcendence, and butterflies are often associated with death, resurrection or rebirth, and immortality (Cooper, 1978).

The red brick walk begins in the upper right quadrant and winds across the page to the lower left quadrant. Bach (1990) has found that such movement appears in drawings of patients who have, or will have, a "downhill trend" in health (p. 39). The red brick walk contains 30 red *X*s. These were clearly drawn. The patient began at the bottom of the walk, at the far left edge of the paper, and worked upward towards the right side of the paper. This left to right movement can suggest a progression from the past to the future.

On a colorless background, the patient made 31 *X*s. The final *X*, at the top right edge of the walk, was faintly drawn and partially shaded over with the same shade of red. Burns and Kaufman (1972) observed in their research with kinetic family drawings that *X*s are associated with "force . . . and counterforce . . . defining areas of conflict," and particularly with attempts to control conflict or impulse (p. 108). Possibly the *X*s refer to the tension between living and dying, but other life stresses might be reflected here.

What is missing from this drawing is people. The pale blue sky shows that it is daytime, and grass and flowers in full bloom suggest pleasant weather. We might expect to see children playing here. (She made this drawing in early April.) This observation caused me to question whether the absence of human life might be a foreboding that the woman's own life is leaving her. Considering the *X*s of her path, might it be that she holds somewhere a sense that her life's path has just 30 periods of time – with an additional faint period – before it ends?

I deliberated whether her 7 flowers might reflect the number of time segments remaining for her life to flower before fading and withering away; counting in months, this would take her 7 months beyond her birthday and into her 31st year. The barely discernible 31st *X* suggests another possibility; her life might end just before or shortly after her 31st birthday, and furthermore, that this period might find her in a coma (suggested by the *X* that was barely there). I regarded this to be a strong possibility, having known several CF patients who had become comatose preceding death.

Seven months after making this drawing, the woman died, on the 7th day of the month, at the age of 30 years and 7 months. (Recall that there were 7 flowers blooming.) Looking back upon her picture, I could understand how the faint, 31st *X* on her path and her 7 flowers might well represent those 7 critical months beyond her 30th birthday. I noted, also that for the last several days of her life, the woman was comatose.

There were other number combinations to consider, namely 3 orange flowers and 4 yellow ones, 4 sections of the carrousel, the grouping of 4 birds, 1 additional bird isolated in the upper left corner, and 1 cloud.

Bach (1990) says that the use of orange represents a decline of energy or a time of "suspense . . . between life and death" (p. 48) when it appears in drawings made by critically ill patients. I have already noted that the woman colored 3 of her blossoms orange. In retrospect, I could see that this number (and the repeated use of the color orange) corresponded to the 3 seasons this woman had remaining to live.

I could not find any similar correlations for the number four or four plus one. Cooper (1978) relates that four can symbolize completion, totality, and wholeness; that five can also symbolize the whole, composed of four cardinal points plus the center, which is thought to be the meeting point of heaven and earth; and the number one may represent isolation as well as unity. This symbolism, which reverberates in the collective unconscious, amplifies her drawing. It was in her isolated, comatose state that the woman experienced the completion of life and the wholeness granted by death.

Before moving to other examples that reveal experiences of living and dying with CF, I wish to clarify further some Jungian concepts about the unconscious process and how it manifests itself symbolically. I do this primarily for readers who are not of Jungian persuasion and for whom the concepts still may be foreign or confusing.

According to C. G. Jung, archetypes are universal influences upon our thoughts, feelings, and responses to life's experiences. Jung hypothesized that archetypes reside in the inherited part of our psyche where they are accessible to all humankind despite age or culture. Research on dream content and world mythologies provides persuasive evidence that archetypes do exist and create underlying, universal patterns of human behavior. Even people with no knowledge of another culture's myths or religious practices might duplicate these or dream of them.

We are preconditioned to call upon these inherent patterns for thinking, feeling, and acting. Jung observed that such behavior results whenever we respond emotionally to some image or mythic stimulus that represents a particular archetype. The image of a Madonna may call forth the experience of motherhood, or a gravestone may evoke associations with death. Should this process of association prompt striking behavioral responses, it is likely that either a distressing or challenging period of our life calls for and critically needs a new or broadened attitude.

Jung maintains that the particular archetype that needs to be activated will repeatedly project itself to the conscious mind as a symbol that will eventually be felt as an illumination or revelation. Through this operation, an archetype can be manifested, albeit indirectly.

Although archetypes in themselves are not representable, according to Jung, there are many images that convey the energy, power, or essence of a particular archetype. For example, the archetype of rebirth or regeneration may appear in a dream as a stream of water, a baptism, crossing a river, an egg, sprouting bulbs, a snake (which sheds its skin), or other images.

Jung observed that archetypal images spontaneously emerge in creative activity such as drawing or painting; this makes such activity particularly effective for promoting the transcendent function mentioned in the Introduction. In other words, an archetype expressed in a drawing will offer a bridge for reconciliation of the ego with personal reality if this union has been at least partially denied or resisted. (We will examine this later.)

To understand the psychological principles on which this work is grounded, it is important that we not confuse the archetype, *per se*, with symbols that represent it. Jacobi (1959) explained that:

> When the archetype manifests itself in "the here and now" of space and time it can be perceived in some form by the conscious mind. Then we speak of a symbol . . . . But an archetype is not necessarily identical with a symbol . . . . As . . . an "invisible center of energy," [the archetype] is always a potential symbol, and whenever . . . a suitable condition of consciousness is present, its "dynamic nucleus" is ready to actualize itself and manifest itself as a symbol. (p. 74)

This process can be revealed through various forms of art, through the words of prophets, and through dreams and drawings of everyday people. All these presentations have potential to bind the knowledge and experiences of past generations to those of future ones.

Jung spent most of his career developing and refining the concept of the archetype and the collective unconscious. Sigmund Freud acknowledged and wrote about "archaic remnants," which he believed to be mythological motifs spontaneously enacted in individuals' lives. But Jung was the one who developed the concept of the archetype and the collective unconscious (objective psyche) as its container.

As early as 1912, Jung began to expand his views about psychology and to go beyond the frontier of psychoanalytic theory by publishing his *Psychology of the Unconscious* (later revised and published as *Symbols of Transformation*, CW Vol. 5). In 1920, Jung's publication of *Psychological Types* (republished in 1971 by Princeton University Press) introduced his ideas about the collective unconscious that contributed to his split with Freud.

One's first encounter with C. G. Jung's teachings might cause confusion about what is *inherited* concerning archetypes and their symbols. Jung stresses that what we inherit is the archetypal forms and not the content (symbolic material) that expresses these forms. Although we all inherit the same forms, our individual, personal experiences will determine the content we use to fill those forms.

Jung (1976a) explains that what we inherit is a human nature that prompts us to conceive of thought patterns that are similar to "identical psychic structures common to all men" (p. 158, par. 224). While Jung did not mean that there was a universal or undisputed symbol for each archetype, it seems that symbols representing a particular archetype often do share characteristics.

We must recognize how this inherited disposition relates to our experiences and prompts our imaging of archetypal symbols. This inheritance that bonds all humans is why it is possible, as we shall see in Chapter 11, for a dying 5-year-old to represent the archetype of death-rebirth. His drawing contains a human figure standing on the edge of a shore, with beckoning arms reaching up and outward; this image mirrors the souls who beckon the ferryman Charon to take them across the River Styx to the other shore beyond. Instead of a ferry, the child imagines a "flying car."

Similarly, in Chapter 5 we find an older adolescent presenting manifestations of the objective psyche in the struggle to assert his masculinity. He represents the archetype of the Self by drawing a water serpent guarding an underwater treasure and symbolizing some threatening power that must be confronted before the "treasure," i.e., the regulating Self, can be redeemed. In his Tavistock lecture series, Jung (1968) refers to the ancient motif of a serpent in a cave of water guarding a treasure. This mythical motif goes back to pre-Christian cults. Understanding the collective unconscious helps us comprehend the significance of parallels between certain images in a patient's drawing and those of ancient civilizations whose beliefs and practices may be unknown to the patient.

Having viewed the archetype as the tendency to form typical images, we might notice that a representative image varies considerably from one individual to another. Two different individuals may need to become conscious of the Devouring Mother archetype that has too much influence in their lives; they might dream of being tangled in a spider's web. The entrapping web is the common image in both dreams; each dreamer's web, and the specific way that it involves the dreamers, will differ in many details. Thus, common images or structures may serve two or more people as representative of a particular archetype, but the individual way that these images are visualized by each person will vary.

Let us return now to the question of what it is exactly, according to Jung, that we inherit with respect to archetypes and their images. If it were images that we inherited, then the images in everyone's dreams, imaginations, fantasies, etc., would be identical in every detail. (The dreamers in the example above, would have identical dreams of entrapment, whether conveyed by a spider's web, a prison cell, or whatever.) That does not happen, but we do find the same archetypal structures arising and maintaining their unique features or content. Jung points out that an archetype cannot reach consciousness but that it has effects that make enactment of it possible.

The relationship between an archetype, archetypal image, and its variation of the image from subject to subject reminds me of a poster I saw in a veterinarian's clinic. The poster depicts various breeds of dogs; each breed bears distinctive characteristics in body structure, size, and fur, yet they are all part of the same species – *canis familiaris*. The different breeds, from airedale to whippet, might represent individual archetypal images. Although you and I make use of the same archetype (dog), yours might be a Jack Russell terrier and mine a greyhound. The archetype itself (the dog in our metaphor) is the "invisible center of energy" that is conveyed by the image.

What we inherit is a *disposition to express archetypes by organizing them into structures (images)* that are available to us through the collective unconscious. The collective unconscious contains humanity's experiences since the beginning of time; Jung calls it our objective psyche. (See Appendix B.)

AMPLIFICATION

Dreams and drawings are not rational constructs. They mix metaphors; these metaphors must be accepted and used "as is" in order to understand their contents. Mary Ann Mattoon (1978) says, "a dream cannot be interpreted from its text alone, . . . its symbolism must be translated like an unknown language . . ." (pp. 53-54). This advice applies to drawings – especially those made at critical periods of one's life. A drawing cannot be interpreted by its content alone; it must be considered in terms of what the content might symbolize. This approach to understanding the meaning of dreams or drawings is part of what Jung called amplification.

For Jung, amplification included not only looking at the possible archetypal motifs, but also examining the dreamer's own associations to the dream material and the dreamer's life experiences at the time of the dream. Broadly defined, Jung's concept of amplification involves three procedures: (1) consideration of what the dreamer associates with an image, (2) looking for relationships between the image and the dreamer's actual environment, and (3) identifying ways that the image reflects mythology, folklore, anthropology, archeology, and religions.

The first two procedures involve personal amplification; the last one incorporates archetypal amplification, which may bring enlightenment not only to the individual, but to a society or all of humankind. Finally, we may also look for any commonality between personal and archetypal amplifications.

All that has been said of dream amplification can be applied to drawings – especially those made at a significant time in one's life. Consequently, in working with patients' drawings, we must not fail to look at personal history and what is happening in the patients' lives physically, intellectually, emotionally, and spiritually. (I would not begin there, however, for fear that such information might distract me from prognostic clues that had no known connection to the patient's personal life.)

It is at the end of the analysis that we must ask whether the drawings reflect accurately both the personal reality and that of the situation at the time of the drawing. (For instance, if a drawing made in July contains a Christmas tree, which does not reflect the current situation, we should ponder why the person needs Christmas now.) We look at each symbol in a drawing as a possible representation of the individual's personal life and present condition, and also as a representation of archetypal symbols from other cultures and civilizations.

Let us examine some ideas that provide a foundation for archetypal amplification. Archetypes influence unconscious psychic processes formally, causing them to organize into patterns of behavior. Certain events and experiences, for instance, may call forth heroic behavior. A movie, play, myth, or fairy tale may serve to awaken some latent energy that needs to be activated to counterbalance some attitude or trait. This is archetypal energy.

Bruno Bettleheim (1977) and Marie-Louise von Franz (1970a, 1972, 1974, 1976, 1997) have written about the use of fairy tales in triggering our consciousness to respond to whatever archetype has been evoked deep within the psyche. The archetype generates the particular energy needed to adapt to a changing or threatening situation.

Life is composed of a series of changes, which Jung (1976a) says are not infinitely variable but are limited in number and can be classified into "more or less typical patterns that repeat themselves [with variations] over and over again" (p. 294). These changes invariably reproduce their corresponding archetypes, which seek to pull into consciousness those ideas that will carry the spirit of the archetype and help bring to consciousness a new reality. Those ideas are conveyed by symbols, images, and motifs.

This activity describes the work of the transcendent function, referred to earlier, and it is a basic component of the Self-regulating process of the psyche. The transcendent function is the human feat of expanding conscious understanding to reach a broader, more accurate perspective of life; it is stimulated by an insatiable hunger and striving for wholeness.

Unfortunately, many parents today do not understand the value of fairy tales in helping children to relate to the archetypal energies they need at critical periods of change in their development. Parents censor these wonderful old tales on the grounds of their being too gory or scary. Yet, many allow their children to engage in thematically brutal video games, to watch all kinds of violence on television, often disguised as animated cartoons, and to purchase toys that invite shockingly violent and gory fantasy play. Our contemporary, rational society has great difficulty appreciating the metaphor in folk and fairy tales, and in relating personal psychology to the tale's characters and to situations presented.

This lack of appreciation and understanding of the value of folk and fairy tales was dramatically displayed in 1987. Some citizens of Brixton, a section of south London, were successful in getting Grimm's fairy tale, "Snow White," banned from the school's library. Families of African descent claimed that the story supported the idea that whites are superior to blacks (or "coloured British"). In reality, "Snow White" is a tale of a classic, problematic mother-daughter relationship in which the daughter experiences the vampiric, devouring aspect of the mother. The story teaches us what it is like when a parent is overcome with narcissism and cannot bear for the child to have her own thoughts when she becomes old enough to do so or to distinguish herself as an individual. But as the story points out, children are also narcissistic by nature, and must learn to transcend this destructive form of self-absorption. Recall that Snow White almost loses her life twice by giving in to the queen's luring offers to make her more beautiful. The tale goes on to relate what we need for independence and maturity, which is to confront life's difficulties, take on appropriate tasks, contribute to the maintenance of one's household, and to learn to enjoy being responsible. Additionally, the story teaches us other lessons about relationships of various kinds. The story has nothing to do, of course, with racism, of advancing the idea that whites are superior, more favorable, or better than blacks.

The valuable symbolism in myth, folk, and fairy tales is mostly lost on our modern society possessed, as it is, with a commitment to honor only that which is scientific, rational, objective, and practical. We tend to suspect anything that cannot be taken at face-value, or anything that is said to be more than it seems. But try as we may, we cannot rid life of its mystery. And one of the mysteries of life is what Carl Jung recognized as the Self-regulatory function whereby archetypal energies penetrate our consciousness through a symbol that leads to transformation of attitude (the transcendent function).

Symbols such as rainbows, birds, serpents, or trees might be examined in drawings and paintings by focusing on a particular symbol as the representation of a specific archetype. This approach is one that was taken by Susan Bach. Bach's empirical research of unconscious symbols in art, spanned more than thirty years. It included the tracking of particular symbols (for example, the bird as motif for the soul) that have appeared in drawings or paintings by patients and by famous artists (Bach, 1980a; 1990).

An alternate approach is to study the function of a particular archetype in one individual's experience, and see how it is expressed in the symbolic language of the person's drawings. Here we might observe different images that one uses to portray a particular archetype in a series of expressions exhibited in a variety of media. The task is to comprehend in what way the individual identifies with the reflected archetype(s) and to recognize what type of impact this archetypal experience appears to have on the individual's life. By using this approach, I have learned the value of the Hero or Warrior, the Self, the Journey, and Rebirth as archetypes that appear especially to help dying patients cope with their destiny.

Sometimes the motifs or symbols will be repeated in the portrayal of the archetype from one expressive work to another. Other times, however, quite different images project the archetype, just as may happen in dreams. Consider the animus (defined by Ursula Bomholt [1990] as a woman's psychic energy that allows her to gain knowledge and focus on things she already knows innately). A woman might dream of her animus as two angry men threatening her; weeks or months later, when she is increasingly integrating this energy and is in better working relationship with her animus, it might return in another dream as an exotic lover or as an admiring, supportive male from a foreign country.

Among therapists of Jungian persuasion, there are those who believe that amplification of images in a dream or drawing robs the dream or drawing of its true power and meaning. They insist that if we name what it is, the magic and mystery are gone and that soul is diminished by delimiting its expression through an "interpretation."

I agree that there is a danger in over-analyzing and intellectualizing about a dream or drawing and possibly killing its transforming energy. We can rush or push an individual into conscious considerations only to shut down the unconscious, healing process. When rational headwork is forced upon us, our soul withdraws.

The purpose of amplification is to enrich the essence of the dream or drawing; we do this by pointing out relationships between their lives and the images they have created. Amplification also shows how the lives of others, such as the therapist or society as a whole, are related to the images presented. Contrary to robbing a dream or a drawing of its true power, meaning, magic, and mystery, amplification can enhance all these qualities.

Amplification is not an attempt to point out "the meaning" of a dream or drawing; it points up the meaning and power of an individual's life. Amplification relates the therapist or even a community to some archetypal energy generated by the image-maker. To amplify an image in a drawing, it is neither necessary nor reasonable to attempt matching the life of its creator to all the ways the image has been used by various cultures or belief systems. The particular symbology an observer selects might reflect the way the observer relates to the image-maker and his or her life (or death) issues.

Chapter 1 Notes

1. As pointed out in the Introduction, Self is capitalized when referring to the primary, archetypal Self that contains both conscious and unconscious psyche; but not capitalized when referring to the conscious, ego self.

Chapter 2

REFLECTIONS OF PSYCHE AND SOMA

Increasingly, clinicians recognize the interrelatedness of soul (or psyche) and body. Studies reveal that patients' drawings can express more than past and current conditions of the body and the psyche; they might even reveal somatic conditions before they can be found clinically (Bach 1969, 1974/75, 1990; Kiepenheuer, 1980, 1990; Furth 1988; & Williams 1981, 1985). Thus, drawings, like dreams, can reflect our present condition, and reveal a prospective course—a prognosis.

I speak, of course, of drawings that the individual produces at will or in response to an invitation to "draw whatever you wish." These are in contrast to drawings of an assigned subject, such as the House-Tree-Person series, requested for diagnostic purposes. Even if unassigned drawings are consciously planned, their input is not confined to the conscious ego. Preconscious knowledge of both our psychological and physical conditions can be reflected in our drawing.

Early in my cystic fibrosis (CF) study (between 1978 and 1979) I found blue-shaded clouds to be a common feature of drawings made when patients were retaining fluid from pulmonary edema, sinusitis, or peripheral tissue edema. Marilyn Leonhart's (1984) studies corroborated that shaded-in clouds correlate with respiratory congestion. (In CF, a disorder in the cells' use of sodium and chloride causes the lungs to absorb too much water.)

Besides the somatic implication of the blue-shaded cloud, the water-filled cloud, obviously, also suggests held-back tears. Many CF patients, particularly in the more severe stages of the disease, appear to experience grief mixed with fear and they express this symbolically. Patients might suppress such feelings just to protect themselves and their families from the discomfort they believe an overt expression would impose. The blue-shaded cloud is one of several nonverbal expressions that reveal symbolically what the psyche feels. Thus we see how one symbol, a blue-shaded cloud, might represent both psyche and soma simultaneously.

Using drawings as a tool for understanding the realities of psyche and soma is an awesome undertaking that requires stamina of body, mind, and soul. My colleagues and I have often wanted to deny certain prognostic signs and have found ourselves rationalizing why clues of a foreboding nature can be read as promising signs. We might fool ourselves, but the pictures speak the truth. Even when patients are not consciously aware of the course their life is taking, as Bach often said to those of us who studied with her, "'It' knows inside of us." There is another piece of advice from Bach (1974/1975): "If what the children tell us in their drawings awes you and you would rather not have it true, be assured that we too who have worked on them for so many years still find our hair stand on end and breathless silence befall us" (p. 102).

It is difficult for professional artists, art educators, and art critics to accept that drawings can lend themselves to such analytical and clinical scrutiny as I have suggested thus far. This is because they consider art a conscious construct. Professional artists, and others, argue that a particular color combination, object, shape, or placement is chosen for "artistic reasons" only – to give a certain balance, rhythm, or aesthetic value to the picture.

I believe we choose consciously to draw a picture one way instead of another – that certain objects, shapes, shadings, or placements on the paper will be preferable to their omission or an alternate way of including them. But I also maintain that our conscious choice is linked to unconscious issues and attitudes as well as to conscious ones. The art therapist and teacher Shaun McNiff stresses the importance of letting an image speak to our receptive soul instead of imposing upon the image a limited meaning that comes entirely from our conscious, ego self.

An art therapist in one of my workshops announced that he knew we would view the absence of a ground line in his painting as an expression of insecurity or of not being grounded to reality. He then claimed that he *chose* to paint it that way because he knew, as an artist, that it was far more aesthetically pleasing. His ego declared what the image was (an aesthetic expression) and it rejected any message from the unconscious that might have been carried by the image.

Despite the clinical training and experience this art therapist possessed, his rational ego-consciousness prevented his looking beyond his explanation of the drawing. He could not admit that his unconscious functioning could influence his aesthetic choices. He was so sure of his psychological and physical stability that he took it for granted; he failed to see that his painted flowers floating in midair, might be suggesting to him (1) the absence of nurture with respect to some aspect of his physical or emotional well-being; (2) some kind of loss; (3) the development of an inflated attitude to compensate for something; (4) some rejection of reality in favor of fantasy; or (5) a dissociation from some natural, instinctual aspect of life. (Of course, no single picture can be taken as an accurate, summary view of its artist.)

We all have parts that our egos do not wish to face, so we trot along wearing blinders to shield ourselves from things we fear or find annoying on our paths. In the film, *The Way of the Dream*, Marie-Louise von Franz expresses this idea in relation to the meaning of our dreams (Boa, 1987). She says that we cannot interpret our own dreams because we cannot see what is on our back side. Similarly, it is very difficult to interpret our own drawings, or even the drawings of someone to whom we are very close. When we are emotionally close to someone we may choose to ignore certain characteristics or complexes that are too painful to confront.

This idea meets widespread resistance despite data supporting the concept that drawings are a valid expression of conscious and unconscious conditions of psyche and soma (Bach 1990; Weber 1980; Furth 1988; Kiepenheuer 1980, 1990; Williams 1981, 1985). The renowned art educator Rhoda Kellogg (1969/1970) believes that children's art is primarily an expression of their aesthetic feelings; she dismisses it as an expression of any condition related either to the personal or collective unconscious. Jung had explained to Kellogg (1969/1970) that children draw mandalas spontaneously, worldwide, around age 3 and that they are inborn images that appear occasionally in conscious imagination.

Analytical psychology understands these mandala drawings to coincide with a need to restore inner balance, bring order to chaos, or to achieve a reintegration involving relationship between the ego and the Self. Kellogg (1969/1970) recognizes the mandala as an image that each individual develops through scribbling experiences, but shows no interest in crediting this stage as providing a possible manifestation of ego development moving towards self/Self identity.

Joel Ryce-Menuhin (1988) describes circle drawings made by children at ages 1 and 2. Apparently, these drawings initiate ego emergence from Self, freedom to act on ego impulse, sense of individuality and wholeness. At times, they also initiate union of (whole) Self and ego, however transitory that state is for the child involved.

Kellogg (1969/1970) also comments that all children go through a phase of drawing humans without arms, and that they do so after they can draw them with arms. She believes this omission is not because of forgetfulness or immaturity; she claims that once the child has made the head and legs in certain proportions the human just looks better to the child with the arms omitted.

I support Kellogg's belief that it is not forgetfulness or immaturity that accounts for this drawing style, which is most typically seen in drawings by preschoolers around the age of four. However, considering the empirical research on unconscious manifestations in drawings, I suspect there is an additional reason preschoolers omit arms in drawings of humans.

Even though they are still largely egocentric, at this age children increasingly develop understanding of the limitations on their energies, although they are still largely egocentric. Children's awareness of their own vulnerability inevitably catches up with their self confidence gained through the mastery of various skills. Roughly, between the ages of three and four, children waver on a seesaw of conquests and surrenders, fluctuating between experiences of autonomy and dependency.

A 2-year-old child speaks so often of "me," "my," and "mine" and loudly protests any demands to curb his or her power and control. This self-centeredness gradually gives way to a shyer, less than confident, 4-year-old person. The brash ego of the 2-year-old grows to be more submissive by the age of 4. An ego's struggle for power over parents, siblings, and peers becomes a conflict of competition. The blossoming assertiveness and initiative of preschoolers might push them too far until they find themselves in trouble and overcome with guilt. To spare their consciences from hurting and to gain a feeling of acceptance, they might suppress their actions to the point of overcontrol.

I suggest that a reason many children around the age of four occasionally begin omitting arms (or legs) from drawings is owing to the situation their ego experiences. The 4-year-old ego suffers periods of feeling defeated, guilt-ridden, or lacking situational control. At this age, children become aware of being manipulated more than they can manipulate either their environment or the people in it. Further, children who have from birth not experienced sufficient nurturing and positive mirroring will have a deficient ego. Such deprivation will be apparent by age 4. Their drawings of humans without arms can both complement and compensate their personal ego experience.

Four-year-olds might prefer to draw armless humans partly because their conscious and unconscious ideas agree about their lack of power to handle life (the unconscious *complements* powerlessness in such drawings). Four-year-olds might also need to restrain physical aggressiveness that leads them into trouble. The unconscious *compensates* for this in their drawings of armless humans. Therefore, armless humans may be taken as symbolic expressions of how young children, particularly around age four, feel about themselves and their environment.

Insisting that one draws or paints something a certain way just because of aesthetic preferences, acknowledges only the conscious level of functioning. Such reasoning ignores the question *why* a person believes a particular choice is aesthetically correct. Several years ago an amateur artist who had been diagnosed with carcinoma gave his grown daughter one of his recent paintings. It depicted a watermelon peddler driving his mule-drawn cart of melons, but there was no ground line for the cart or mule; instead, a mist or fog obscured the ground. This man had responded to therapy and achieved remission.

A few years later, still in remission, he visited his daughter's home where the painting had been hung; he seemed to notice for the first time the absence of a ground line and became very displeased with his painting. It did not look right to him; he was so distressed by the absence of a road to support the cart and mule that he insisted on retouching the painting to put ground under the cart's wheels and the animal's feet. Though he had taken pride earlier in presenting it as a gift, he was now dissatisfied with what he saw. Something about this painting was no longer *his* picture; he could not claim it as it was.

We could take his reaction to mean that because his life was now less threatened and his personal path of life made more solid by the remission of his cancer, he felt it appropriate for the objects in his painting to be grounded as a way of affirming his increased stability. On the other hand, the man also knew that there was a good possibility his cancer could recur. His insistence upon adding the ground line may have reflected an urge to deny that instability was potentially a part of his life's picture. Adding a ground line could also reflect a desire to connect with the earth and to be nurtured to health – to thrive instead of fading away. (This man was an avid gardener.)

Considering my own and my clinical colleagues, interpretative experience with drawings, it is difficult for me to regard the dramatic change in this man's preference for a ground line as unrelated to the influence of cancer in his life. Had this incident happened with the painting of a young school-aged child, I would probably attribute the change in artistic taste to the child's maturation – improvement in skill and increased sophistication.

However, this painting was made by a retired but active man who had painted as a hobby for most of his life. The sequence of events related to this man's painting of a melon cart are persuasive that he had expressed, whether knowingly or not, the importance of reaffirming life at a time so critical for him.

A few years before I began my CF study, I collected from an eleven-year-old cancer patient a drawing that contains a remarkable expression of psyche and soma. Two years earlier, Franklin was diagnosed with bone cancer (rhabdosarcoma) in one leg, which eventually led to amputation below the knee. An athletic boy, Franklin adapted quickly to his prosthesis and became a star player on his school's baseball team. Unfortunately, the cancer returned in his lungs, requiring pulmonary surgery twice.

Now he had come back to the hospital for staging of the cancer – radiological testing to find possible recurrence and location of new cancer growth. While waiting for his trip to the x-ray unit, Franklin decided to draw a picture of a football player (Fig. 2). He explained to me that this was the quarterback and that he had been in a rough game. He chose to use the purple coloring pencil for his entire drawing, regardless that he had a full range of colors available.

In Bach's (1990) study of drawings by cancer patients, she noted that whenever the patient used purple (Bach called it mauve) there were issues or aspects of control involved in the following ways. Their symptoms frequently included either seizures or spastic conditions, or the illness would seize the patient critically, as occurs with a metastasis. This color occasionally expressed psychologically a feeling of being supported (positively or negatively) or it suggested a control issue – the need to be in control, to possess, or to be controlled or possessed.

The face of Franklin's quarterback tells us that this game was an injurious one. Previous games may have left their mark, too; there is a scar with nine sutures on the right side of the player's face. Finishing the face, Franklin complained that the paper was not large enough to draw the whole figure. I suggested taping on another sheet of paper so he could continue. We did this and had to add three more sheets in all to allow him to draw the entire figure.

Even then, he was not satisfied; he explained that he needed to draw the football field and the audience in the stands. With the fifth and sixth sheets added horizontally, Franklin's drawing took on the shape of a cross, reminding me of the burdensome cross his progressing illness required him to bear. How crucified he must have felt from having to endure so many treatments and surgeries!

The finished drawing reveals that Franklin's quarterback is a professional player in the National Football League. He is "number one"; as quarterback, he directs the offense for his team. All these characteristics about Franklin's football player describe remarkably his valiant fight to overcome cancer. They also suggest how highly this boy valued his life.

When he finished his drawing, he sat back to examine it. Suddenly, he declared, "He's not dirty enough," and with this remark he picked up the purple pencil again and shaded an area on the lower left side (right side on the drawing) of the quarterback's chest. In clinical slang, "dirty" is a word sometimes used to refer to infection or a lesion detected by X-ray. Almost immediately after adding this "dirty" spot on his drawing, Franklin was called to the X-ray unit. It was nearly time for the activity room to close, so I told Franklin I would keep his drawing in my office until the next day.

The following morning when I arrived for work, I saw Franklin's oncologist perusing his chart at the nursing station. I quickly retrieved Franklin's "dirty quarterback" from my office and showed it to the oncologist, explaining that he had drawn this while waiting for his call to x-ray. When I reported Franklin's comment about the additional "dirty" shading to her, she caught her breath and exclaimed, "Oh my God, that's exactly where his X-rays show the cancer to be now!"

Bach (1969) concluded from her observations of drawings by severely ill children that children project their physical condition directly onto the drawing paper so that the drawing mirrors the body. The right side of the drawing mirrors the condition of the right side of the body, and vice versa. However, Bach (1980b) also said that with schooling, a child eventually corrected for the "mirror image" projected in their drawings and rendered them "objectively" (p. 8).

I find that when older school-age children (from about age nine onward) project somatic content into a picture, they usually correct the mirror image. Franklin's purple shading on the right side of the quarterback from our viewpoint, corresponded to the metastasis found in his lower left lung.

My experience in evaluating drawings tells me that unconscious influences blend with our conscious intentions when we draw from the imagination. This blending of conscious and unconscious thoughts allows our own life and environment to reveal itself in our decisions and actions in the creation of our picture. The attitude and rationalizations of those artists and educators who belittle *unconscious* influences in the composition of a drawing or painting would suggest that creative imagination and its expression is under conscious control – that the artist is complete master of the canvas or drawing paper.

The fact is, the ego enjoys persuading one to believe that the conscious self is the all powerful, controlling energy of one's whole psyche. In reality, the ego manages just the *conscious* element; it has no control over the *unconscious*. This truth is frequently displayed to us by what Freud (1913-14) classified as a parapraxis – the phenomenon of "forgetting words and names . . . [or] what one intends to do . . . [and by] slips of the tongue and pen . . . [and various] instances of 'absentmindedness' . . ." (pp. 166-167). Freud explains such "accidents" as situations in which the unconscious betrays the conscious attitude.

The point I have made about unconscious influences might apply even in a situation where one is required to draw something in a very specific way. However, when a botany student's assignment is to draw the underground network of a rhizome, or a medical illustrator is asked to draw a particular anatomical formation, the unconscious influences will be inhibited and difficult to detect. Detection of unconscious functioning in freely drawn pictures or in subjects chosen to be drawn by the artist is a much easier task.

A person's style of adapting, coping, interacting with others, and processing life's experiences is cast early in life. A drawing can mirror one's personal rhythm of life in a symbolic way. Very compulsive individuals may be compelled to have perfect balance in their drawings, so that whatever is on the right side – a tree, flower, bird, or certain other things – will be repeated on the left side.

A person who suffers from tension headaches might be suppressing anger; this suppression can convert anger to tension. Tension can potentially produce vascular constriction and ultimately a headache. My colleagues and I have learned that people who adapt by suppressing anger often draw pictures that are mostly colorless, even when all colors are available to use. The refusal to "show one's true colors" is a reflection of the psyche-soma relationship in which denied anger (felt by psyche) has produced a constriction of the circulation of blood (a somatic experience).

This event often causes paleness of the face, painful throbbing in the head, and sometimes even fainting. Thus, one may produce a pale or faintly-drawn picture because it is that person's nature to withhold expression. This does not mean, of course, that if you or I draw colorless pictures we must have a headache, be angry, repress feelings, or lack energy! No single characteristic in a drawing can be relied upon to depict the human condition; we must consider every image in relation to the whole picture.

Might healthy persons and those who are seriously ill include the same figures and motifs in their drawings? The answer is a qualified "yes." Susan Bach (1990) gives examples of drawings with the same motif drawn by both ill and healthy children. She points out important differences between the way the motif is developed by the ill children and the way it is developed by the healthy ones. In one instance, two boys close in age, one healthy, the other one ill, had drawn pictures of a woodpecker. The boys neither knew each other nor saw the other's drawing. Bach evaluated their drawings without knowing which boy was the healthy one. She showed how she evaluated the details in each picture to learn which picture fit a profile of illness and which one conveyed an image of health.

Another case Bach (1990) reports on concerned identical twins, 8-years-old; one had leukemia, the other was healthy. They decided to draw pictures of the cherry harvest. The twin with cancer drew his picture while hospitalized; the other twin drew his picture at home. Neither of them saw the other's picture. Differences in the two pictures are striking – particularly in the way the ill twin colored the cherries. Bach finds that healthy children's drawings generally contain fewer oddities; they have fewer colors out of place and fewer omissions of essential items.

Furth's (1973) study compared and contrasted drawings by three groups: healthy children, leukemic children, and children who were sick but not seriously so. The most omissions were in the drawings by the leukemic children. He observed that the healthy children tended to draw the sun with a face and that the other two categories of children tended not to put this feature on their suns.

It is inevitable that our drawings will contain some reference to the happenings in our lives – however veiled in symbolism that reference may be. Drawings and dreams are very much alike and can be analyzed in much the same way.

I have already mentioned the disdain art educators and critics have for a Jungian, archetypal approach to art. There are people who ridicule any kind of drawing analysis that seeks to shed light on an individual's physical or psychological state or the relationship to his or her environment; this is especially so if such analysis is based on the premise that the unconscious might play a responsible role.

I believe most artists will readily admit, however, that their art reflects their total personality. Furthermore, most artists, art educators, and critics recognize that there are certain characteristics each artist develops as a part of personal style. Nevertheless, it is customary for artists, art educators, or critics to regard all such elements in art in a formal, aesthetic way without relating them to any symbolic function.

In discussing this cultural bias, Dougherty (1996) states, "When aesthetic principles define art in sharp separation from life, then the role of the artist is similarly separated" (p. 2). We and the artist are deprived of the artwork's "ability to transmit meaning in the life of either the... [artist] or the community" (Dougherty, 1996, p. 1). Considering the common practice of analyzing art apart from any human experience, is it any wonder that artists, art educators, and critics deny that spontaneous art can communicate something from the body or the psyche?

There is a widespread fear of unconscious influence in one's life. If art educators and critics were to acknowledge that artists can unconsciously project conditions of the psyche and soma into their paintings, they would have to admit that the same process might just as well apply to them.

Similarly, I have seen parents deny clinical evaluations of their child's personality and behavior based on the child's drawings. They reject the psychological inventory with rationalizations why their child drew things a certain way ("He drew a man chopping down trees because his grandpa was clearing some woods last month" –"Oh, she always draws females that way"–"He saw the movie three times and has been obsessed by that character").

The desire to negate or trivialize their child's uncomfortable psychic state blinds parents from seeing the motif their child was moved to use and its possible symbolic or metaphorical significance to the child's present situation. The simple fact is, most of us are either scared witless or painfully embarrassed by facing the naked truth about ourselves – or our children!

Kellogg (1969/1970) says that it mystifies her "why adults insist that a child's work is a report on his life experiences, when even the most talented adult artists find difficulty in portraying emotional experiences in art" (p. 149). It seems to me, with all due respect for Ms. Kellogg and her truly remarkable work, she confuses conscious and unconscious expressions in one's art. Children, adults, and professional or amateur artists may fail to portray to their satisfaction a particular mood, or the enchanted feelings a scene evoked in them. But there is great possibility their pictures will contain features that reflect certain idiosyncrasies of their personality, particular effects of their life experiences, and clues about the state of their health. This may be so even when the reflections have nothing to do with what the artist *consciously* set out to express.

The unconscious can exert influence even when we "copy" a picture of something or choose to draw something "from life." This influence is exerted partly in our choice of the subject, but also in subtle, and sometimes blatant, alterations or deviations from the original subject. Bach gives an example of a leukemia patient whose deviation from a photograph she "copied" relates significantly to both her psychological and somatic state.

Bach (1974/75) published her report originally in an international journal and included an edited version of the article in her book, *Life Paints Its Own Span* (1990). She tells us that the patient was a 17-year-old girl who chose to copy from a magazine a colored photograph of an owl perched on a branch of a pine tree. However, deviations from the magazine picture that appeared in the girl's drawing suggested to Bach parallels with the girl's health.

These deviations included, among other things, strikingly sparse pine needles, a worm-eaten and rotting bough that made an insecure perch for the owl, eyes drawn such that one appeared to be removed, black shading around just the owl and the tree, a blank and colorless background, and omission of the wooded background in the original picture.

We cannot prove that the owl's precarious perch upon a diseased branch expresses the girl's foreboding of an uncertain foothold on life, that the sparse pine needles reflect the girl's loss of hair owing to anticancer therapy. We cannot insist that her owl (a bird that sees in the dark), which seems blind in one eye, represents her fear of looking into the dark unknown – perhaps not wishing to see the possibility of death – or that her colorless background reveals that she withholds her true feelings (anger?). We *can* see that these obvious deviations present remarkable coincidences with the girl's somatic and psychological state. Bach's study teaches us that even when a picture is "copied" the uniqueness of one's situation proclaims itself symbolically, wittingly or not.

DEALING WITH CF

Several years ago, a young child with CF overheard his parents and the doctor discussing the child's diagnosis. The words, "cystic fibrosis," were so foreign to him that he thought they were talking about "sixty-five roses." He must have thought it puzzling why everyone thought "sixty-five roses" was a serious problem! Word of the child's amusing mispronunciation of the disease spread through the network of CF centers.

"Sixty-five Roses" eventually became the title of an educational film about CF. Later, the name was adopted by a baseball club organized to raise money for CF research and The 65 Roses Sports Club expanded to include other sports clubs throughout the country, including basketball, soccer, hockey, and football. These clubs have raised thousands of dollars throughout the years for the CF Foundation.

Unfortunately, having CF is nothing like a bed of roses. Before viewing the experiences of living and dying with CF as revealed in patients' drawings, it might be helpful to the reader to review some facts about the disease. CF is a genetic disease of the exocrine glands; it is still incurable in 1998. The disease is inherited, supposedly, according to the genetic laws of the nineteenth century scientist and monk, Gregor Mendel.

However, in 1990, genetic researchers stumbled over some new evidence concerning DNA. They discovered that genes can mutate, that both members of a pair of chromosomes can come from *one* parent, and that the gene from one parent can have an effect on the fetus that is markedly different from the same gene of the other parent. This has canceled all the rules on which genetic counseling had relied.

It used to be thought that CF could be transmitted only if both parents were carriers of the CF gene – where the sperm and the egg that it fertilized each carried the CF gene. It was understood that unless both the sperm and the egg carried the CF gene, the child could not even inherit the CF gene as a carrier – much less be born with the disease. Now we know that when a child gets both copies of the CF gene from a mother who is a carrier there is no possibility for a healthy gene from the father to overcome the CF gene. The sperm's gene is rejected because no extra DNA is needed for that particular pair of chromosomes. In such a case, a child having a double quota of maternal DNA would be born with CF – regardless that the father does not even carry the recessive gene.

This is a rare occurrence, but it explains why a few parents who were counseled that they couldn't have a child with CF eventually had one. (At the time of this writing, the CF Foundation does not give the public this ominous genetic update in their distribution of information concerning the CF inheritance factor. This is most likely because of its rarity.)

CF makes life very unpleasant. The body's mucus secretions are abnormally sticky; it causes bronchial tubes to clog. Impaired breathing is the result, and it provides an ideal culture where trapped bacteria can multiply and spread throughout the respiratory system. This same gluey mucus plugs openings from the pancreas so that enzymes needed for digestion are blocked from entering the small intestine. The latter disorder requires aggressive treatment to prevent poor growth, a ravenous appetite, and abnormal stools (Professional Education Committee, Cystic Fibrosis Foundation, 1980).

Chronic obstructive pulmonary disease (COPD) appears in the advanced stages of CF in most patients; it presents the most serious complication in CF. Among other symptoms and changes, patients with COPD experience shortness of breath on exertion, anatomical changes in the chest making the patient look pigeon breasted or barrel chested, clubbing of the toes and fingers owing to decreased oxygen in the blood, a noisy, wheezing respiration, a marked decrease in appetite resulting in severe weight loss, muscular weakness, rounding of the shoulders and poor posture, a stunting of growth, and a chronic, paroxysmal, productive cough that may also cause vomiting (Professional Education Committee, CF Foundation, 1980). One can imagine how these symptoms have a negative influence on the patient's self-image.

CF affects the liver in many patients and it does so in various ways. Older patients with CF frequently have diabetes mellitus. Males usually suffer atrophy of the Wolffian ducts owing to the thick mucus that blocks them; ultimately this results in sterility but with no impairment to sexual functioning. Although female CF patients have no similar anatomical anomalies related to the reproductive system, infertility is high and conception difficult because of peculiar cervical and vaginal secretions (Professional Education Committee, CF Foundation, 1980).

Advancements in therapy have extended the life expectancy of individuals with CF so that it can no longer be thought of as a disease that afflicts children only. By the 1980s, many CF patients lived into their twenties, and some even into their forties.

Clinicians who treat patients with CF, particularly patients having an advanced stage of the disease, cannot fail to observe certain sources of stress that these patients commonly experience. These include (1) feeling victimized, (2) being aware that death might come soon, and (3) carrying the physical characteristics of advanced CF that most always result in a negative self-image.

Presently, we will look at three cases, all of whom had developed COPD. Dennis, the oldest, also had a gastric ulcer. We will examine a series of drawings by each patient to observe both unconscious and conscious reflections of somatic and psychic conditions. Additionally, we will see in these drawings the reconciliatory function of the symbol as the representative of an archetype.

Before proceeding, however, I wish to make clear my role and how it was limited with respect to the CF patients in my study. I was responsible for helping hospitalized patients cope emotionally with their hospital experience, and for providing activities to help compensate for the interruption that hospitalization imposed upon their psychosocial growth and development.

In the outpatient clinic, my role was to offer activities to relieve stress caused by physical examinations or clinical tests. Frequently, I introduced various art activities in both inpatient and outpatient settings, but I did not function as an art therapist. Nor did I function as a primary counselor to these CF patients; I had no contact with them away from the hospital or the outpatient clinic.

For that matter, I know of no patients in my study who did have a primary mental health counselor to help them and their families with the emotionally trying aspects of living and dying with CF. This service is one that I have found sadly underrated and generally discounted as unnecessary by CF treatment centers throughout the U.S.; I base this judgment on the exchange of information at regional and national CF conferences.

These centers emphasize various services that are beneficial to the patients' physical condition or financial situation. But with few exceptions, the *psychic* pain that the patient and the family unquestionably experience is generally overlooked; it is not deemed significant enough to provide a course of play therapy or family counseling that would give the patient and the family emotional support and teach them coping skills.

Chapter 3

SORTING GRAINS

As I examine the details of a pictorial expression and follow C. G. Jung's model for amplifying dream images, I find wordless but valid and reliable communications from patients suspended between life and death. I recall the resistance my audiences have shown towards accepting pictorial representations of psyche and soma; I imagine skeptical readers will accuse me of reading into the drawings things that are not there.

Such skeptics would argue that I can't *prove* the reliability of such communications. They might rationalize that the painter did his work in a particular way by intent or conscious knowledge, or merely from some remembered experience. I realize it is difficult to accept the existence of something that cannot be measured, weighed, or touched. It is impossible for some persons to accept the suggestion that an image might represent something not affirmed by the patient.

To understand these kinds of pictorial expressions requires one to use separately both masculine and feminine consciousness. One must begin with feminine consciousness. This means receiving, welcoming, relating, intuiting, sorting through details, and having patience.

Susan Bach pointed out forcefully to me the importance of the feminine attitude towards doing this work. While I was studying drawings under her supervision, Bach questioned me about details of a particular feature in one of my patient's drawings. I told her what I knew, but she pushed me to go deeper.

"And what is that about?" Her question took me by surprise. I thought I had already expounded sufficiently on details in the drawing. Apparently I had missed something, because she continued her inquest.

"What do you see *there?*" She tapped the picture with the thin pointer she used to avoid touching the drawing with her finger. (She was

36

fanatically dedicated to preserving each drawing and she opposed touching one any more than absolutely necessary.) I leaned forward, carefully scrutinizing the drawing for whatever I had missed. I still drew a blank, but she was not giving up with me.

"Where did that come from? To what could that be related?" I met her persistent questions with a long silence. Having gone as far as I knew how, I could think of nothing more to say.

She broke the silence. "Well, what is it?" She insisted that I attend to her probing about the feature!

In exasperation I blurted out, "I don't know!"

"Of course, you don't *know*; but what do you *feel?*" she queried, like Aristotle.

Only then did I realize that I had been caught up too much in intellectualizing about the drawing. I had to get back into my soul – get out of my head and into my heart – so that I could begin to feel what the patient experienced.

Masculine consciousness (by no means limited to gender) expresses itself in rational thought, clarification, definition, and judgment; these are essential later in the analysis. One must put complete faith in the unconscious process and trust the ability of the human psyche and soma to communicate symbolically – perhaps subliminally. Such an attitude leads one to view drawings with great respect, to absorb and to consume every detail, to ponder and embrace their meaning.

In many Cinderella tales, and in the *Amor and Psyche* myth, the heroine must laboriously separate grains – the good from the bad. Similarly, we must sort patiently through the elements of these drawings – count all repeated objects, and note which colors are used. We must know what is present and what is absent that might usually be included in such a picture. These reveal the truth of the drawing. As Marie-Louise von Franz (1972) points out:

> separating . . . grains is a work of patience, which can neither be rushed into nor speeded up. . . . it is a work of careful, detailed discrimination, but not discrimination as done by the male logos. . . .
> The feminine principle . . . has its way of seeing clearly . . . by the selection of innumerable details, showing that this is this and that is that . . . . (p. 156)

Indeed, women can be painfully boring by their insistence on going into detail about things – describing what one was wearing or reporting on what was served at a meal, etc. Some people take this quality to mean that women are gossipy and interested only in petty things.

Part of the feminine "grain sorting" in the evaluation of a drawing is to make a detailed inventory of every object, including the characteristics of every mark and color forming each feature. Bach required us to put tracing paper over the drawing and to trace every line and all the shading. This made us aware of the minute details that feminine consciousness relies upon.

Feminine consciousness enables both men and women to experience the wholeness of important images. It does this by considering recurring elements or themes, contrasting elements or themes, and how these might be related. This is one kind of meaning. Masculine consciousness allows us to consolidate all components of a drawing or painting and to extract an encompassing, general message from it. This may appear to contradict the idea of the feminine and masculine approach presented by Sullivan (1989), who says the concern of the feminine is "with meaning rather than with facts . . ." (p. 23), but Sullivan and I are really advancing the same idea.

The feminine or Yin[1] way involves absorbing every detail of the image, including amplifications that yield several possible meanings. These meanings are organized and further clarified by the masculine or Yang consciousness so as to energize an archetype that can give meaning to the picture. Yin (soul) brings unconscious material to light through an image; Yang (spirit) distills and organizes the new material to give it meaning. (Soul/anima and spirit/animus are defined and discussed more completely in Chapters 5 and 10.) It should be clear that each gender contains both anima/soul and animus/spirit. It takes the ordering and action of the spirit to advance the dreams of the soul. (This concept is discussed further in Chapter 10.)

Many would prefer to bypass the tedious "grain sorting" aspect of picture analysis and head straight for the whole meaning. (As my dear husband complained to me once when I was sharing an anonymous patient's drawings with him, "I don't want to try to keep all those picky details in my head – just get to the bottom line!") We find meaning only when we go into the depths of a drawing and contact its essence. Soul finding requires the painstaking sorting of grains; there is no escaping the tedium. Nowhere is this method better illustrated than in C. G. Jung's writings on interpreting dreams.

As we attempt to understand what pictures have to say, we must remind ourselves that we cannot hope to grasp the complete meaning of a drawing. Just as the meaning of a dream is never completely exhausted, so it is with a drawing rendered at a significant time in a patient's life. This explains why I am tentative and equivocal in discussing what a drawing expresses. I often caution my students that *drawings cannot give answers, but they can show us which questions we need to consider.* Readers will find further possible meanings for the pictures I present as they apply additional amplification. The inferences that I find in a patient's drawing reflect partly my knowledge of and relationship with that patient.

IMAGES AND IMAGE-MAKERS

This book concentrates mainly on what a patient's drawings may have to say about the patient's experience or condition. It is not intended to be a primer on how to read drawings. (See Appendix A for major features of Bach's model.) Bach (1969; 1990) and Furth (1988) have already covered this ground. Bertoia (1993) provides a list of Furth's "focal points" to consider in analyzing drawings and a case study to show their applications.

The attitude we bring to the image is an important aspect in reading patients' drawings. Both invited and spontaneous drawings should be viewed as messengers bearing gifts from the psyche. This perspective is both valid and needed because these pictures reflect and affirm meaningful realities just as dreams do. It is important to honor the images and all that they bring to light, both through the patient's associations and through amplification. Images serve as a mediator between the ego and both the personal unconscious and the objective psyche (collective unconscious).

Jungian dream analysis emphasizes "sticking with the image" instead of using free association. With the latter, it is easy to read into dreams or drawings meanings that are not actually there. To stay with an image, we must walk around it, as it were, to view its various facets. We begin this process by considering first what the image means to, or evokes within, the person who produced it. After that, we can further amplify what message the image may have for the individual, or what further way the individual and image may be related.

We amplify by considering the image as it appears in a mythological or anthropological framework. The latter type of amplification is

especially helpful and revealing when the individual makes no particular association with an image. People will often include something in
their drawing and later comment that they don't know why they drew
it; they may say that they added it just because it seemed to be the
right thing to put there, or because they find it attractive or fascinating
in some way.

Amplification of images, however, presents problems just as free
association with them does. It is tempting to get caught up in an analyzation of the image that is so intellectual and academic it severs the
image's connection to the feelings and personality of the image-maker.
At this point, I call upon the principles of analytical psychology that
lead us to understand purpose and value of the image. These principles have nothing to do with what the image stands for of itself or what
we think it might mean. It is, in fact, what the image-maker takes it to
be because of some meaning the image evoked within. It is easy to
misinterpret what this is unless we have some knowledge of and relationship with the image-maker.

This fact was impressed upon me in a shocking way by a CF support and counseling group. One of the group's members, an acquain-
tance, asked if she might use some of my patients' drawings to illustrate a proposed brochure about their services. Having permission
from the parents for this kind of use, I consented to this request only
to regret it. I was aghast to discover that they printed in the brochure
erroneous information about drawings by one of the patients.
Someone had taken license to include in the brochure their own *blun-
dered* conclusions (based on one or two drawings) of how the patient
experienced his dying. Their writer had never known him nor had
even studied his case history!

An essential condition to understanding pictorial messages is to be
in relationship with the image-maker. Without that relatedness, important nuances go undetected and we run the risk of incorrectly translating the message. Furthermore, without this relationship to the image-
maker, we can be lost when it comes to understanding how archetypal content is particularly related to the individual's psyche – at either
a personal or a cultural level. To paraphrase Hippocrates, it is more
important to know what sort of person is ill than to know what sort of
illness a person has.

This alliance with the patient is important because it creates a safe
container that can be trusted to hold the patient's imaging that leads

ultimately to transcendence. Within this sacred container – the relationship – the image evokes a response from both patient and therapist. It is in this context of soul-moving images and a trusting relationship that growth and psychic transformation take place.

It is not even necessary for the therapist to use the patient's drawings as a tool for counseling; the act of drawing is itself therapeutic – apart from the therapist's efforts. It is only necessary for the therapist to trust the power of the image and the functioning of the patient's unconscious. We know that dreams work on the psyche in a mysterious way, and that only the dreamer can come to know truly what one's dream really says. Similarly, drawings that are produced at critical times in a person's life work mysteriously to aid the psyche. Their images and motifs have special meanings that are gradually assimilated by the individual who created them.

Patients' pictures often possess an energy that connects in a remarkable way with both patient and therapist. This energy is archetypal; it embodies transference and countertransference that arises from the therapeutic relationship. Schaverien (1992) recognizes that patients' pictures "have the potential to seduce the viewer by the power of fascination which . . . archetypal material exerts. The therapist has a responsibility not to be arrested by such material, but to enable its full expression" (p. 195). Schaverien (1992) further states, "The therapist may well be 'drawn in' to an intimate form of relating through such pictures as the therapeutic relationship deepens" (p. 195).

A therapist may be moved by the symbols of death and rebirth drawn by patients who are only partly conscious of impending death. The picture carries a message for which there are no words – at least not yet. Schaverien (1992) described this feature of transference and countertransference as a therapist and patient "sharing the 'secret' knowledge of his inner world, as revealed in the pictures" (p. 206). At this stage, verbal translation of the picture would be premature. The picture's symbols and their meanings are yet inseparable. Patients need a little time to live with a picture before assimilation and reintegration can occur.

A first and most important step for the therapist is to hold and honor, with deepest respect, any drawings that a patient may produce. Second, the therapist must relate to the patient at a feeling level, and not limit the relationship to a ritual of intellectualization and rational discussions. It is well if a therapist can grasp some meaning from a patient's drawing by applying various forms of amplification. When both therapist and patient revere a drawing's images and the mystery they unfold, their therapeutic alliance will create the necessary, sacred temenos for transformation to take place. This is true no matter how much is verbalized or even consciously known.

At some level, we must get into the lives of the patients with whom we work. Clinicians in both the medical and counseling fields have been warned in their training to avoid emotional involvement with patients. We do need to take care that we not become enmeshed with our patients' lives to the extent that we abandon necessary boundaries, fail to function rationally, or to make objective evaluations. We must complete enough analysis of our personal psychology to avoid becoming emotionally hooked by a patient's complexes – bound in a web of unconscious countertransference. However, unless we can relate to our patients on a *feeling* level and facilitate their becoming conscious of what they feel, we cannot begin an honest communion with the images that our patients produce.

The image bridges what is repressed, denied, or latent and its acceptance into full consciousness. For a patient to cross this bridge, a therapist must allow the patient's ego sufficient time to accept these images as emissaries from the other side. We must be careful not to rush this process. It is one thing for the patient to acknowledge what the image has to say, but quite another to embody that message.

There are times when a patient's drawings contain messages that are meant for one's society, just as one may have a dream containing an important message for "the whole tribe." Dreams and drawings of terminally ill patients can carry such messages. It is possible to look at patients' drawings and "read" them as we would read a letter, to learn what the patient is experiencing, and to share with the patient a profound understanding of living and dying. I will attempt to read the drawings that follow so we can learn how they relate to the individual's own situation and can grasp their universal message. Ultimately, I believe, patient's drawings move both patient and caregiver to a closer relationship with soul.

Chapter 3 Notes

1. In ancient Chinese philosophy and religion, Yin (feminine) and Yang (masculine) were two principles thought to influence the destiny of life and matter.

Chapter 4

IN THE BEGINNING

Dennis was the second of three surviving children born to the Brownings.[1] Another child had died in infancy with CF. Dennis, his older brother, and his little sister were just a few years apart in age; only Dennis had CF. He passionately hoped that medical science would find a cure for CF in time to save his life. But it was not until 1989, eight years after his death, that a breakthrough occurred – the CF gene was isolated.

This gene inhibits cells from properly expelling chloride ions and it prevents production of a particular protein. Experiments in 1990 with the CF gene were fruitful. Researchers corrected this defective gene in the laboratory by introducing a normal gene. Then they inserted the repaired CF gene into a test tube of malfunctioning CF cells; this caused the cells to function normally. That discovery has suggested new areas for experimentation with gene therapy and new kinds of medication. Such a milestone in CF research has brought hope for a CF cure within a few years.

It is too late for the potential rewards of this research achievement to benefit Dennis and the other patients whose drawings are presented in this book. These patients, along with approximately 30,000 other CF patients in the U.S. alone, had to live with an incurable disease during the years of my CF study.

When I asked Dennis for permission to publish his drawings, I explained that for the sake of his family's anonymity, his surname would not be used. However, Dennis was so enthusiastic about my study that he insisted I could use his whole name.

Dennis said he would be proud for people to know that he had contributed to my research and hoped that his drawings would help people understand better the experience and needs of one who is born with CF. I feel an enormous responsibility to Dennis as I attempt to fulfill the latter part of his wish, and pray that I will do justice to his life and to his dying.

Should the hereafter sustain Dennis's consciousness in some form, I believe that he would be excited to learn of the discoveries about CF since his death in 1981. He would also be pleased to know that his drawings that I collected over a three-year period are being used to teach people what it means to live and die with an incurable disease.

Dennis was 18 when we first met in 1978. He was hospitalized for a collapsed lung (pneumothorax) and for failure to gain weight. (He weighed just 57 pounds.) Besides his malnutrition and pneumothorax, he had bronchopneumonia and a viral infection (pseudomonas). He went to surgery for a procedure to bolster pulmonary recovery, and the doctors hoped this operation would also make him less vulnerable to future pneumothoraces.

Dennis experienced cardiac arrest at the end of this operation and was quickly revived without ill effect. He did well after surgery except that the pneumothorax remained. (An open chest tube was inserted to remedy the accumulation of air above the left diaphragm.)

About two weeks into his postoperative period, the doctor ordered hyperalimentation to address the nutritional problem. (Hyperalimentation consists of inserting a feeding tube venously to insure immediate absorption of food by the blood stream.) This procedure enabled Dennis to gain three pounds in two weeks. He was dismissed from the hospital after thirty-five days. The hyperalimentation continued a while longer at home. His open chest tube was monitored and eventually removed by his local, primary physician. The surgery appeared to have helped; Dennis went for a little more than eighteen months before requiring further hospitalization; this was the longest period he had ever managed to go without being hospitalized.

Research on near-death experiences (such as Dennis had on the operating table when his heart ceased beating) reveals some experiences these individuals share. These include a sense of being in the presence of bright, comforting light, often surrounded by caring people, and of enjoying the bliss of the experience; they do not wish to return to life. When they are revived, they feel a deeper appreciation for life and no longer fear or dread death. Frequently, their experience also includes seeing a beautiful landscape, as if one were viewing paradise.

In the 1970s, Raymond Moody, M.D., started interviewing people who had almost died and he began researching seriously the near-death experience (which he called NDE). Years later, pediatrician Melvin Morse, M.D., directed a distinguished research team in a study of the NDEs of children. His study sought to answer (1) whether near-death is required to have the so-called near-death experience, and (2) whether near-death experiences are hallucinations caused by drugs or lack of oxygen in the blood.

Morse's findings were published in the *American Journal of Diseases of Children* (1986), coauthored with P. Castillo, D. Venecia, J. Milstein, and D. C. Tyler, and in his bestseller book, *Closer To The Light.* Morse (1990) reported that one does need to be near death to have this experience; neither sleep deprivation, anesthetic agents, Dilantin, phenobarbital, mannitol, morphine, Valium, Thorazine, Haldol, antidepressants, mood elevators, codeine or other pain killers, nor oxygen deprivation states resulting in hallucinations could produce the typical NDE experiences. Morse never alleged that his Seattle study was proof of life after death; he took pains to see that the study results were never sensationalized in any way.

Jungian analyst and writer Nathan Schwartz-Salant says near-death events are numinous experiences for those individuals to whom they occur. He describes the event just before these patients feel pulled back into their bodies as the period when they have "that numinous experience of light and never say a word about it to anybody, and then twenty years later might uncover it in analysis as *the* crucial element" (personal communication, February 24, 1998).

Schwartz-Salant describes that highly charged, mysterious experience as terrifying to patients. Characteristically, it produces a sense of being incarnated with God and of feeling whole, in perfect harmony with Self and the universe. Patients often repress the numinous NDE, or at least keep it a secret because, as Schwartz-Salant puts it, "they are too terrified to let [such an experience] get into space and time" (same source as above). They fear the pain of loss that their recall would produce. (See also N. Swartz-Salant's *Narcissism and Character Transformation,* pp. 12-14; 18-21; 27, 169.) They fear attacks of envy about this experience. This fear is a projection of their own envy. They crave that numinous near-death state because it was perfect – they were connected with the secret core of the Self. Envy arises because they know the fullness of the experience can be neither captured nor contained.

Children are usually more trusting than adults and it is their nature to be naive, egocentric, and naturally more honest than adults. This explains partly why Dr. Morse encountered so many children who were eager to tell of their NDE. Dennis never reported any NDE sensations after his brush with death on the operating table. However, many of his drawings afterwards bear remarkable motifs suggesting a numinosity, hope, and optimism completely incompatible with the severely critical physical condition that prevailed at the time he drew them.

During the last three years of his life, Dennis spontaneously produced three pictures on three occasions when he was gravely ill; these pictures contained features that suggest what people describe who have had NDEs. I speculate that while Dennis was clinically dead during pulmonary surgery, he, too, experienced that seeming preview of heaven described by so many of Morse's pediatric patients who were near death.

I believe that it was precisely this numinous experience that sustained Dennis's psyche as he relapsed somatically time and again during the three years leading to his actual death. That Dennis never reported things from his brief brush with death might be because he was either afraid to mention them, or else he might never have allowed them to surface at his conscious, ego level. Nonetheless, they would be contained in his personal unconscious and therefore available to his psyche for support at critical times in his illness.

By the time these drawings began to occur ten months later, I had forgotten about Dennis's cardiac arrest, perhaps because it brought no negative results. It was not until after his death, when I began comparing his drawings with his medical history, that I could put together the pieces applicable to his NDE. Several observations concerning Dennis's pictures that I share here came only after allowing these images to incubate a few years while I gained more experience in understanding the symbolic language of drawings. Though I missed some of the messages in Dennis's pictures while he was still alive (and doubt seriously that he was conscious of all that they meant), I sensed strongly that we both understood intuitively how portentous these pictorial expressions were.

By keeping his drawings in a secure file, by showing respect and reverence for all they represented, and by continuing my relationship with Dennis, I could provide a "safe container" (corresponding with the covered vessel in alchemy) in which conscious and unconscious content could merge and transform. In this mysterious, alchemical way, Dennis gradually transcended his old attitude concerning life and death and adopted a broader, more fitting one.

Jung's study of alchemy led him to discover that the alchemists were writing in symbols that matched those of Gnosticism, and that their alchemical texts paralleled one's psychological experience of life (Jung, 1965). Later, we will look at more drawings from an alchemical perspective.

Three weeks after the pulmonary surgery previously described, I collected my first drawing from Dennis while he was still hospitalized. It was an extemporaneous pencil and crayon drawing he titled, "In The Beginning" (Fig. 3). He said of it, "This is when God created the world." The drawing includes, among other features, two snow-capped mountains on the right side of the page; the one in the foreground (with black smoke billowing out of its flat peak) is obviously a volcano. (Possibly the other, smokeless mountain is a volcano, too, but that was not clarified.) Dennis had never seen a volcano nor had he visited any place where volcanos existed.

While the emphasis in this picture (amplified by Dennis's comments about it) is on the creation of life, one cannot ignore the potential destruction represented by the smoldering volcano. Considering this feature as a possible reflection of the condition of the psyche, we might wonder what smoldering issue could erupt in this late adolescent's life. Given that CF had restricted Dennis in several different ways physically, he had ample reason to grieve and vent anger about being deprived of a body that looked healthy and functioned normally. Viewing the volcano as a possible somatic reflection should cause us to search for symptoms such as burning, eruptive episodes that Dennis might experience.

Approximately twenty-one months later, the volcano appeared again in one of Dennis's drawings (Fig. 9); it loomed from a pinkish-red ground line (an inappropriate color for either ground, rock, or grass.) This color caused me to ponder whether some inflammation could be present or "on the horizon." I noticed also that the volcano's billowing smoke was much more pronounced than in his first drawing (Fig. 2).

This volcano was drawn at a routine outpatient clinic visit for maintenance of the CF. I showed the drawing to Dennis's CF specialist in the clinic and asked him, "What do you suppose is about to 'erupt' in Dennis?" The physician replied that he did not anticipate any distress from the CF because Dennis's physical examination had revealed the disease to be well maintained. However, he reminded me that Dennis also had a gastric ulcer and admitted it would be no surprise if that "erupted" soon. Fourteen days later, Dennis came for emergency admission for gastric ulcer exacerbation.

Could the erosion of the stomach's inner wall, caused by bacterium working havoc with gastric acids, be related to one's inner world of repressed strife – to feelings of helplessness and suppressed anger? At the time of this emergency admission, Dennis was evidently anxious and depressed over the recurring health problems that had caused him to drop out of community college. He had been studying business and accounting with a dream of becoming his mother's manager and accountant for her home business in interior decorating; now, his career goal was denied. His ulcer incident seemed to express both his physical and emotional profiles.[2]

We should return to the first drawing, "In The Beginning," to consider some more of its features. C. G. Jung observed that water is a common symbol for the unconscious; the water in Dennis's picture, lapping half way up the mountainside like a tidal wave, suggests strongly that something from the unconscious is pushing for integration. In the lower right corner (opposite the water) Dennis printed his first and last names (the latter blacked out here for confidentiality) and the date of the picture, using the same blue he used for the water. The blue water on the left might suggest what is unconscious; Dennis's name in the same blue on the right might signify that he is ready for or preparing to bring some psychic content to consciousness and accept it.

After telling me what his picture represented, he remarked, "Something's in the drawing that really shouldn't be there . . . it's the birds." (There were 6.) He explained that there were no birds in the beginning, but added that this could be the sixth day. (According to the account of creation in Genesis, birds appeared on the fifth day.) Possibly Dennis thought he recalled the scriptures to say that birds were created on the *sixth* day, or else his comment related to the scriptural affirmation that the birds were already here since "yesterday."

The important point is that Dennis was defensive about including birds prematurely with respect to the title he gave the picture.

Obviously, it was important to Dennis to include the birds. Black birds appeared in 9 of the 20 drawings I collected from him. In each drawing, Dennis's black birds are an integral part of his pictorial statement.

Nowadays, black is often associated with death or negative characteristics. But it was not always so. In Paleolithic times, black was associated with the life-giving Goddess of fertility, who rises and dies with plant life (Gimbutas, 1989). In old, European times, black was still associated with the Earth Mother and fertile soil. Gimbutas (1989) reminds us of the many shrines that feature black Madonnas throughout the world. Miracles are attributed to these icons; they are visited and revered by devout pilgrims. Their blackness inspired archetypal associations that evoked a numinous experience for these pilgrims. Could Dennis's black birds possibly relate to some mysterious beginning for him? We will see in two of his later drawings that Dennis seems to address this very question.

It may also be worth noting, considering both his title, "In the Beginning," and his 6 black birds, that 6 months later Dennis celebrated another birthday. By then he had survived the NDE during his pulmonary surgery, had lived yet another year, dared to put behind him the fear of a premature death, and to look towards and hope for manhood.

Both folklore and religion contain many references to birds and angels as messengers from God; they often bring life-saving advice and direction. Vincent van Gogh's last painting, *Wheatfield With Crows*, (Fig. 4) depicts fields of grain (sometimes a symbol of fertility or new life) divided by a central path. In the foreground there is a path to the left and one to the right. Black birds swoop down from the sky, presumably to feed on the grain. Might a preconscious knowledge of his approaching death (suicide) have caused van Gogh to consider a life he had yet to live beyond death? Did he unconsciously and symbolically represent this with the life-giving grain field, ready for harvest, together with reference to a decision about his life's path he felt moved to take? Could the black birds, robbing the field of its harvest to sustain their own life and reproduce, represent both death and new life?

Bach (1990) refers to the black birds in van Gogh's last painting as ravens or crows; she points out that in European folklore they are an "omen of death and disaster," and that in this painting the artist forecast his early death (p. 90).

Might Dennis's black birds similarly represent a harbinger preparing his soul for death, or for "birth of the life . . . yet to live," as Marion Woodman (1985, p. 14) expresses it? Dennis's intuitive sense that the black birds had entered his drawing prematurely could mean he sensed it was too early for him to die. We might say he tried to die on the operating table but was compelled to survive. At a conscious, rational level, he excused the so-called mistake in his drawing by saying, "Oh well, I suppose it could be the sixth day." The birds could be reminders to his unconscious psyche that, for him, life is still beginning; he is coming out of adolescence, eager to become a man and to experience all that manhood implies for him before he dies.

Viewing Dennis's birds in all of the ways just discussed, and taking them in context with the rest of this drawing, we see that "in the beginning" of Dennis's manhood his future is threatened by CF. However, we also see that with this threat comes hope for new life.

I have already mentioned Dennis's fervent hope that a cure for CF would come in time to save his life. Although Dennis held this hope consciously, it is possible that preconsciously he was preparing for a new life only death could bring. It is a life he may have glimpsed briefly when his heart failed him on the operating table.

We see many signs of life that are accompanied by a shadow of death (represented by the volcano). This picture represents a state in which the unconscious reflects the psychic condition. The unconscious and conscious thoughts have agreed; the symbolic expressions in the drawing reflect and emphasize their agreement.

Thus, "In The Beginning" seems to say that although God created life, living with CF is like living in the valley below an active volcano – in the valley of the shadow of death, where destruction of life is inevitable. Acceptance of the reality of both life and death is expressed here. The adolescent boyhood fantasy of being indestructible – being immortal – does not appear here.

Compare this picture, the first of 20 collected from Dennis, to the first dream or sandtray arrangement (an expressive therapy medium) that an analysand presents to the analyst; in such instances the unconscious commonly presents the current situation and a possible outcome. Dennis's "In The Beginning" states graphically that there is physical life now; however, it is clearly destined to meet its destruction in just a matter of time. Meanwhile, Dennis can choose to identify some previously latent aspect of himself.

Dennis had daydreams and longings that could never be realized –
potential that would remain buried. Despite the small improvement
caused by Dennis's pulmonary surgery, he could not free himself of
the threatening illness.

Chapter 4 Notes

1. A pseudonym. Other family facts have been varied to further maintain the family's anonymity.
2. Although helicobacter pylori are the root cause of most gastric ulcers, stress that compromises immunity can, conceivably, increase susceptibility to infection.

Chapter 5

"TREASURE HARD TO ATTAIN"

Four months after making his drawing, "In The Beginning," Dennis drew an invited picture for me during a routine visit to the CF Outpatient Clinic. I call this untitled picture "The Sunken Treasure" (Fig. 5). It shows a treasure chest on the bottom of the ocean floor with a sea serpent swimming over it. The treasure and snake are reminiscent of the search for one's own true nature, the undiscovered, authentic self/Self with its guardian serpent or dragon hovering near it. (See Lecture Four in C. G. Jung's *Analytical Psychology*, the Tavistock lectures; he discusses the dream of a room of water under the cathedral of Toledo, and a serpent guarding a treasure.) Jung referred to this motif – a treasure with its guardian serpent or dragon that must be overcome – as the "treasure hard to attain." It represents the attainment of individuation by separating from the mother. Jung wrote about several myths that reflect through this motif the universal dilemma in the mother-son relationship (Jung 1968; 1976a).

Jung (1976a) informs us that the snake and water are both presented as "mother attributes" in the Miller fantasy about Hiawatha (p. 350). A son's spirit insists that he distinguish himself from his mother, but a childish wistfulness for her impedes the action he needs to take. This process leads the son to develop various anxieties that make it even more difficult for him to separate and travel his own path. The more he holds back and clings to the mother, instead of adapting to nature and following his instinct, the more impotent his psyche becomes. This makes him even more anxious.

When a boy is born with an illness such as CF, the mother-son relationship becomes even more complex because of the son's dependency upon the mother's solicitous concern for his health. Any conscientious mother in such a situation will show special concern, give extra nurture, and be more available than she would be to a healthy son.

This maternal absorption might act as a bewitchment upon the son, heightening his dependency, and strengthening his loyalty to the mother.

The courage to distinguish oneself from the mother is enhanced through the power of the father. A father must support his son and thus empower him to step into the masculine role. A father's responsibility is to transform the mother's boy into a man. He must break the mother's "spell" upon the boy and liberate him from eternal childhood. In primitive rites for initiating boys into manhood, the first step is separation from the mother. The father must equip the young hero; this paternal task is a major theme in Robert Bly's work with men's groups. In this context, I should note that Dennis's parents had separated two years previously, and had just recently reconciled and reunited. Dennis blamed his father for the separation and still felt some bitterness towards him.

At the top of the drawing we find a bright yellow, paper-chopped sun near the left corner. Its lightly-shaded rays shine outward in all directions, but no ray touches, must less penetrates, the surface of the water. This solar power is comparable to masculine consciousness, the psyche's spirited aspect that has the energy to penetrate the outer world. This masculine consciousness was mostly out of reach for Dennis. The light of the sun symbolizes consciousness. The sun is commonly linked with the father archetype; it can represent the human father, the Great Father, or the Heavenly Father. Dennis might have felt that what he needed at this time was not yet obtainable either from his human father, his Great Father within, or the Heavenly Father.

Dennis's water snake was colored earth brown and shaded over with dark green. We might consider this coloration as a relationship to Mother Earth and the regeneration of life. C. G. Jung (1976a) observed that a man's unconscious femininity, that is, his "inner woman" or the soul attributes of his psyche (referred to by Jung as the "anima"), was frequently a snake in his patients' images. Remember that in distinguishing himself from the mother, the boy must redeem the feminine – the hero must rescue the damsel. The task is to free himself from the mother without severing himself from his own inner feminine, or soul.

The serpent or snake is a complex symbol with myriad meanings, many of which are antithetic. A creature that sheds and renews its skin, the snake symbolizes death and regeneration. (For a more complete discussion of snake or serpent symbolism the reader should consult reference books on symbols and sacred images.)

One peculiar feature of Dennis's snake is its tail; it widens at the very end. Medical personnel who saw this picture tended to associate this unusual widening with clinical tools such as the stethoscope or bronchoscope used diagnostically in Dennis's medical care. With some imagination, we can also view this feature anthropomorphically as the snake's vulva; as such, it is dilated as though preparing to give birth (birth of a new ego — a new persona? — the rebirth of Self?).

Part of a sculpture preserved from 19th century South India includes a minor female goddess with a phallic-like creature, perceived to be a "serpent of creative energy," bounding out from her vulva (photographed in Cooper, 1978, p. 149). The phallus, or linga, as it is known in Hindu, is an ancient, sacred symbol in Indian culture (Gimbutas, 1989). The linga represents the masculine creative principle, cosmic creation and renewal of life. Male psychic energy needs to flow outward to connect a boy with his objective reality while simultaneously finding relatedness and meaning via his kinship with the feminine principle. When male psychic energy is projected back into the mother, the son remains separated from, and unconscious of, his true nature.

Dennis's snake has both masculine and feminine qualities, spirit and soul. Is the snake thus an unconscious compensation for what Dennis lacks and needs, a differentiation and then an integration of the masculine ego with the feminine principle? Symbology associates the presence of a snake with pregnancy. Dennis may be laboring to bring about a new "birth" which would undoubtedly assure him of attaining the treasure of the authentic self — a personality differentiated from his parents.

As Jung (1968) pointed out in his fourth Tavistock lecture, there is something very mysterious about the nature of the treasure. "It is connected with the serpent in a strange way; the peculiar nature of the serpent denotes the character of the treasure as though the two things were one" (p. 132).

A man's anima — his so-called feminine, soul side — emerges from his impressions of various females who influence his life. In childhood, the anima is formulated largely by his associations with his mother. The male's soul quality, which includes his concept of feminine nature, is largely unconscious in a male; this is especially so in his early life. But, if a man can somehow reach within himself to embrace his internal mother, she can function for him as a guide to other unconscious contents and mediate between the ego and the whole Self.

Therefore, the anima is an important tool in a man's individuation process. His individuation calls for distinguishing himself from the physical mother. Until this task is accomplished a man will project his unconscious feminine nature onto his own mother, and quite possibly on to other women (as mother types).

By not differentiating and integrating his "feminine aspect," a man's relationship with women might be freighted with paranoid feelings of being devoured, overpowered, or possessed by his female contacts. This situation is particularly threatening to a romantic friendship; it blocks a man's ability to make a commitment. When a woman is ready to make a commitment she expects this readiness to be reciprocated. Unfortunately, the man perceives her readiness as an attempt to devour the masculine spirit. The man then feels a love-hate relationship to the woman not unlike the love-hate a boy feels towards his mother when he needs to distinguish himself from her.

Admittedly, the simplified description I have given is just one of many forms a mother-complex may assume – and its effects on the psyche of an incomplete, immature male can vary. Furthermore, I have concentrated on the traditional viewpoints without attempting to apply fascinating and controversial post-Jungian theories. It is not my purpose to examine masculine psychology in depth; I intend only to make the reader aware of the problematic nature of the mother-son relationship. We will consider this issue from the vantage point of the mytho-poetic Men's Movement, which studies and amplifies the poignant drama of a boy's coming of age. Robert Bly, Michael Meade, and others articulate this psychological development from a standpoint of analytical psychology.

If no marked pathology owing to abuse or deprivation exists in the mother-son relationship, a boy's love for his mother will be evoked by the positive maternal attributes that have nurtured and protected him; his hate originates from the threat or fear of being forever bound to mother so that he must give up his own way, that is, sacrifice himself. If he does not allow the mother to "die," then he will "die." This is when the hero is needed.

I use the term hero in a broad, archetypal and classical sense to represent the courageous man who sacrifices his life to rescue and preserve "the good and the true" from "the evil, false, or destructive." However, the mytho-poetic Men's Movement generally refers to the hero as an immature characteristic of the boy, a transitional phase that, in a healthy psyche, develops into the "warrior." The Men's Movement uses the term "warrior" in the sense of "hero" as we find it in most literature and in the works of C. G. Jung.

If the ego, the conscious mind, cannot accept the need to integrate masculine spirit with feminine soul, it regresses back to the mother, to unconsciousness. So long as the son is unconscious of his unique self, his psychic energy is possessed by the mother.

The snake in Dennis's drawing contains symbolically the unconscious state and the poison of self-doubt that prevents the son from obeying instinct. Failure of the hero to emerge may result in, among other possibilities, a state of perpetual adolescence – the *Puer Aeternus* (Eternal Child) entrapment. (See von Franz's *Puer Aeternus: The Problem of the Puer Aeternus* and R. Moore's and D. Gillette's *King, Warrior, Magician, Lover.*) In its immature form (refusal to take responsibility for one's own life, to find one's own soul and to differentiate from the mother), we can observe in the male only the negative shadow of the puer. Without the positive aspects of the puer, the Divine Child, a man lacks imagination and the spirit of play.

According to C. G. Jung (1976a), snake dreams suggest a disagreement between the ego and the instinctual aspect of the Self; the snake characterizes the foreboding facet of the conflict. But Jung (1976a) also refers to the snake as the hero – "the sacrificer and the sacrificed." He reminds us of early traces of hero-snake identities such as the ancient myth of Cecrops, in which the hero Cecrops is half snake and half man (p. 382). Hillman (1973) comments on the serpent's mythological meanings in writing about the Puer problem:

> [The serpent] is a power, a numinosity, a primordiality of religion. Its meanings renew with its skin and peel off as we try to grasp hold . . . . The slippery flow of meanings make it possible for Great Goddess and *daimon* to merge, to lose their distinction, so that by means of the serpent . . . the mother gets at the puer and brings his fall into heroism. She tempts him into the fight for deliverance from her (p. 112).

All this information illustrates the complexity of the serpent symbol and its myriad associations and meanings. In the repository of the collective unconscious there are many archetypes that may be portrayed by the serpent. (One can easily get carried away by such archetypal symbols; they can constrict our thoughts and devour us – like a serpent!) Let us be content with our exploration of the widening of the snake's tail as an image of giving birth. We have covered enough material to show that this unusual feature in Dennis's drawing is meaningful.

Another peculiar feature of Dennis's snake is the tiny protrusion near its throat. Might this be a beard? Dead heroes cast as bearded snakes were worshiped in ancient Greece. Some bearded snakes were reported to be gods. (I have been asked whether Dennis ever had a tracheoscopy or tracheostomy; he never had either.)

We do not know whether Dennis consciously made this mark at the snake's throat or whether the unusual tail was a conscious intention; could they be accidents? Analytical psychology argues that there are no accidents! As Furth (1988) points out, we need to consider every "accident" in a drawing as a form of parapraxis. (He borrows Freud's term for slips of the tongue and the sudden forgetfulness of names or other information with which we are normally quite familiar.) Furth says that under every so-called "accident" or error in a drawing a repression exists (p. 17). A particular pattern of psychic energy wants to come to consciousness through such "accidents." These are quite common in both spontaneous and invited drawings.

If we view Dennis's snake anthropomorphically, we might take the protrusion in question to suggest the Adam's apple. According to the creation myth, Adam ate the fruit of the Tree of Knowledge of Good and Evil that Eve offered. A morsel of the forbidden fruit stuck in Adam's throat – hence "Adam's apple." Adam was intended to be immortal, according to the more traditional creation myth, but eating the fruit from the Tree of Knowledge brought Adam consciousness, and with it mortality. The Adam's apple is regarded as a physical reminder of man's human nature and his instinctive hunger to understand the mysteries of life.

It is not the godlike heroism from Greek mythology that is needed to bring about ego-consciousness and individuation; it is done by human ego strength that honors instinct. The main objective of all hero myths is the development of ego-consciousness. Human beings must become aware of their own strengths and weaknesses so that they can adapt to the many challenges of life (Jung, von Franz, Henderson, Jacobi, & Jaffe, 1964).

In the upper right quadrant of Dennis's drawing, we count 10 black birds above the surface of the water where the sky is sparsely and faintly shaded with pale blue. Ten is reported to be the perfect number, the number that contains all numbers. It represents all things and all possibilities. Ten is also associated with completeness and perfection. God gave Moses ten commandments. In Greek mythology, ten is the number of journeys completed and the return to origins by the hero, as in the myths of Odysseus and Troy (Cooper, 1978).

Sandplay therapists observe that figures placed in opposite corners often represent what needs to be integrated. Because Dennis's birds give an aesthetic balance to the underwater serpent, we should study these two components – birds of the sky and chthonic serpent – to discover how these opposites relate to each other. Do they complement each other or is their relationship compensatory?

Before attempting to answer that question, we should consider a commonality between Dennis's birds and his sea serpent; both can live in two environments. The snake adapts equally to water and land; the birds take to earth and air. This characteristic is a universal clue denoting the animals as symbols of transcendence. That birds are symbols of release and liberation reiterates their transcendental character in symbolic expression. Dennis portrayed this fifteen months later in one of his drawings ("Free." See Chapter 6, Fig. 7). Birds are sometimes represented as a spiritual guide, like angels, that give advice to the hero. In some tales, birds are carriers of the truth, as in the Grimm's story of "The Three Little Birds." Spiritual guidance and truth support transcendence.

The snake suggests descending into the depths of the unconscious, into our chthonic, instinctual nature. From here we can bring to consciousness that which would enable us to confront the inner realities of shadow and of soul and spirit. As the ego mingles with this congregation of psychic parts, the individual can ascend to further spiritual heights, as represented by the birds.

We have answered our question whether the birds and snake are complementary or compensatory. Dennis's birds and snake are complementary aspects of transcendence. These images introduce an element of suspense: for Dennis, that first heroic step towards individuation and transcendence is to leave his childish attachment to Mother. It is a formidable task for one who is facing death! He cannot avoid his own death, but by simply regressing, he can keep alive his bonding with Mother and therefore a sense of being anchored in a safe harbor. Which way will he choose? Will the treasure remain lost forever at the bottom of the ocean? Will Dennis's potential as a man remain in the depths of the sea of unconsciousness?

Dennis was trying to transcend his dependency on the feminine realm for sustenance and to identify more closely with the masculine way of life his older brother (a successful photo journalist) had already begun. But Dennis's attitude towards maternal dependency (doubtless more critical because of his disease) was not the only change taking place. Dennis was already coming close to the end of his life.

We see that he drew the mud or sand bottom under the water in a narrow section stretching across the bottom of the page. In the middle we find an object that Dennis described as a piece of coral, heavily outlined with black and filled in with red. Additional black markings on this object suggest rocklike contours. Because coral is the skeletal remains of anthozoic animals, we might view it as a symbol of death, or of a previous life.

There is another interesting parallel between coral and CF. The tissue of certain corals is known to fill with water. Similarly, in one afflicted with CF, certain human tissue retains fluid and the sinuses congest with mucous. Further, when coral is exposed to air during a low tide, like CF, it produces mucous.

Additionally, beautiful coral is a highly prized specimen of the sea – a treasure from the ocean. In some ways, the coral might be a more accurate representation of Dennis's life than the treasure chest. The coral depicts the treasure of Dennis's life; it is a life made vulnerable by CF. The treasure chest seems to correspond more appropriately to Dennis's dream of a life cured of the disease – a treasure extremely hard, if even possible, to attain in Dennis's lifetime.

Close by the coral, to the left as perceived by the viewer, we see the chest of red jewels (a color representing life and passion) on a purple background. There is a string of light blue jewels hanging over one side (the side nearest the coral). Purple is a royal color befitting the lining of such a precious "treasure hard to attain." Bach (1990) tells us that pale blue, seen in the overhanging beads, might "reflect loss of vitality," or that we might see it as a "color of distance" (p. 50). There is no dispute that the hospitalization, when this drawing was made, marked a time when Dennis's vitality was low. Did Dennis feel compelled to withdraw from his present environment in anticipation of death?

Joan Kellogg (1984) points out that pale blue is the body chakras' color for the throat. She says this chakra is associated emotionally with the sustaining birth waters and the "ideal mother which each of us deserved and none of us got, the mother who . . . supplies our every need and requires nothing in return" (p. 78). The pale blue appears on a piece of jewelry worn around the neck, bearing out its association with the throat chakra; CF is a disease that chokes one. We have already considered the smothering aspects of the negative mother complex; that brings us back to Bach's view of blue as a color of distance.

Dennis needs to distance himself psychologically from his mother while relying on her to help with some of his home treatments. The lifeblood red jewels and pale blue necklace sybolize the tension Dennis experiences in his struggle to individuate and in his struggle to hold on to life in the battle with CF.

The lid of the treasure chest is open; it is pale yellow and has dark green shading on either side. Dennis referred to this green part as "that junk that grows on things under the water." One cannot fail to associate this statement with the "junk" – the infections – that frequently grows in Dennis's own "chest" (lungs)! This verbiage is not unlike the play on words that often appear in dreams.

The treasure chest has a heavily-colored yellow mark, shaped like part of a circle, at the middle of the top edge of the lid. Dennis said this was the clasp that locked the chest. We have seen another part of a circle in the same shade of yellow, which Dennis used to depict his (paper-chopped) sun. If we dare regard this part of the chest as complementing what is missing from the sun, we could say that the father archetype, in the depths of the unconscious, is the key for unlocking the treasure for Dennis.

In summary, it is soul-relatedness supported by his masculine nature that will help Dennis experience his true, natural self. We see that quite possibly Dennis is trying to take responsibility for his own life, as evidenced by the unlocked chest and the treasure that is exposed (at least under water). Retrieving the treasure, bringing it up out of the water, is yet another task and a tricky one at that. The son must help himself without offending the mother, who is always ready to pamper him. He must do this by calling upon the masculine energy that lies deep within himself. It is this energy that will empower the boy to define himself as an individual and to relate simultaneously to his creative spirit and his nurturing soul.

We noted earlier that the rays of his sun do not penetrate the water. This feature recalls that recent period when Dennis's father was absent. If a son is wounded by his father's absence, the boy may have to find his own way to connect with the life-giving masculine energy. To do this he must experience and activate the masculine archetype contained in the objective psyche (the collective unconscious). This manner of initiating masculine individuation is extremely difficult, particularly when not aided by a strong male role-model or a professional counselor.

We see in Dennis's picture an array of underwater plants, some dark green, some a pale yellow-green. Two have combinations of yellow-green and brown, and one has heavily applied brown. The stems and all the branches of the tallest, centrally-located plant lean towards the right. This is the same direction that the snake is heading. The branches of this plant rise almost above the water line. The darker green might be interpreted as representing healthy growth. Yellow-green, the weaker hue, usually appears when health is declining or returning from a low condition (Bach, 1969).

The underwater growth represents both Dennis's physical and psychological growth. From the physical perspective, the section of dark green "seaweed" (as Dennis called it) on the left corresponds to a previous time of better health. The plants' stringy quality reminds one of Dennis's skinny frame. He was always underweight and appeared undernourished; this is a typical symptom of advanced CF.

Dennis's decline in health, with more frequent relapses (expressed by the lighter shade of green?), marks an emotionally stressful period for him. It is a period beset with frequent ups and downs, progression and regression, hope and depression in sympathetic response to his physical episodes of stabilization and relapse. At times, he seemed to be reconciled with life's nearing its close and accepting his fate courageously. Other times, he appeared to deny that his life was ending. This vacillation continued until about eight months before he died.

The left side of a drawing frequently corresponds psychologically to one's past life or to the unconscious; the right side often refers to the present or the future, or perhaps to what is already conscious or just entering consciousness. We can almost feel the impressive plant in approximately the center of the page (next to the coral) being pushed to the right by the strong flow of the water. We might take this plant to suggest a move towards consciousness, or possibly looking to the future, intently anticipating what is yet to come. The coral just to the right of this plant has already been mentioned as a symbol of death or as a metaphor for the fluid retention Dennis often experienced and for his esteem for both his personal self and his inner Self.

Dennis desperately wished to be a hero who could survive the ordeal of CF and thus live to claim the "treasure hard to attain." Perhaps he believed that if he could only overcome the disease and grow normally the victory would automatically enable him to individuate into manhood – to distinguish himself from his mother and even outshine his father. As it was, the threats CF imposed on his development restrained his adolescence. His dependency on his family, especially his mother, for both physical and moral help made growing up an especially difficult challenge.

C. G. Jung (1976a) referred to the dual aspects of the mother, which Samuels (1985) says can be understood as either (1) the duality between one's personal mother and one's mother archetype, or (2) the duality between the good and bad revelations of either the biological or archetypal mother.

I submit that a child with CF may unconsciously project the "bad mother" (witch or vampire) onto the disease. CF might even encourage such a projection; it is a genetically inherited disease that can, by virtue of the mother's transmitting both members of the pair of chromosomes, make her solely responsible for the affliction. This situation could lead a boy with CF to feel that he has a double battle to fight: the destructive power of CF and the enchanting powers of the comforting mother. The "enchantress mother" who wants to hold on to her child represents the shadow side of the good mother.

Failure to overcome CF means physical death; failure to overcome his infantile desire to be with his mother means sacrificial death of the authentic self/Self. Further, a boy's anxiety over separation from his mother would be compounded by hospitalizations, particularly if they occur during the first two or three years of his life.

Jung's description of the mother's duality might well be expanded for patients with CF (or other life-threatening genetic disorders). This expanded concept recognizes a duality between the enchanting powers of the human mother (and the temptation to identify with her) and the inescapable "spell" of the evil, genetically-inherited disease. It springs from the child's instinct to split the mother into "good" and "bad" parts. The "CF witch mother" is forever working to pull the child into her underworld of death, while the "enchantress mother" competes with her to keep the child alive by holding on to her child.

This duality between an enchanting, possessive mother and a witchy (or vampiric), possessive mother can be experienced by girls as well as by boys. I believe this duality presents a uniquely critical barrier to the development of the masculine ego; as such, it imprisons males in the darkness of unconsciousness. (Feminine individuation would also be negatively affected, but not in the same way. For now, we confine our study to the masculine individuation process as experienced by Dennis.)

These dual states are experienced initially through the primitive psyche of a child. Beyond experiencing bad and good aspects of the human mother, the subject with CF (or any disease inherited from the mother) posits the enchantress, shadow side of the "good" mother; for the "bad" mother the subject posits a profoundly evil aspect – the passing of the "bad gene" – that is life-threatening. While this clash of "CF witch mother" with "enchantress mother" is applicable to the human, personal mother, it is conceivable that this dynamic could even influence one's sense of the archetypal mother.

The personification of CF as a witch mother (a much greater evil than the seemingly benign enchantress mother whom one can hardly bear to leave) does not imply that children with CF consciously resent and blame their mothers for wickedly imposing the disease on them. Possibly, there is a primordial tendency to hold the mother more responsible than the father for giving life and nurture. This might be related to primitive bonding begun in utero and reinforced for the newborn by the familiar sound of the mother's voice experienced before the actual birth. The infant's pre- and postnatal maternal experiences thus seem to predispose an irrational tendency to hold the mother responsible for whatever life brings. For this reason, children with CF may unconsciously link their mother with their disease, (and even consciously associate mother as the giver of life and with it the disease). Although maturity and sophistication may bring some conscious resentment and anger towards both parents for bearing the gene that so unfairly seals the child's fate, such feelings, whenever they exist, are most often repressed.

A 9-year-old female patient in my London study could not directly confront her mother with her emotions related to her CF; she slipped notes to her, on the mother's bed pillow, expressing her anguish and insinuating that her mother was responsible for the disease and its out-come. She drew an octagon on one such note. According to Cooper (1978), this is a symbol of regeneration and rebirth. In Christian churches, the baptismal font is often built in the shape of an octagon. Inside the octagon she wrote: "Cystic Fibrosis – I am cystic." Beneath this drawing she added:

> I am cystic. Why did you bring me up like this? I hate it having fissieo [*sic*]. ["Physio" was the term used at Great Ormond Street to designate bronchial drainage treatments to the chest given by the physiotherapists]. I want to be like the others. Some cystics can't fite [*sic*] desieses [*sic*]. Everyone asks me why I'm cystic. i [*sic*] hate it. Mum help me. You no [*sic*] I hate it. I'm even crying about this letter I'm writing to you. Help me please, [Here she signed her name], Your cystic child. by[e] SOB SOB cry

Inside each letter *O* in "SOB SOB," she drew faces with turned-down mouths, added ears to the sides, and on the tops of these "heads," drew hair standing on end.

The closest Dennis ever came to revealing such feelings in his draw-ings happened two years later in a cartoon-style drawing. It employed gallows humor to depict his impending death. We will consider that picture in a later chapter.

Figure 1. Drawing by a 30-year-old woman.

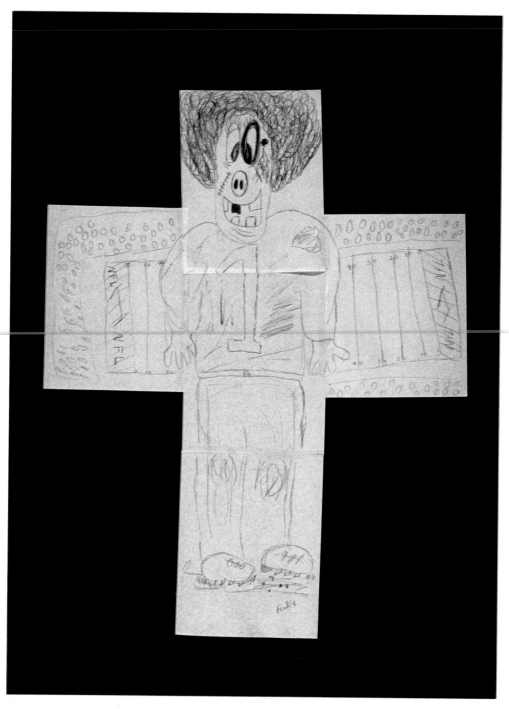

Figure 2. Dirty Quarterback.

Figure 3. In the Beginning.

Figure 4. Wheatfield With Crows (Vincent van Gogh)
Amsterdam, Van Gogh Museum (Vincent van Gogh Foundation).

Figure 5. Sunken Treasure.

Figure 6. Remembrance.

Figure 7. Free.

Figure 8. Bad Lands.

Figure 9. Smoking Volcano.

Figure 10. Beginning.

Figure 11. Ended.

Figure 12. Mountain and Cactus.

Figure 13. The "red" Bud.

Figure 14. Setting a Record.

Figure 15. Life Begins.

Figure 16. Fence and Barn.

Figure 17. Energy.

Figure 18. Budding Rose.

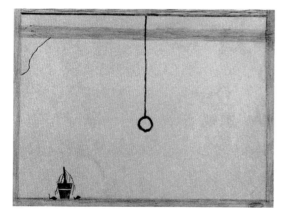

Figure 19. Imagine.

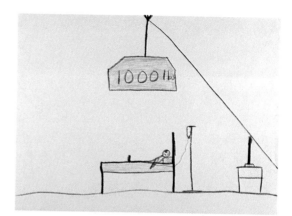

Figure 20. Self Portrait, cartoon style.

Figure 21. The Sun.

Figure 22. Life Ending.

Figure 23. Shamrock.

Figure 24. Leprechaun's Hat.

Figure 25. Easter.

Figure 26. Ronda, An Angel!

Figure 27. Cat, Dog, and Mysterious Boy.

Figure 28. Flying Car.

Figure 29. Batman and Superman.

Figure 30. In Final Battle.

Figure 31. All New.

Chapter 6

FREE AS A BIRD

Dennis produced his next picture at the third of his clinic visits, which occurred once every six weeks. (I was in London studying with Susan Bach during his first two visits.) His picture was an invited drawing he titled "Remembrance" (Fig. 6). He told me he gave the picture this title because he had recently noticed a tree with a nest of newly hatched baby birds. He didn't know why, but this scene deeply touched him and he said he always wanted to remember it.

As Dennis shared his feelings with me on seeing the birds' nest, it seemed that he wished to make permanent the memory of a season he might never see again. I recalled how difficult it is to say goodbye to something we love; it hurts to realize we might never see this person or place again. At such times' we savor and cherish all our memories associated with the place or the ones we are leaving. We yearn to hold on to what we are about to lose; we soak up what we see like taking in a big, thirsty gulp of water. All our senses become so acute that we seem to experience for the first time what we already know and have often sensed. This emotional experience is a form of anticipatory grief.

Twenty-three months after drawing his "Remembrance," death separated Dennis from life on earth. Surely other meaningful things and special people brought happiness to Dennis's life. He would want to remember them as much as the birds' nest. Why did a tree containing a bird's nest and its nestlings strike such a sentimental chord?

The egg that hatches new life is a symbol of death and rebirth. The death-rebirth archetype is a prominent theme throughout Dennis's series of 20 drawings. I found it recurring also in other CF patients' drawings. The idea of rebirth gives meaning to life, and hope for what awaits one beyond death. I have found consistently that persons who believe in life after death face dying with more peace and reconciliation than those do who lack such a faith. I believe that by relating to the archetype of rebirth, one provides compensation to the psyche. This compensation is the hope that sustains the soul during the dying process. When the spirit embraces the death-rebirth epiphany, the soul finds contentment.

The baby birds, hungry beaks open, are dependent upon their parents to bring back food to nourish them. They have not learned to fly and forage by themselves. This dependent aspect of the birds characterizes Dennis's dependency upon his own parents – especially his mother. Will it soon be time for Dennis to leave the nest and fly? Will this kind of freedom leave Dennis feeling lonely, with wistful memories of how Mother made life feel so safe and good? Consciously, Dennis is seriously aware of his physical deterioration and he knows (at least *unconsciously*) that he has very little time left. When he saw the baby birds in their nest, he may well have wondered whether he would live to see another spring.

His unconscious psyche may be impressed with this scene, but for a different reason. Dennis's illness had prolonged his adolescence. *Unconsciously*, he may have sensed that there is not much time to work through the task of leaving the nest because his days are numbered.

Psychological literature takes notice of the ambivalence of the adolescent male who wishes to live independently from his mother, to distance himself from her, and simultaneously fears doing that very thing (discussed in Chapter 4). If Dennis cannot free himself from his mother he will never become conscious of who he really is. If he cannot free himself from CF he cannot live to become who he has a potential to be. Either dilemma is pressure enough for one in Dennis's shoes; adolescence is a chaotic, stormy road to travel.

Health care providers forget all too often the double burden that a life-threatening illness imposes on a young person's psyche. I believe that those of us who understand the psychological ramifications of a life-threatening illness with children and adolescents have a responsibility to stir up the medical profession's interest in this issue. It seems to me that the emotional-spiritual needs of dying children and adolescents have been mostly ignored by the medical profession, at least in the USA. Exceptions might be sensitive pediatric oncologists and a few other atypical physicians or surgeons.

There are yet other features in this drawing that deserve mention. Dennis's tree, with its two arm-like branches cradling the birds' nest, gives the drawing a maternal characteristic. J. C. Cooper (1978) tells us that the tree symbolizes "the feminine principle, the nourishing, sheltering, protecting, supporting aspect of the Great Mother . . ." (p. 176). The tree seems to bring us back to the mother-son relationship.

Dennis's tree is paper-chopped at both the bottom and the top edges. Psychologically, paper-chopping at the bottom suggests that one is especially reality-bound or perhaps feeling insecure and needing support. Paper-chopping at the top suggests high aspirations along with a tendency to fantasize about what has not been achieved or has otherwise been denied. The chopping at the bottom of Dennis's tree is an exaggeration of the grounding of its base. This would express Dennis's knowledge that he is gradually losing a hold on life and his need to feel secure about his life support. The paper-chopped branches at the top remind me of Dennis's fantasy that a cure for CF would come in time to save his life.

The right side of the tree reaches for the golden rays of the sun. Dennis's sun, also paper-chopped in the upper right corner, radiates eight large rays and nine smaller rays that shine even farther out from the sun. At the time I received this drawing, I could not find the numbers eight or nine related to any unit of time significant in Dennis's life; I still have not done so. (I would like to have known in which month Dennis's parents reunited.)

J. C. Cooper (1978) reports that eight is the number for new beginnings (like octaves repeating the musical scale) and is also the number for "paradise regained . . . regeneration; resurrection . . . ," and that both eight and nine signify completion (p. 118). Moreover, nine represents "fulfillment; attainment; beginning and end; the whole . . . ," as well as "the Earthly Paradise" (p. 118). Furthermore, odd numbers are held to be Yang or masculine, and the even ones to be Yin, or feminine. I have noted earlier the relationship between the sun and the father archetype, and that the sun can also be considered to represent God the Father.

Dennis's tree might thus be viewed as joining opposites: heaven and earth, father and mother, spirit and soul, masculine and feminine, or death and birth. These opposites suggest that Dennis's individuation process requires him to join his masculine spirit to his feminine soul. He must descend into unconscious depths to learn both his strengths and his weaknesses, his limitations and his potential. Through this experience, he will become enlightened about his true nature. Such an experience will empower him to take his place beside his father; he will no longer have to live "through" his mother by identifying with or projecting onto her.

This process represents death of the old, underdeveloped ego and birth of the new, enlightened ego. Unconsciously, Dennis is striving to transcend boyhood and become a man. The golden sun is a metaphor for the treasure of the authentic self/Self; Dennis's Tree of Life reaches to be nourished by this treasure. The roots of the tree must penetrate the earth, the symbol of man's anima (defined in Chapter 5), and thereby find the "gold" that is buried deep within.

Connection with his outer world and the father archetype gives Dennis opportunity to encounter his masculine spirit. Connection with his inner world, the world of the soul, provides Dennis a healthy fusion of feminine feeling with masculine spirit and instinct. We can say that he is rewarded by gold (what is treasured) from above and from below, from his outer and inner reality, and that this reward can transform his life.

The pallid leaves on his tree outnumber the healthy green ones. About eight months later, there was a remarkable decline in Dennis's health, and during the following six months he had to be hospitalized four times.

The black bird (raven?) is also prominent here; it appears to fly towards the upper left corner, just beyond the tree. If we consider this location of the bird to be the place of the western horizon where the sun sets, we can equate this position with the ending of life – when the "sun will set" for Dennis. Susan Bach's empirical studies (1990) reveal that movement of objects or figures into the upper left corner, "upwards to the beyond . . ." and "where the sun is last seen . . ." (p. 39), often relates to a patient's illness that is taking him or her slowly out of life; she says that such findings can be read as forecasting signs.[1] However, by completing what is missing of the circle of Dennis's full sun, we observe that most of it has not yet come into his picture. (It was eight more months before Dennis's health made it impossible for him to continue his college education.)

It is quite possible that Dennis consciously intended the raven to be the mother of the nestlings. If that is so, we must note that his placement of the bird and his heavy application of the black crayon suggest an unconscious sense that his attitude towards his mother (prime nourisher and protector) must die. The raven's flight into the upper left corner shows how one symbol can simultaneously express conditions of both soma and psyche (the mother complex and the approach of physical death).

Is it possible that this scene moved Dennis because of nostalgia? To anticipate saying goodbye to childhood and goodbye to one's earthly life must surely evoke a huge sense of loss and intense remembrance of what one is leaving behind.

Dennis completed his drawing, "Remembrance," by printing the letters of his title slanted towards the sun; he used the red crayon – the color of life-giving blood and a color representing strong feelings.

Early the following winter, when Dennis was 20 years old, he was hospitalized for a relapse of CF. On the last day of January, he drew a picture he titled "Free" (Fig. 7), and said of it, "This is water and a bird flying overhead, and there is a bright sun. I named it 'Free' because I thought if they came up with a cure for CF, then I would be as free as this bird." Dennis's bird is black, as usual; so is his title in the upper right corner. He printed his name and added the date, in pencil, on the reverse side of this corner. The final "*E*" of "Free" is superimposed on the first three letters of "Dennis;" we can see this if we hold the reverse side to the light. I believe we can regard this positioning of Dennis's name as an unconscious way of showing his conscious, strong desire to claim the freedom from CF that Dennis fantasizes. But there is another freedom that Dennis's psyche is moving towards and he might not be aware of this; it is his movement towards freedom from childhood and dependency on his mother.

The partial sun in the upper left corner is vibrant with red-orange layered over golden yellow. Pale yellow rays come down from the sun and nearly touch the water. Pale yellow is blended into the blue water, possibly intended to represent the sun's rays. (Dennis used the yellow drawing pencil here, but its mixing with the blue gives a greenish cast.) A faint, horizontal shading in blue suggests the sky. Color has been applied most strongly on the bird and the sun, and next, on the title "Free." This aspect suggests that the masculine spirit needs to "shine" (be activated) to free Dennis from his childish desire to stay with his mother.

What a frightfully difficult task it is for a young man so critically ill to attempt independence. Given his present condition and grim physical outlook, he can easily rationalize the impracticality of moving in this direction. This picture seems to summarize Dennis's continuing struggle since adolescence to overcome what hinders his becoming a man. On the one hand, this hindrance is a dependency on mother and feminine domination of his personality. On the other hand, it is CF that threatens to take his life before he can achieve full manhood.

It was now the winter of 1980. Two days after drawing "Free," and while still hospitalized, Dennis volunteered to draw another picture he called "Bad Lands" (Fig. 8). The title suggests parallels with Dennis's diseased life. The term badlands refers to barren, eroded soil, like the badlands of South Dakota and parts of Nebraska. Besides being literally barren (sterile), Dennis does not yet have a sense of accomplishment as a man. Moreover, his lungs have been increasingly eroded by infections.

His picture contains a desert-like foreground with a large brown rock in the lower left side; on the right side, an animal's skull with horns appears to be propped on a stick erected on the ground. On the horizon, which is a little more than two-thirds of the way up the paper, 2 mountains are centered with the sun rising between them.

Upon finishing this drawing, Dennis commented, "This [drawing] correlates with my disease. The 'bad lands' represent the rough times I've had with CF and the fact that with this disease I've not been able to do too much. The two mountains I think of as being the hurdles that I so often have to overcome in fighting my disease. I put a little green growth on them because I thought that even though I've been unhealthy, there have been some times that it's not been all bad — times when I have been healthy. So, I thought that there should be at least *some* foliage, some life thriving." Then he went on to say "The sun is rising." When I asked Dennis to tell me all that he could about the figure in the lower right side, he simply said that it was an animal skull.

The sun is brightly colored; just like the sun in the previous picture, it has orange blended over a golden yellow. Pale yellow rays create a continuous band of color spreading from the sun and rising over the tops of the mountains. Dennis informed me that he liked to put suns in his pictures. I wonder whether Dennis's affinity for the sun related unconsciously to a vision experienced during his near-death episode, or if it signaled his need to bring more light and energy to his masculine ego.

Upon completing the picture, he used a pencil to print the title, "Bad Lands," in the upper left corner. (Dennis also used the pencil to print his name and the date on the back of the paper. He placed it right

beside the animal skull that shines through from the front.) Art therapists have noticed that items drawn with pencil often suggest something that is impermanent.

We might take the animal skull as a sign of death or of a life that has
already been lived and ended. The skull, the rock to the left, and the
sun, stand out as the most heavily colored objects in the drawing. The
rock and the skull demand our attention not only because they are in
the foreground, but because there are no other objects in the barren
land that stretches behind them. Moreover, the skull appears to be a
sign or a memorial; it is purposely propped on the stick (bone?) stuck
in the ground.

A student called my attention to the similarity between Dennis's animal skull on the stick and a Cheyenne Indian ritual rattle with horns,
pictured in J. C. Cooper's symbols encyclopedia (1978, p. 85.) The
Indian ritual rattle was used for demon exorcism, for shamanistic and
puberty rites, and for rites for the dead (Leach & Fried, Eds., 1972).
Traditionally, the head of the rattle was made of gourd or a wood carving filled with maize kernels or seeds. The stick or phallic staff on a rattle designated it as the male type; the female type was usually made of
cocoons and bells. "The male type [of ritual rattle] is associated with
the vision quest for renewed life and cure . . ." (Leach & Fried, 1972,
p. 927).

If we look carefully at the skull, we can see a design between the
dark eye sockets; it vaguely resembles a flower or an ear of corn.
Dennis drew it with a graphite pencil – an erasable medium. This tentative rendering suggests some ambiguity facing Dennis. He did not
admit to associating any particular animal with the skull, but it appears
without question to be a member of the bovine family.

Let us now consider what these three objects – sun, bull or ox skull,
and rock – have in common, and how this commonality might relate
to Dennis. We must first consider some pre-Christian beliefs. Several
thousand centuries before the birth of Jesus, goddess-centered religion
was practiced in a large part of the world. According to Gimbutas
(1989), goddess worship lasted much longer than the Indo-European
and Christian religions, and thus our Western psyche seems to have
been permanently imprinted by this historical period.

Practices and images from ancient cultures often emerge from the
collective unconscious in the dreams and visions of contemporary
folk. Jung illustrated this fact dramatically by reporting the accounts of

a vision and a dream. A schizophrenic patient reported his vision to Jung (1976a). In this vision, he saw an erect penis on the sun, and when he moved his head from side to side, the sun's penis moved also; it showed the changing directions of wind. Jung was puzzled over this bizarre hallucination until he read about some visions in an ancient, recovered text presumed to pertain to the Mithraic liturgy.

The text refers to a tube that hangs down from the disc of the sun; this is said to be the origin of the creative, fruitful wind. The ancient writing said that the tube's turning generated a corresponding wind. When it turned eastward, a boundless west wind blew; if it turned westward, the corresponding east wind blew. Jung discovered that the insane man's vision coincided astonishingly with the description of the tube's movement in this Mithraic text. However, Jung could not understand how this patient, who had no more than a secondary school education, could have any knowledge of the solar phallus, its movement, and the origin of the wind described in the Mithraic text.

Jung (1976a) observed that the first edition of this mythological text appeared several years after the patient had been hospitalized; he concluded that this case represented "not a question of inherited ideas, but of an inborn disposition to produce parallel thought-formations, or of identical psychic structures common to all men . . ." (pp. 157-158). Such identical structures, common to all humankind, comprise what Jung called the collective unconscious.

An uneducated African-American man, whom Jung met in the U.S., told Jung (1976b) that he dreamed of a man being crucified on a wheel. It would not be unusual for this man to dream of a crucifixion on a cross, but this dream was most uncommon. Jung immediately recognized the image of the ancient sun-wheel on which a man is crucified as sacrifice to conciliate the sun-god. This type of crucifixion is portrayed in the Greek myth of Ixion, whose evil deeds against men and gods are punished; Zeus had Ixion fastened to a perpetually turning wheel. Jung could not prove the American man had never been exposed to Greek mythology or seen a drawing of Ixion's crucifixion before dreaming of it, but it was highly doubtful that the man had any conscious model for this idea. This case taught Jung that there are no cultural or racial barriers in the collective unconscious.

When I point out the correspondence between a motif in a child's drawing and an ancient myth, students will protest that the child couldn't possibly be acquainted with the obscure myth. I then tell them about these two incidents from Jung's practice and experience. Thus, we will continue here to examine mythology and ancient religions as they might relate to Dennis's drawing, "Bad Lands."

As late as the sixteenth century A.D., Simon Grunau's Old Prussian Chronicle recorded a belief about an ox whose body is made partly of plants (Gimbutas, 1989). This astonishing ox gives birth to plants when he is killed. Gimbutas (1989) reports that Mycenaean art often depicts flowers growing between a bull's horns. Instead of appearing lifelike, these flowers are stylized – sometimes with horn-shaped buds. Gimbutas (1989) tells us that from the body of the sacrificed bull the goddess manifested herself as a "flower, tree, column of watery substance, bee, or butterfly" (p. 265); she says that the bull was not an actual deity, but "a symbol of becoming" (pp. 265-266).

If we view the head and horns of the bull as the female uterus and fallopian tubes, we can understand the association of the bucranium (an ornament having the shape of the skull of an ox) with the creation of new life. (Gimbutas [1989] gives a drawing to illustrate this [p. 265].)

The ancient Persian religion of Mithraism rivaled Christianity from the early second century A.D. until the fourth century. According to Mithraic belief, Mithra, the god of light, truth, and justice, was born of a rock. He rivaled the sun in strength, but eventually made peace with it. His next significant task was to slay the primeval ox. The shedding of the ox's blood, and the dismemberment of his limbs, are what brought forth all of the animals and the useful herbs; the ox's soul went to heaven where it became a guardian of the animals (Leach & Fried, 1972).

Identified with the Persian Mithra, Mitra is a sun god in Vedic mythology and is thought to have been a manifestation of the valuable attributes of the sun. Evidence shows that Mitra was worshiped by a culture in Northern Mesopotamia as early as the fourteenth century B.C. Mithra, however, seems to have been a more popular deity, particularly in Iran. At the time of the prophet Zarathustra, Mithra fell out of favor; after the period of Zarathustra, he was restored as one of the mightiest of the Persian deities.

For many centuries, Mithra was a penetrating influence upon other religions and mythologies over a wide geographical area. He was apparently a remarkably adaptable deity; he appeared in India as god of daylight, and as "lord of wide pastures" in latter-day Zoroastrianism (Leach & Fried, 1972, pp. 732-733). Afterwards, he appeared as "a

Persian rock-born god of the middle zone between heaven and hell..."
and later, as "a cave-dwelling bull-slaying hero-god of the Roman
legions" (Leach & Fried, 1972, p. 733). In the fourth century A.D., he
was again revered as the sun god, and was worshiped by the Emperor,
Julian, much to the chagrin of the Christians.

According to Leach and Fried (1972), Mithraism "had much in common with Christian beliefs, symbols, and practices; such as baptism for
the remission of sins, a symbolic meal of communion including con-
secrated wine, the sign on the brow, redemption, salvation, sacramen-
tary [sic] grace, rebirth in the spirit, confirmation, and the promise of
eternal life" (p. 733). Furthermore, the birth of Mithra is celebrated on
the twenty-fifth of December and his rebirth is acclaimed at the spring
equinox, which closely approximates Easter (Leach & Fried, 1972). In
its early history, Christianity had to be practiced secretly, owing to
political pressure, and worship was conducted in underground caves.
Similarly, Mithraism was practiced in underground caves as a secret
religion (Leach & Fried, 1972).

In all Mithraic underground sanctuaries bas-reliefs show Mithra as
a young man slaying a bull. With his left hand, he holds the animal's
head back by the nostrils or by the horns; with his right hand he stabs
a dagger into its throat. Usually, the carving shows a crow, some trees
or plants, and an ear of corn sprouting from the bull's tail. This symbolic picture is usually interpreted as a revelation of the drama of
death and rebirth, "in which the divine bull by its great generative
power and sacrificial death promote[s] the fertility of vegetable and
animal life, and assure[s] . . . annual renewal on the earth" (Leach &
Fried, 1972, p. 733).

Thus, archeology, mythology, religion, and history amplify for us
how Dennis's "Bad Lands" might represent a marvelous regeneration
of life. It contains a bright sun and a prominent rock (birth rock?) anal-
ogous to the birth of the sun god, Mithras, who slays the ox (represented by Dennis's bucranium perched on a staff), which in turn brings
assurance that life on earth will be renewed. If there is any question
whether the energy of this picture is directed towards the emergence
of new life, notice Dennis's stylized plant design (made with a graphite
pencil) on the front of the skull. This motif resembles both a budding
flower and an ear of corn; it underscores the idea of generating life,
however dubious Dennis may have been about this idea at the time.

Dennis was quite articulate about the upper part of his picture that
makes up the background – especially the mountains, and to a lesser

extent the sun. However, he had practically nothing to say about the foreground in the bottom half and he apparently had no particular conscious associations with a bucranium. This absence of association and lack of commentary, together with his equivocal flora design, suggests strongly that his unconscious wants something to come to light and that it might be on the threshold of consciousness. Some aspect of psyche or soma may be seeking validation.

Consequently, I chose to amplify the bucranium and the rock and to relate them to the strongly colored sun that Dennis says is "rising." By so evaluating his "unconscious foreground," and relating it to his "conscious background," we might understand better how this young man's psyche relates to his dying process. The signs of rebirth in the foreground reflect a strong will to celebrate life. Is this life a physical or spiritual one, or could it somehow be both that he celebrates?

Two other components of this drawing deserve special mention. The desert environment and the mountains both suggest an association with spiritual growth. One may wander into the desert or climb a mountain to contemplate spiritual truth and meet God.

A short time after this drawing was made, Dennis was sufficiently stabilized to be discharged from the hospital. At his outpatient follow-up visit, our treatment team learned he had dropped out of college. His previous two hospitalizations (in January and February) had prevented his returning in time for his second semester; he had decided that his all too frequent relapses would now make it impractical to try to continue the college work. It was at this clinic visit that he drew the volcano (Fig. 9), already discussed; the drawing appeared to foretell of the gastric ulcer "eruption" that would occur in just two weeks.

I have been particularly interested in studies from the past ten or so years that show a significant link between long-lasting stress and weakening of the immune system. In the book *Who Gets Sick?* (1987), Blair Justice refers to Frankenhaeuser's studies that reveal a rise in stress hormones and, in turn, a depression of the immune system in those workers who believe they have no control over their job (Chapter 10, note 10, p. 361).

Justice (1987) reports on a paper Levy presented about a study of women with breast cancer. Levy found a significant correlation between the degree of distress or helplessness these women felt and the activity of the natural killer cells in their immune system (see Justice, 1987, Chapter 10, note 9, pp. 360-361). Justice (1987) says the body's biological sensitivities are the most likely areas to respond to psychosocial factors in producing certain somatic disorders. He suggests that there are people who "may have gastrointestinal tracts that overreact or [who] are 'nasal and respiratory responders'" (p. 40).

We know, of course, that Dennis's digestive and pulmonary systems were both weakened by CF. Considering all these findings, it is evident that Dennis's pulmonary infections could be related to a weakened immune system, and the gastric ulcer symptoms might be his body's way of communicating stress.

The winter that Dennis had to drop out of college, the period when he drew "Free," "Bad Lands," and the "Smoking Volcano," was a depressing time for him. Quitting college ended one of Dennis's important goals and there is no doubt that this event brought him much grief. After a few days of treatment for his gastric ulcer condition, Dennis was discharged from the hospital only to be readmitted the following month owing to a recurring episode with the ulcer.

The body and psyche are not separate; they function as one entity. This thread runs through all of Susan Bach's work – also in the teachings and practice of the British dermatologist and Jungian analyst, Anne Maguire. Readers might also recognize this premise as central to the work of attitudinal healing and therapeutic imagery.

Fredrick (1976-1977), Schleifer, Keller, Camerino, Thornton & Stein (1983), and Helsing, Szklo, and Comstock (1981) found that prolonged grief suppresses the body's immune system and, consequently, renders the human system increasingly vulnerable to external pathogens.

Chapter 6 Notes

1. Studies by Kiepenheuer (1980) substantiate this finding; a study by Furth (1973) failed to provide significant evidence to support it.

Chapter 7

BIRDS FLY OVER THE RAINBOW

I urge you to be patient and remain steadfast as we pursue our study of the messages in Dennis's drawings. I could make it much simpler by omitting details; however, that would deprive you of learning how we get from "A" to "B," and would rob those who are clinicians of the practical experience of using a model to understand how patients' drawings can be evaluated. We will apply the feminine principle of sorting grains as we pick carefully through the many features of these drawings to amplify the nuances of psyche and soma. It is in the sorting, rather than having them sorted, that we gain insight.

Soon after his admission to the hospital (March 2, 1980), Dennis developed severe headaches and vomiting. Although he suffered intermittently with sinusitis, a disorder common to CF and known to produce headaches, Dennis's physicians did not attribute his headaches entirely to this cause. His physicians believed that his gastric ulcer and migraine headaches might be somatic expressions of an inner fear still too painful to integrate. They had observed that Dennis was remarkably aware of his physical condition and well read and informed about CF.

Dennis realized that the critical state of his health did not hold much promise for prolonging his life; he had expressed some of his anxiety concerning this to certain members of the CF team. I don't believe Dennis was afraid of death itself; he was afraid his time would run out before he could feel some sense of accomplishment as a man.

Two days after this hospital admission, Dennis used coloring pencils to draw a spontaneous picture of a rainbow, which he titled, "Beginning" (Fig. 10). The picture contains a level ground across the bottom of the paper; it is filled in with both shades of green mixed with dark brown. On the right side of the ground, Dennis drew what he later identified as a "sapling" with 4 sprouts.

He drew part of a rainbow and connected its right side to the ground at the center of the page. The rainbow's top arc extends to the left edge of the paper – a little more than half way up. The rainbow's bands are colored (beginning from the ground side) red, light green, orange, and pale blue.

Two birds in flight, colored black, are in the upper left corner. The upper right corner contains just a small portion of a radiant sun; it extends below to fill nearly all the remaining space of the upper right quadrant. (Borrowing from Susan Bach's observations, we note that a sun in this eastern position is rising.) Dennis drew only a small part of the sun's full circle; therefore, we might wonder whether it will be quite some time before the sun follows its full course and sets for him.

Dennis lettered the title, "Beginning," in black pencil on the back of the paper in the corner. This is the corner the sun occupies on the front of the paper. Besides this statement in his title, we are fortunate to have Dennis's verbal comments about his drawing. He described it as containing "a rainbow, a sun, and a sapling just beginning to bud." When I asked what he associated with a rainbow he responded, "I think of a rainbow in terms of what is at the end – you know, a pot of gold. In other words, I think of it as representing hope." Dennis made no comments, however, about the birds in the picture, but it was only two months ago that he had drawn his picture, "Free," depicting the large black bird flying over the ocean. That was when he commented, "if they came up with a cure for CF, then I would be as free as this bird."

The bird motif appears in 9 of the 20 drawings collected from Dennis. The motif of new growth or rebirth, which we see in his sapling, is also contained in 10 of his drawings. Hope for a cure (that would bring a new "beginning" to his frail body and set him "free as a bird") is a prominent theme throughout his series of drawings. I have already commented on the possibility of a double meaning concerning this freedom; while he consciously wished to be free of CF, unconsciously he was striving for psychological freedom from his mother and becoming the man he had the potential to be.

We would want to know what Dennis associated with the picture's title, "Beginning." Could it be a new beginning after some kind of "storm," or a new day, a new growth, a new life? Could it be the beginning of a new ego and the budding of manhood, or was it quite another kind of beginning that Dennis had in mind?

He gave titles to 13 of his 20 drawings. He made 9 drawings that were titled with either the graphite pencil or the black coloring pencil;

I always offered him the standard set of colors. (More commonly, along with using a pencil, the CF patients titled their pictures with red, green, blue, purple, pink, brown, and orange.) Dennis titled in black 7 of the 9 pictures he drew during those periods when his health was in danger. He drew the remaining two at times shortly before his health worsened.

After considering this remarkable use of black titles, and finding the black title, "Beginning," on the back of the paper's corner occupied by Dennis's sun, we must ponder the possible significance of the front and back juxtaposition of this black title and the bright sun. Could there be some threatening element about this "beginning" – whatever it might have signified for Dennis?

His sun appears to hold lots of power and energy; it might symbolize the affirmation of life – a strong will to live that could sustain him for some time to come. Then we might consider his black "beginning" to represent both the hope for life, which is thematic throughout his series of drawings, and an inner knowledge that a "beginning" will not be a part of his experience on earth. A real "beginning" would require the cure for CF that Dennis fantasized. The truth might be shown in his very small sapling whose *barren* sprouts Dennis called "buds" – a possible foreboding that Dennis's life will not last long enough for him to blossom.

Some of my colleagues questioned whether the sun in this drawing might be viewed as menacing, owing to its closeness to the earth and the intense radiation it emits. Could so much solar power be too much for the tender, young plant? I have already expressed the belief that some of Dennis's pictures reflect his near-death experience, which would in all likelihood have included a positive relationship with a bright, comforting light. Is it possible that his psyche would cause him to recall this comforting light during times of severe physical distress?

Jungian psychology stresses the importance of balancing opposites in our lives. This task urges us to avoid one-sidedness and to strive for wholeness. Our dreams often exaggerate what is either missing or out of balance; they bring a more authentic orientation to consciousness. Perhaps the exaggerated sun represents an energetic, spirited, "masculine consciousness" needed to balance the soulful, "feminine consciousness" Dennis developed through the close relationship to his nurturing, supportive mother.

Alchemically, this fiery sun could represent a *rubedo* phase. This is the sunrise that follows the dawning of light: *albedo*. But before that, all is dark. The initial phase is *nigredo*; psychologically, it is the black night of depression, melancholy, and despair. The whole cycle, from *nigredo* to *rubedo*, represents the death of an inadequate ego in which consciousness leads to a new life or a new perspective. In the individuation of a personality, this cycle is perpetuated throughout life. Thus, this drawing coincides with a *rubedo* period in Dennis's life, a period of new awareness. We can expect next that he will experience another *nigredo* phase; he will feel a loss of self and will need reintegration. This process represents the steps of the spiral path towards individuation.

Despite his burdensome situation and distressing symptoms, Dennis was a courageous young man who never seemed to give up hope. He associated the rainbow with hope, and seemed to emphasize this thought with his very radiant sun on the eastern horizon. He also affirmed hope with his young sapling "just beginning to bud," and with his title, "Beginning" (however precarious that "beginning" might be). Dennis's rainbow is a reminder of God's promise to man. Noah had trusted in God, survived the great flood, and received God's wondrous covenant. Like Noah, Dennis was also in danger of a destructive "flood" – the critical accumulation of mucous secretions characteristic of CF that posed such a threat to his pulmonary functioning.

Dennis made this drawing *before* responding positively to treatment. This fact makes the hope he conveys even more impressive. We might wonder from whence such undaunted hope comes, especially in one so knowledgeable about his disease. My sense is that Noah's God was also very real and alive for Dennis; perhaps he sensed communion with God during his near-death episode.

After putting his title in black on the back of the drawing (on the back of the sun) Dennis turned the paper 180 degrees and with black pencil wrote his name and the date in the corner diagonally opposite his title. On the picture side, this is the lower left corner, under his rainbow of hope.

We might take this pictorial statement from Dennis to express both his conscious hope for survival and his unconscious or preconscious knowledge that his great hope–freedom from CF – would be found only through death. Possibly, the hope that can be found only through death is symbolized by the "pot of gold," buried at the other end of the rainbow. We cannot see the end of the rainbow because Dennis did not include it in his picture – even though he commented on it.

About three weeks after making this drawing, Dennis was suffi-ciently stabilized to be discharged and followed as an outpatient. We experience an astonishing emotional impact when we look at such a picture composed of so few objects. It grips us by the perseverance and vulnerability it polarizes. Although the picture evokes feelings of barrenness and loneliness, it also radiates beauty and peace that warm our souls. Such pictures can teach us to bear with patients, in a deep-er, more meaningful way, their feelings about critical issues of life. Dennis died thirteen months later at the age of 21 years and 5 months.[1]

The following day, Dennis made another spontaneous drawing with colored pencils; he titled it "Ended" (Fig. 11). We see a sunken sailboat (paper-chopped on the right side of the page, bow pointing towards the center of the page) sitting on the bottom of the ocean floor. There is a huge hole with sharp jagged edges in the side of the boat. The mast has fallen and is leaning towards the bow at a forty-five degree angle. The top part of the mast is paper-chopped at the top center edge of the page. A black arrow extends upward from the tip of the bow where figureheads are sometimes attached. (This arrow extends slightly past the center of the page.) Three ropes dangle from the mast. The ropes, mast, side of the boat, and arrow on the bow all have something green clinging to them; it looks like some kind of underwater growth. (Somatically, we might associate this green feature with coughed spu-tum that often harbors the growth of microorganisms. Recall also Dennis's comment about the green "junk" growing on his underwater treasure chest in Fig. 5.)

On the side of the boat, we see the name, "S.S. Sword." In maritime jargon, "S.S." stands for steamship; though Dennis's ship is obviously a sailboat, we could say, metaphorically, that it has lost its steam. There is no sign of the sail that the mast carried. Might the hole in the boat's side represent the tendency for Dennis's lungs to collapse (owing to COPD), and rob him of his energy ("steam")? The name, "Sword," and the arrow of the bowsprit are related by the masculine characteristics they share. We could also take the mast to be a phallic symbol. (I will return to these features in a moment.)

A brown ocean floor forms the base for this picture. It extends the full width of the drawing but occupies not quite one and a half mm of the total 21.5 mm of the side of the paper). To the left of center on the ocean floor, Dennis drew what he identified as a "rock," outlined in black, colored red and partly overlaid with brown. Considered somatically, this coloration suggests the residual, dried, encrusted blood sometimes found in nasal passages in cases of severe sinusitis. Susan Bach (1969) found this color used by cancer patients with hematomas.

On the far left side of the ocean floor, a bed of green "sea grass," as Dennis called it, has grown to the height of the bowsprit of the sailboat. This sea grass, like the green growth on the sailboat, is both light and dark green. Bach (1974/75) observed that when leukemia patients used both shades of green on the same object, they had anemia that resulted from a corresponding chemical imbalance in the blood. We might consider this color combination somatically for CF, but without application to the blood. In CF, a much more common chemical imbalance occurs with the electrolytes – especially with the measurement of sodium and chloride ions. In CF, the cells absorb too much sodium and release too little chloride. (Interestingly, the prefix chlor means green.)

In the upper left quadrant, a golden yellow and orange creature, which Dennis said was a "jellyfish," swims towards the upper left corner. The rest of the picture is filled in lightly with horizontal blue strokes to suggest the sea water that completes this underwater scene.

Dennis titled the drawing "Ended." Using the black coloring pencil, he printed and underlined this title on the back side of the paper. It appears in the corner just above the spot where the jellyfish swims on the picture side. He then turned the paper vertically (still on the back side) and with a plain pencil printed his first and last names and the date, March 5, 1980; this appears in the lower left corner that has, on the picture side, the sea grass in the lower left quadrant.

Recall Furth's (1988) practice of viewing objects or figures at the edge of the paper as relating to "hedging" about something – committed to neither one side or the other, but perhaps struggling in a state of conflict. We might ask what it could be that puts Dennis in a conflict. Is there something he wishes to avoid? Certainly, he wants to avoid death, at least until he can celebrate his 21st birthday. Is it significant that it is the stern instead of the bow that Dennis cannot bring into his picture? Is that which is to follow, the end, the part to which Dennis is uneasy committing himself?

We want to know what messages the images in this drawing could possibly tell from Dennis's inner world. In the lower right corner, we see the sunken ship's gaping black hole, and in the opposite, upper left corner, the jellyfish. "Black Hole" is an expression that suggests imprisonment; it refers to the deadly, eighteenth century Black Hole of Calcutta. "Jellyfish" is also an expression denoting one who lacks stamina and strength, or who is indecisive.

CF had so imprisoned Dennis's life that he could not live out his masculine potential (symbolized by the mast, the erect arrow on the bow, the phallic shape of the jellyfish, and the name, "S.S. Sword"). His hopes and dreams for this life were sunk; all his plans were ended. (When asked what happened to the ship, he replied, "I don't know; it just went under.") Recall that two months earlier, he had to abandon his college studies — his preparation for life in the future.

His drawing on the previous day, "Beginning," relates to this picture by revealing the appropriateness of his psychic stance with respect to his somatic condition. The bright light will illuminate the way to a new life, where he will obtain the treasure that could not be realized in this life. Dennis appears to be integrating his limitations in this life with the possibilities of a new life after death.

The alchemical process needs to be considered here as well. We already saw that the drawing, "Beginning," corresponded to a *rubedo* phase for Dennis — a period when he could envision a new day or a new life. It follows that to continue his journey of individuation Dennis must return to a *nigredo* phase and confront the darkness that is not yet brought to light. We can see many images of the *nigredo* in the drawing, "Ended." (The more progress we make in bringing unconscious issues to light and integrating them, the more our psyche pushes at other preconscious issues we need to bring to the surface.)

The tall sea grass on the lower right side of Dennis's drawing has two shades of green; one is strong, the other is weak (pale). It suggests the life that Dennis has lived and the precariousness CF has imposed on his electrolytes.

The image of a rock appears in 3 of Dennis's drawings. We first encountered it in his drawing, "Bad Lands," where it suggested the birth rock of Mithra, the sun god who regenerates life. In this drawing of a sunken ship, Dennis merely identified the object as "a rock." Having no particular associations to guide us, we turn once again to other available sources to amplify its meaning in Dennis's picture. Similarities between Mithraism and Christianity have already been mentioned. The rock symbolizes St. Peter and Christ is also called the rock. Rock symbolizes permanence, stability, strength, steadfastness, and the source of the waters of life. "The Living Rock is man's primordial self" (Cooper, 1978, p. 140).

All these meanings are in sharp contrast to the connotations of a "jellyfish," the figure in the quadrant just above. This paradox can be viewed as projecting both of Dennis's aspects. Somatically, he is lacking in strength and stamina, but his psyche staunchly endures life with fortitude.

We cannot see what is above the surface of the water in this drawing as we could in Dennis's previous underwater scene. Everything here is underwater. We could take this as an emphasis of the underworld or death, the birth waters of a new life, or as unconscious content approaching the ego.

After making this drawing, Dennis displayed for me an interesting discovery he had made about this picture and the one from the previous day. When this one is placed on top of the other, the rainbow fits perfectly over the sea grass and the rock and under the jellyfish; the sun fits in the top right corner with its beams just touching the displaced mast. Dennis commented that it looked as though he had purposely left room for the rainbow and the sun!

Four days after drawing the sunken sailboat, while still hospitalized and complaining of headaches and vomiting ("I think I have a bug," Dennis said to me), he nevertheless opted to do another drawing (Fig. 12). In the center of his paper, filling almost the whole picture, Dennis drew a mountain. The mountain has two shades of brown; the darker brown is layered over parts of the lighter brown. Part of the right side of the mountain has two shades of green and some brown. Dennis said this was "a mountain with foliage growing on one side."

The top of the mountain is flat; about two-thirds of a bright yellow sun appears behind it. A heavy, black line denotes the base of the mountain; this ground line is shaded towards the foreground with a dark green that fades to paler green further towards the foreground. The pale green gives way quickly to a pale brown foreground with very light shadings of black that results in gray.

A small patch of yellow-green overlaid with two sections of the lush, dark green interrupts the gray foreground. This little green area supports a cactus (so identified by Dennis) heavily colored with dark green and brown. Directly above the cactus, in the upper right corner, 4 black birds are in flight – "a family of blackbirds," Dennis informed me.

Mountains appeared in 6 of Dennis's drawings. Dennis lived in a flat region of Indiana where one sees fields of corn, wheat, or soy beans for miles. To my knowledge, he had never visited any mountainous areas. Clearly he admired the beauty and majesty of mountains and hills, which represented a compensation for the monotonous, flat fields of the area where he lived. Mountains are rich in symbolism. Among other things, they represent a meeting place for heaven and earth, eternity, constancy, firmness, and stillness. Mountains are associated with the spiritual and sacred. A mountain top symbolizes the state of full consciousness (Cooper, 1978). Mountains sometimes represent hurdles or challenges to overcome. It is no wonder that a young man with CF should be so drawn to the imagery of mountains.

As a reflection of psyche, we can we can see Dennis's psychic strength portrayed by the mountain. The rising sun coming over the top represents a new consciousness: acceptance of the reality of life, death, and rebirth. This idea was also suggested by his two previous pictures.

The earth colors of the cactus bring us to somatic reflection. A succulent, the cactus is a somatic representation of the fluid retention Dennis experiences as pulmonary and sinus congestion. The scene Dennis has produced here is a barren one; it points up the fact that the outlook for Dennis is also a barren one. (Recall, too, that CF has rendered him sterile.) This drawing evokes a feeling of tranquility but also one of isolation (similar to his drawing, "Beginning," done five days earlier). Perhaps the maturation of Dennis's ego consciousness has blessed him with a sense of tranquility in spite of his being barred from a normal, healthy life.

It is instructive for us to examine as a series Dennis's three most recent drawings – those made during hospitalization approximately two months after his withdrawal from college. (The barren quality of "Bad Lands," reflects his loss of opportunity for fruitfulness through a vocation.) Serial drawings can give a more complete picture of one's life than a single, isolated drawing can. This picture series begins at a time when Dennis was experiencing simultaneously a severe setback in his illness and an emotional depression.

New experiences confronting psyche and soma strengthen and buoy our ego and a sense of wholeness prevails if we can relate to them comfortably and internalize them. If we can find no constructive way to adjust to new experience so that the ego (conscious self) integrates it, our sense of (whole) Self is fragmented or weakened. (I refer here to the process of ego/Self [self/Self] functioning without mental pathology such as autism, schizophrenia, severe brain damage or deterioration, or personality disorders. Content that is overwhelmingly threatening to the ego is automatically repressed.)

This process of Self-constellation, generated by a series of dilemmas-recoveries, begins at birth and continues throughout life. Michael Fordham (a major contributor to Jungian child therapy) referred to this cyclical phenomenon as deintegration-reintegration. His theory concerning this process was further refined and expanded by Joel Ryce-Menuhin (1988), who maintains that the deintegrative process applies to life development from cradle to grave, and that deintegration and reintegration continually take place through ego growth and relationship to the Self.

While he was producing the picture series under discussion, Dennis was in the advanced stages of his illness; he knew from his critical symptoms that his life was threatened. It is possible that his NDE two years previously helped him to endure and integrate these difficult episodes of his illness. Compare his very radiant sun in the first picture of this series to the classical "bright light" typically reported in NDEs, and consider that Dennis's sun gives him hope for a new life to bloom. This reintegration could serve not only to maintain his ego/Self position, but to prepare him for the ultimate deintegrative-reintegrative experience – death.

Deintegration returns the following day, expressed by his drawing of a sunken sailboat. In spite of his ever-failing physical condition, he achieves reintegration again. This is revealed by his drawing four days later of a mountain with the sun rising over its peak.

Dennis told me that the sun in his mountain picture (Fig. 11) was "rising" – compatible with the *rubedo* in alchemy. The alchemical process corresponds with the deintegration-reintegration process of individuation. Thus, the last three drawings, made over a period of five days, seem to reflect a remarkable union of opposites: beginning and end; gain and loss ("a sapling just beginning to bud," a new day, green growth on the mountain, and the cactus contrasted with the sunken "S.S. Sword"); *rubedo* and *nigredo*; deintegration-reintegration. All these are metaphors for life and death.

Although Dennis made several descriptive comments about his mountain picture, he did not choose to give it a title or to sign his name to it. The sun still has a way to go before the full light of day. At this point, a conversation with Dennis might lead one to describe him as naively optimistic concerning his faith in eventually overcoming CF with the help of advancements in medical research. Dennis's drawings seem to reveal him in a much broader way. I believe that drawings are often ahead of our conscious, ego self.

His drawings clearly show how related he is to nature. Moreover, there is a spiritual quality about many of his drawings. Some are graphic illustrations of contemplation, of tranquil inner peace. Nurturing rebirth is a prominent theme. We can see his soul longing with constant hope for another day, a new beginning, another time, another life, another chance. Simultaneously, his spirit urges him onward, to rise like the undying sun when he feels sunken and over-whelmed, to rise above the burden of his disease and persevere to become "free." We are not to be fooled by his cheerful, sunny disposition. Underneath that persona is a solemn warrior eager to defend his life. But before his warrior can act, Dennis must first find his life. Who is he, and where will he find what he is seeking?

Chapter 7 Notes

1. If we consider certain numbers in this drawing prognostically, might the 2 birds in the Western corner signify that after 2 more solstices – summer and winter – Dennis will die and be "free as a bird" that flies over the rainbow? As a matter of fact, he died the 15th of April, and his rainbow picture was drawn the 4th of March, 1980. Observing that his death came in the 4th month, could we take the 4 colors in his rainbow and the 4 sprouts in his sapling to anticipate this event?

Chapter 8

BECOMING A MAN

Not long after he drew the mountain, cactus, and rising sun, Dennis was sufficiently stabilized to be discharged again and maintained as an outpatient. At his next CF clinic visit, three weeks into spring, Dennis drew a striking invited picture (Fig. 13) titled, "The red Bud" [sic]. It features, in the center of the page, a redbud tree with dark green grass growing around its base. A narrow gray ground extends horizontally across the bottom edge of the paper. Above this gray the ground is light and dark brown. To the right of the tree, another green patch gives rise to 5 heavily-shaded brown mushrooms or toadstools. To the right of these, a faint yellow-green blends into the gray ground; it underlines a bushy, fan-shaped plant that is brown, dark green, and yellow-green.

On the left side of the drawing, paper-chopped at the bottom edge of the paper, we find a large, dark brown, dead stump with black markings that suggest charring. Moss, colored both dark and yellow green, flanks both sides of the stump. The tree trunk in the center (only about one-fifth the breadth of the stump to its left) is dark brown and has a black streak running its whole length. Forty-two thin, dark brown branches extend from each side of the tree trunk. There are 21 bright red "buds" on each side of the tree.

An apparently empty bird's nest is at the top of the tree. It is heavily colored with both shades of brown and a few black markings. In the background, pale blue, horizontal lines suggest the sky. Pale yellow rays of light, fanning from the right corner, sweep across the entire picture.

After finishing the drawing, Dennis wrote on the back, in red, "The red Bud" – lower case *r*, upper case *B*. (This title is overlaid on the picture side by the fan-shaped, bushy plant.) He then added black quotation marks around this title and started to add his name (with black pencil) in the corner below the title. (This is the back side of the picture's upper right corner where the yellow rays appear to originate.) However, after printing "D-E-N," Dennis switched to a regular (erasable) pencil, turned the paper ninety degrees, and printed his formal name with the date in the corner opposite and below "Den." Thus, he signed his picture (in block letters) on the back of the picture's upper left corner (the one opposite the corner from which the light rays appear to emanate). His signature (on this reverse side of the picture) is diagonally opposite his title, "The red Bud."

As a way of viewing the complementary facets of one's life situation, Susan Bach taught us to hold pictures up to the light and look through them to see what was placed on the reverse side. Dennis's title, in lifeblood red, affirms the vigorous life depicted by the plant that overlays it on the picture side. This suggests the hope and the grit he has to survive until his 21st birthday.

Diagonally opposite this life corner, his formal name shows through to the picture side in the upper left corner. Bach (1990) labeled this space the corner "where the sun is last seen" (p. 39). Dennis's incomplete name shows through from the upper right corner, closer to the place where the light rays originate. Knowing that his life is nearing its close, Dennis could be showing that he is beginning to relate to eternal light – perhaps the light experienced in his NDE – and one to which he feels he will ultimately join.

Dennis offered no thoughts about this scene that is in keeping with the season (made on April 4, 1980). Several thoughts occur to me. I was particularly struck by the very bright red buds; they remind me more of droplets of blood than buds on a tree – the "red blood tree." (1) There are 21 buds repeated on each side; Dennis would be 21 on his birthday seven months away and would nominally enter manhood. (2) The spring-blooming redbud tree is symbolic of a *rubedo*,[1] blooming period. (3) He emphasized the new life by capitalizing the *B* of Bud while using a lower case r for red. Regarding these letters yet another way, the lower case *r* could represent a lowering of vitality or diminishing of human life and the upper case *B* emphasizing new life, perhaps an afterlife.

Reviewing these thoughts, I wonder whether these features expressed a hope of holding on to his life to enter manhood. This prompts us to recall Dennis's tree in "Remembrance," (Fig. 6) and to take note of von Franz's remark that the tree is a symbol for "death's mysterious relation to life" (von Franz, 1987, p. 25). He had drawn "Remembrance" eleven months earlier; that drawing raised the question at that time whether Dennis wondered if he would live to see another spring. Now he might wonder whether he will reach manhood.

What is important about the bird's nest in "The red Bud" drawing? Early April is a bit too soon in Dennis's part of the country for baby birds to have already abandoned their nest. Are the eggs still in the nest, or have they not been laid yet? Does the potential life expressed here refer to Dennis's physical life on earth, or to a spiritual life into which the encompassing light can usher him? There are no birds in this drawing. Though Dennis drew birds frequently, he put only a nest here. Has it been abandoned prematurely? Does Dennis feel an urge to leave the nest psychologically before his monumental birthday? On the other hand, has the nest been robbed? Does Dennis have a sense that his life is being snatched away before he can fully realize his manhood?

The redbud is a deciduous tree; it is a metaphor for "the world in constant renewal and regeneration" (Cooper, 1978, p. 176). The tree has many meanings as a symbol; it is the Great Mother, the Tree of Life, the feminine principle, and the Tree of Knowledge, to name only a few of its many representations.

Death-rebirth is symbolized by the moss growing on the dead tree stump. What about the black streak down the right side of the living tree? This is the side facing the light; the black cannot be taken to represent the dark, shadow side of the tree. Could it represent a scar — dead bark, perhaps, from a strike of lightning? Regardless what the black streak signifies, the tree repeats the death-rebirth motif; it provides a foundation for new life (represented by the nest).

Ryce-Menuhin's model of Self/ego (1988) is especially appropriate here as we attempt to learn how the psyche responds to critical somatic changes; his model is grounded on the Self theory of Carl Jung and Michael Fordham. As I understand Ryce-Menhuin's theoretical model, reintegration is aided by a clustering pattern of "ego subsystems that he calls con-integrates (p. 8). Con-integrates are psychic preservations of personal experiences that help the ego, when it recognizes them, to differentiate from the Self. Con-integrates, through their relationship to the objective psyche (collective unconscious), enable an ego-match with archetypal images.

Matching an archetypal image with a con-integrate validates the individual sense of Self. During the deintegrative stage, the developing ego identifies with the archetype, resulting in a temporary loss of Self. Con-integrates generate a *relationship* with the archetype; this results in reintegration (pp. 196-212).

For both children and adults, individuation involves relationship with the Self; it is an ongoing movement towards realization of one's fullest potential. When Fordham published *The Life of Childhood* in 1944, he showed that archetypes function essentially the same way for children as they do for adults. Adults are more likely than children, however, to grasp the meaning of symbols of the Self. Archetypal symbols contribute significantly to the deintegration-reintegration process and thus to maturation.

Children of Christian heritage often depict the birth of Jesus in the sandtray at times other than Christmas; this coincides with an integrative phase in which their ego (sense of self) becomes stronger. On the other hand, the child might put a treasure chest in the center of the tray. Selecting either object (Treasure or Divine Child) reflects an increasing integration of various parts of the personality.

These symbols of the Self and of the ego are not understood as such by children engaging in sandplay, but the symbols evoke within them a recognition of and relationship to the esteem of the miniature object. The figure of the Christ Child, or the treasure chest, found on the playroom shelf, connects with an internal awareness of divine potential – a treasure hard to attain. An adult might dream of a baby or a treasure chest and, particularly if familiar with dream interpretation, immediately recognize the image as a symbol for the valuable potential of the self/Self that needs to be nurtured and brought to light.

What possible significance could mushrooms or toadstools (fungi) have in "The red Bud?" They are things that grow and spread very quickly. Sometimes they are poisonous. If we were to find these in the drawing of a cancer patient, we might expect metastasis, but how would rapid, mushrooming growth apply to Dennis and his illness? The infections in his lungs were becoming more difficult to overcome. His regimen now included a highly toxic, experimental antibiotic. We can identify a somatic connection between the rapid, wild growth of poisonous mushrooms, and the invading lung infection together with the "poison" Dennis was taking to kill the infection.

This picture has 5 mushrooms. Do they suggest that in 5 units of time Dennis will experience a period of rapid physical decline, or a time of rapid psychic maturing? This picture was drawn in early April; 5 months later is early September. We must follow his history to see what happens. First, we will examine the 6 drawings that he made from May through August.

Dennis was discharged not long after drawing the redbud tree. The following month he returned to the clinic for his posthospitalization checkup; he offered to make a drawing (not shown here) and said, "This is going to be a quickie." He opened the box of colored pencils, drew a base line overlaid with brown and green; then he drew a brown stem, or trunk, rising from the center and overlaid it with both light and dark shades of green. Near its top he drew branches combining both shades of green. He left the rest of the paper blank; the tree (or whatever plant it might be) is quite isolated. The plant's lack of fruit, buds, or leaves suggests Dennis's struggle for maturity made complicated by his disease and dependency upon his mother's care.

One of my colleagues asked Dennis whether there was anything he wanted to tell about this picture. Dennis replied, as he noticed the CF Clinic's nurse walking over to us, "No – there's not enough time." The nurse announced that Dennis had to take a urine test now, but that he could come back later and finish his drawing. Dennis responded, "It's already finished." Was the picture really finished, or did the nurse's interruption shut down a process just beginning? I often had to remind myself that our patients came to the hospital and the clinic to receive diagnostic and therapeutic treatment and not primarily for expressing their psychic and somatic experiences through drawings!

All clinical data that day showed values within normal range except, of course, for Dennis's pulmonary functioning; it was always below normal because of COPD that had already developed.

Not many weeks after that, Dennis's health declined considerably and he had to be hospitalized again. On the third day of July, I visited at his bedside and he reported that he had experienced a terrible nightmare the previous night. Eagerly, he described it for me.

"I dreamed I was flying, suspended from a hot air balloon. The wind was blowing very strong, lifting me higher and higher. There was nothing I could do to get back down, and the wind was getting even stronger. I was so frightened by the wind that when I woke up I was still scared. In this dream the wind just kept blowing stronger and stronger and I felt completely helpless. I was so afraid it was going to blow me away and I could never get down again."

The desperate feeling this dream gave to Dennis reflects the fear of his conscious ego self; his ego was not ready to accept that he was virtually helpless when it came to holding on to life. But the unconscious psyche knew he was losing ground and tried to prepare him to assimilate this reality.

After relating his dream to me, Dennis decided he wanted to draw a picture to illustrate it. I encouraged him to do so; drawing our dreams is one way of allowing the dream to continue. As we draw images from a dream, we give opportunity for the unconscious to continue interacting (initiated by the dream) with the ego as though there is a conversation between them.

Dennis drew a boy (himself) in the gondola of the hot air balloon just to the left of the center of the paper (Fig. 14). He made large black circles for his eyes, which gave the face an anxious expression; no other facial features are discernible. He gave himself a bright red shirt; we can see only his head and shoulders.

The top of the balloon is dark green; its base is a heavily-applied yellow-green. Two sandbags hang down from the sides of the gondola. The gondola's rope comes over the left edge of the gondola, trailing behind towards the right and nearly touching the pale yellow-green ground below.

A paper-chopped golden yellow sun with a band of lightly-shaded orange rays is in the upper right corner. Analytical psychology recognizes the sun as symbolic of the father. As discussed in Chapter 4, this can be the biological father, the Great Father archetype, or God, the Father, and we see in this drawing that part of Dennis's sun is missing. The tree (also included in Dennis's picture) is symbolic of the mother – biological or archetypal.

One of my colleagues pointed out the similarity of Dennis's balloon to the uterus, and of his rope to an umbilical cord. These comparisons suggest the dependency upon his mother that Dennis's disease imposed upon him. Robert Bly talks about the important role the father has in supporting the son's process of separating from the mother. A young boy needs a good father, or male mentor, who can provide the *patriarchal* nurture that is needed for masculine individuation.

Dennis's parents had separated when Dennis was in his early teens (mentioned in Chapter 5). This event left Dennis feeling that he and his family had been abandoned by his father and it embittered Dennis for a time. By the time Dennis produced this drawing, their relation-

ship had begun healing; more than a year had passed since his parents
were reconciled and reunited.

When Dennis added the tree to his drawing he commented, "There
wasn't a tree in my dream, but I'm adding it so I might be able to wrap
the rope around the tree and get back down." (As noted in the previous chapter, the tree can symbolize death's mysterious relation to life.)
The tree's trunk is a heavy, dark brown color; it has a puffy top of
foliage made with circular motions using both shades of green. Brown
branches appear through the foliage. Dennis's picture contains all of
the tree, but his sun is not all there. It is interesting that the proportions
of these things correspond with the psychological situation.

People who report having had "out-of-body" experiences commonly speak of experiencing some kind of cord attached to their body,
which ultimately pulls them back to earth and into their body again.
Did Dennis experience a sense of such a connecting cord during his
brush with death? Does he, unconsciously at least, associate the rope
in his drawing with this cord?

Blue, sketchy lines from the right edge of the page continue in an
upward direction all the way over to the balloon. Dennis explained
that this coloration represented the force of the wind blowing the balloon upward. The balloon appears to be moving from the right,
ascending towards the upper left corner. This is a movement that
Susan Bach (1990) finds "in the pictures of children and adults whose
illness takes them slowly out of life" (p. 39).

When he finished the drawing, Dennis began to describe what he
had drawn, and it was as though he were telling another dream – as if
he had had two dreams in a series about a hot air balloon: "I'm in a
hot air balloon and afraid I can't get back down." After a brief pause,
he continued, "I'm in a race trying to set a record. The wind is blowing really hard. I'm scared. It's like with my CF – I'm trying to set a
record in overcoming CF. I don't want to be carried away by the disease." He then turned the paper over, and on the back side of the
upper left corner – Bach's "going out of life" corner – printed (with a
regular pencil) "Setting A Record." Below that he added his name, and
"7/3/80, age-20." He completed this nine months before his death.

Preconsciously, Dennis knew that life was ending for him. The
dream's metaphorical meaning of being carried away by the wind was
too threatening for his ego to process. Therefore, Dennis's ego rele-
gated the input of this dream to the personal unconscious. This defen-

sive response is graphically depicted through Dennis's drawing in which he added the tree (mother?) to help his efforts to rescue himself. But the drawing presents a paradox. If Dennis wraps the rope around the tree to stop his ascent, he will lose the race! It is as though the personal unconscious has corrected his unrealistic hope of racing to overcome CF by introducing the tree, an object his ego has fantasized using to help him out of his dilemma.

Let us take a closer look at Dennis's paradox. He adds the tree to introduce a means of taking control of his life; it replaces the fear of the unknown and the desperate feeling of insecurity with the feeling of being anchored to what is familiar. The tree is an anchor to hold him to the ground where he will feel safe. He wants to feel safe and secure, but he also wants to win the race of overcoming CF. This contest, symbolized by a hot air balloon race, is with time − the time it will take to find a cure for CF.

Or, perhaps, it is simply the 4 months to his 21st birthday when he nominally achieves manhood. Coming down to feel safe and racing on to win appear to be converse goals, but they can be explained as actions contributing to the same wish: to survive to reach manhood. His dependency upon the tree represents his dependency upon others to help and support him in bearing the tremendous burden of CF in his arduous journey to reach his goal.

Although I have emphasized Dennis's struggle to detach himself from his mother so as to individuate, it is important to realize the value of supportive relationships that allow for both separateness and connectedness. A good relationship with family and health-caregivers should encourage Dennis to assume appropriate responsibilities for himself, to identify both who and what he needs for help and support, and to develop the interpersonal skills necessary to achieve this goal. Dennis will mature and persevere until he does overcome CF − not physically, but spiritually. His death will conquer CF.

The tree epitomizes the nurturing potential of Dennis's environment and those in it available to him. It is healthy that he can admit his dependency on others, including his mother, for support that is especially crucial at this time in his life. Separation from mother may not be very appropriate as a developmental goal for a young male with a life-threatening, genetically-inherited disease; a much better goal would be to transform the mother-son relationship to one that is more supportive of his life as his own person (S. Quintana & J. Kerr, 1993).

Adaptive patterns of connectedness to family and friends permitted Dennis to receive the nurture he needed along with a sense of being appreciated and validated.

Within the same week that Dennis drew "Setting A Record," he was discharged from the hospital. He did not do very well at home; two weeks later he came back to the CF clinic. Here, he produced a remarkable (invited) drawing that he titled, "Life Begins" (Fig. 15). It is remarkable because of its vegetative motif; it implies rebirth at a time when Dennis's health was in a critical decline. Using the bright red coloring pencil, he wrote the title of the picture, "Life Begins," on the back side of the upper left quadrant of the picture, signed his name underneath, and added the date below his name. The black birds occupy this space on the picture side.

Suppose that the black birds are ravens, birds that are messengers of death in folklore. We have another paradox: on the "other side," Dennis says in the color of life's blood, "Life Begins," but on the side that contains his picture, the ravens prophesy death.

Dennis began drawing in the upper left corner; he drew a mountain or steep hill that moves downward and across to the lower right side. Bach (1990) found such left to right movement to be associated with a return into life, a successful treatment, or a process of recovery, whether permanent or temporary. Indeed, we meet a sign of new life at the foot of the mountain – a sprouting plant colored with both shades of green.

The mountain side is both light and dark brown; the dark brown predominates on the lower side of the slope. There is a strip of light green ground cover on the mountain side and 2 additional patches of ground cover – one light green the other dark green. A stream of water colored with 2 shades of blue and dark green flows down the side of the mountain. The stream disappears around a rise just at the lower center of the picture. The pale brown section to the right of this green area could well be another mountain in the distance. The line at the base of the picture is quite definite and is filled in heavily with the light shade of brown.

A new plant sprouts from a little mound of dark brown earth that rises above the lighter brown base area. (This rich-looking mound of soil tapers down to the right side and another smaller mound crests above the base area before it diminishes to the right edge of the paper.)

Three black birds (which we guessed to be ravens) are flying in the upper left quadrant and appear to be headed for the upper left corner of the paper. Susan Bach (1990) says this place is where "The sun is last seen," and that it represents a direction signified in drawings by "adults and children whose illness takes them slowly out of life" (p. 39). In the upper right corner, a huge red and golden sun rises. We assume this because in the evaluation of drawings we consider right as east and left as west (Bach, 1990). The sun's golden and red rays reach out to almost fill the remainder of the upper right quadrant. This location reflects the present situation of the individual, we have learned empirically.

Let us inventory the positive signs that would suggest healthy aspects related either to the somatic or psychological condition. We find great use of earth brown, and a stream flowing down a mountain where it might ultimately water the rich mound of earth and give life to the young plant. We have a radiant sun in the eastern sky, and might say that it has lots of energy to give before it reaches its setting position. Positive evidence of a progression into the healthy side appears also in the movement from upper left to lower right – leaving the place of the setting sun to return to the place of recovery and life. All these healthy signs are reaffirmed by the young plant that sprouts under the sun, rooted in the rich earth watered by the mountain stream. The title "Life Begins" suggests vigor. Finally, both the title and Dennis's signature are written in blood red; these give vitality to the drawing and to his personal identification with the healthy side of life.

Objects or elements that might be considered less than positive signs include the birds, strongly drawn with black, flying to the left; the presence of pale green in 2 sections on the mountain; and pale green in equal portions to the dark green on the young plant. However, the use of pale green could also signify a return to health, with the aid of treatment, and does not necessarily connote a weakening of either soma or psyche. Could the lighter shade of brown in the base area and pale brown on parts of the mountain (or mountains) imply not only undernourishment and debilitation but a struggle to restore nutrients – to return to the healthy state?

There are no human figures in the drawing; Dennis included human figures in just 2 of the 20 drawings that I obtained. Some persons might interpret this absence as a negative sign. However, positive or healthy colors, movement, and placements outweigh the negative or unhealthy ones – not to mention that the very positive theme of rebirth is a prevailing motif of the picture.

At the time of this drawing, my colleagues and I found such a seemingly healthy pictorial statement hard to accept in the light of Dennis's condition and clinically predicted outcome. Dennis's picture reflected neither what had been happening in his life nor what appeared to be his near destiny. The nurse in the clinic said of this drawing, "He must be referring to and preparing for a life to begin after death." (We knew that Dennis came from a Protestant background with strong convictions about resurrection and life after death.)

Seeing repeated groups of 3 in his plant and his birds made us wonder what might occur in 3 units of time. Possibly, in 3 periods his life on earth would be completed and the next life, the spiritual one that his faith affirms, would begin. Or, it might be that in 3 units of time we would see a remarkable and unexpected turn to a healthy condition.

A severely ill Dennis was admitted to the hospital the following month. (During this time, he produced 4 drawings that we will discuss later.) Dennis became progressively anxious during this period. After about four weeks of hospitalization, he was discharged, but had to be readmitted almost immediately for a collapsed lung. After stabilization and discharge, he was home only a few weeks before the doctor discovered a heart murmur at one of his clinic visits; it required hospitalization in October. The heart murmur was related to the combination of prescription drugs he was taking. After the doctor altered his medication, the heart murmur diminished and finally disappeared; Dennis was discharged again.

We have now progressed nearly to the middle of October, or about three months since he drew "Life Begins," and approximately a month before his 21st birthday. At this time, Dennis felt so desperate about his life situation that (without informing his CF specialist) he took it upon himself to consult a herbal doctor. This doctor analyzed a lock of Dennis's hair in an attempt to find nutritional deficiency in Dennis's body; the analysis resulted in a prescription for large doses of vitamins and herbs. At his next CF clinic visit, around the last of October, we saw a different Dennis! There was no pronounced shortness of breath, he was energetic, had good color, had been eating well, had gained a little weight, and his lungs were much more clear. He was using oxygen only at night.

At first, he had been afraid to tell his CF specialist that he had gone to a herbal doctor, but on second thought decided that his physician should know what additional medicines he was taking; he became concerned about their compatibility with his CF drugs. Thus, he had called the CF specialist a short time before this clinic visit, and had been reassured that if he continued his CF treatment as prescribed, the additional vitamins and herbs would pose no problems. Furthermore, the physician even encouraged Dennis to continue the daily dosage of herbs and vitamins if they seemed to cause an improvement.

When we saw Dennis in the CF clinic at the end of October (3 months after "Life Begins" was drawn), the herbal doctor's prescriptions, or Dennis's faith in them, had effected significant improvement. Whether this was nothing more than a placebo effect was irrelevant. What mattered was that something had advanced his well-being.

Before proceeding further with Dennis's history, we should return to Dennis's summer hospitalization that came early in August, following his July pictorial statement, "Life Begins."

The next picture in Dennis's series is a pencil drawing he titled, "Fence and Barn" (Fig. 16). This was a spontaneous drawing he made in his hospital room at a time when I was not there. He told me that he got the inspiration for it by looking through a book of Andrew Wyeth's paintings that I had lent him. He drew the barn on the right side of the paper; it is paper-chopped in its center and has just half the hayloft door visible. A heavily-drawn phallic-like object, protruding straight upward, appears about halfway down the left side of the roof. It is shaped like an arrow and has a small oval object on its tip. Dennis identified this as a lightning rod. The lightning rod grounds a barn, thus preserving it in case lightning strikes the rod. Beyond its phallic characteristic, the lightning rod resembles a stick figure standing precariously on the edge of the roof.

A barn is a shelter for animals (symbolic of the instincts) containing hay that will nurture the animals during the winter. That the barn is only half way into the picture, may suggest that the ego has not yet taken notice of what is instinctual. Possibly, Dennis knows something instinctively that grounds and sustains him during the stormy episodes of his illness. Could this knowledge be related to the way in which Dennis was affected by his near-death experience?

Comparing this feature with what Furth (1988) refers to as "edging" in a drawing, we might gather that Dennis feels on the edge of life – not yet out of life, but not fully a part of it either. Viewing the lightning rod as a stick figure helps convey this idea.

The ground the barn sits on slopes downward towards the left and disappears just short of the bottom left edge of the paper. (We do not know whether Dennis drew this sloping ground from right to left, or vice-versa.) At the top edge of this sloping ground line, Dennis has drawn a barbed wire fence with 13 fence posts and 3 wires.

Thirteen is often taken as an unlucky number, but in some Christian Lenten rituals thirteen candles, extinguished one by one, symbolize the darkness on earth at Christ's death (Cooper, 1988). The number three holds many meanings in religion, mythology, and folklore. Among other things, three represents "man as body, soul and spirit; birth, life and death; beginning, middle, end; past, present, future" (Cooper, 1988, p. 114). Three can suggest God, Goddess (Sophia), and Holy Spirit, or the Godhead (Father, Mother, Son) that is mirrored in the human family (Cooper, 1978).

In the upper left corner, 6 black birds are in flight. The center of the drawing is empty, as is a good portion of the left side. There are no animals in sight, no farm machinery or tools, and as usual, no people. The barbed wire fence and the lack of color give the picture a harsh quality. It is a stark picture and it conveys a feeling of isolation.

Dennis's phallic lightning rod or stick figure recalls his wish to be grounded in manhood before death strikes or before he falls off the edge. (He penciled the title, with his name and date, on the back of the drawing in the corner occupied on the picture side by the lightning rod. The first letter of Dennis's name is superimposed on the top of the lightning rod.)

By their numbers, the 6 black birds suggest symbolically harmony, balance, completion, and creation (Cooper, 1978). God created the world in 6 days. Dennis was moving towards a better balance of personality as he identified increasingly with his heterosexual manhood. (Incidentally, 6 months later he was admitted to the hospital for the last time.)

Dennis's older brother, who had a successful business and was engaged to be married, was a good model for Dennis. Dennis's relationship with his father was also improving. Earlier in the year, Dennis had a short-lived romantic relationship with a nurse's aide from the hospital. The relationship did not last; Dennis perceived that she was in love with him because she wanted to be needed, and apparently felt that with Dennis's illness he would always need her. Dennis broke off the relationship but still dreamed of finding the right girl.

Back to the 6 birds: 6 is also the number for chance or luck, and in western U.S. gambling, throwing 6 with dice wins. (Cooper, 1978).

Dennis urgently hoped to be lucky enough to celebrate his 21st birthday, signifying the manhood of folklore. What chance did he have of completing that goal?

Besides the heavily drawn lightning rod, the barbed wire fence is the most arresting feature of this drawing. It is a barrier; we should ponder what Dennis wants to prevent from crossing this line. It was clear he wished to hold death at bay and to sustain his life for a few more months.

During these summer months, beginning with Dennis's hot air balloon picture, "Setting A Record," Dennis appeared to be going through a transition and becoming more conscious about his span of life. He fluctuated between periods of remarkable insight and reconciliation and periods of confusion and denial. I regarded his choice to draw his barn picture with a plain, erasable pencil as a sign that he was uncertain whether to relate consciously to some issues this picture suggested symbolically.

After presenting me with this spontaneous picture, he wanted to make another one (Fig. 17) to add to his folder. Using the light brown coloring pencil, he shaded a level area of ground all across the bottom edge of the paper and rising just .5 mm above the edge. A little to the left of the center of this ground line, he drew a bulbous, phallic-like plant with three defined sections of unopened petals budding from the ground. The plant and petals are outlined in red and shaded very faintly with the same red pencil and the regular graphite pencil. This coloration gives the plant a variegated pink and silvery appearance. He added a dark green botanical receptacle at the base of the plant and 2 leaflets – one on either side. Oddly, the receptacle is not wide enough to contain the bottom left side of the bud.

Dennis made a paper-chopped orange sun in the upper left corner, from which a dense band of golden yellow and orange sun rays beam down on the plant below. He completed this drawing by adding yellow sun rays to the left and right of this thick band to completely illuminate the entire picture. The right side of the paper is barren excepting the rays of light and the very small section of ground. On the back side of the picture's upper right corner, Dennis used a graphite pencil to print his name, add the date, and to title the picture, "Energy."

This drawing, like so many others by Dennis, has rebirth as its theme. We could take his phallic-shaped plant as symbolizing the masculine creative principle. Where can Dennis find the energy to become the person he has the nature and potential to be? He has fought hard against the problems of CF and wishes desperately to find his place in the sun where he can bloom. But perhaps this new life, eager to bud, cannot be contained in an earthly form (like the plant's inadequate receptacle).

The drawing's all-encompassing light suggests Dennis's near death experience two years earlier. Although he had long dreamed and fantasized about the cure for CF coming in time to save his life, I believe Dennis was integrating the truth and compensating for the reality of his approaching death, not with fantasy, but by focusing upon a new, transformed life. Possibly, he had previewed this other life two years ago, when he "died" on the operating table. If so, his recalling the image of the bright light and reproducing it in a drawing could have served as a reintegrative aid during those critical times when he felt he was losing ground and Self. Perhaps we see here that an image gave energy to the death-rebirth archetype. It helped Dennis to transcend his old attitude about being cured of CF and to arrive at a new attitude that would include outliving CF in the afterlife.

Three days after Dennis drew "Energy," I visited him in his hospital room. He was too weak to be out of bed, but he expressed gladness for my coming and added that there was something important he had to tell me. He proceeded to describe an incident that occurred two days earlier. "I drew a picture that upset me so much afterwards, that I crumpled it up and threw it into the trash can. Now I wish I hadn't thrown it away, but kept it to give to you, because I think it was important."

Dennis began to tell me all about the drawing. "I drew a large rosebud – just beginning to open." (I thought to myself, rebirth, again.) "The stem had five leaves, except one had wilted and fallen to the ground. This fallen leaf really upset me. I thought: here are five leaves and I'm one of a family of five. But this one leaf had fallen." With an anxious expression, he looked me in the eye. "You know – I thought of the leaves as being all the members of my family, and I was the dead one that had fallen off!" I saw him look down, nervously fidget for a few moments with a sheet of paper on his over-the-bed table, then continue, "I couldn't face it; it upset me so much I just had to throw it away." He looked me in the eye again. "I feel better now that I've told you about it."

Suddenly Dennis had an inspiration and blurted out, "I know what – I'll draw my destroyed picture all over again for you."

Chapter 8 Notes

1. The final stage in alchemy, in which base metal is transformed into gold. C. G. Jung compared it to the phase in individuation that involves reintegration, Self awakening, and uniting opposites.

Chapter 9

LIFE ENDING

Dennis quickly retrieved the drawing pencils from his over-the-bed table and proceeded to redraw the picture he had destroyed (Fig. 18). When he finished, he explained, "This is just the same as the other one except for the new leaf I added." I soon learned, though, that the additional plants on either side of the rose were not in the original drawing.

A black scar on the lower right side of the stem marks the place where the dead leaf had been. There is also a small amount of black on the tip of the fallen leaf's stem. The dead leaf is colored pale green and has light strokes of both shades of brown; it is outlined by the dark green used on its stem. The central vein of the leaf is colored dark brown. The leaf lies on ground colored lightly with a mixture of dark and light brown; this ground is overlaid with a lightly applied black shading to produce dark gray. The ground extends the width of the page and at its tallest point rises about one mm from the bottom edge.

The rose dominates the picture. Rising from the ground in the center, it spans practically the entire height of the page. The dark green stem, overlaid with pale green, bows to the left; its large bud slants toward the upper left corner. Four mature leaves, two on each side of the rose stem, have stems of heavily applied dark green. Dark green outlines the leaves; they are colored lightly with both shades of green. The tiny new leaf on the lower right side is outlined and colored the same way, but just one central vein is visible – colored dark brown.

A curious detail appears in the scar on the side of the stem. A very thin red line, barely perceptible, extends a short distance above and below the scar, just on the edge of the stem. Uncannily, this marking suggests bleeding where the leaf had detached itself. Dennis had already conveyed to me how wounded he felt upon viewing the fallen leaf and what it represented to him.

This feature mirrors the motif of wounding that is a common theme in legends and folk tales. There are many ancient stories in which the wounding initiates the individuation journey. In the Grimm brothers' story of "Iron Hans," a boy steals from his mother the key to the Wild Man's cage and wounds his finger as he unlocks the cage. Later in the tale, one of the king's soldiers stabs the boy in the leg, but the boy proves to be a hero and defender of the kingdom and he marries the king's daughter. To live life completely, one must risk and experience wounding.

Up to now, the road to manhood has been especially formidable for Dennis. We can see that Dennis's rose has no thorns. Does he feel completely defenseless when it comes to confronting CF, or might the absence of thorns reflect a compulsion to deny the pain he has been forced to bear?

The rose has been a popular symbol throughout civilization. Biedermann (1992) reports that the rose symbolizes resurrection and love that transcends death. Consulting J. C. Cooper (1978), we learn that the rose "growing from the drops of Christ's blood at Calvary" portrays martyrdom (p. 142). It is also the flower of paradise and a symbol for the Virgin Mary. Roses were cultivated in Roman funerary gardens to represent eternal life, eternal spring, and resurrection. The rose symbolizes "Time and Eternity, life and death, fertility and virginity . . . perfection . . . completion; the mystery of life . . . the unknown" and the rebirth of the spirit after the death of the body (Cooper, 1978, pp. 141-142).

Another strange characteristic about Dennis's rose is that it does not grow on a bush. Its isolated, independent appearance calls attention to the unique burden and lonely journey that one with a life-threatening illness must endure.

Edward Adamson (1984) remarks that he often finds the black and red color combination in patients' paintings (present in Dennis's rosebud) to predict tragedy. Dennis associated his original picture of the rose with what he saw as the tragedy of his life's ending. Alterations he made to his so-called reproduced picture, however, suggest that a new attitude is burgeoning. I refer, of course, to the tiny new life below the scar and the two small plants sprouting on either side of the rose. New life replaces the dead leaf.

In the spirit of P. B. Shelley's poem "Ode To The West Wind," Dennis expresses pictorially "withered leaves to quicken a new birth."

The two added plants on either side of Dennis's rose counter the idea that the rose is isolated. They suggest that Dennis feels supported by his family and health-care friends, but pairs of anything in dream analysis also suggest a new condition's or attitude's coming into consciousness.

Dennis admitted to being very upset by his original drawing. This countered his stated relief in telling about it and his eagerness to reproduce it. This contrast made me suspect that the original image had released an unconscious archetypal response that generated a reintegrative episode. Such reintegration would represent transcendence of the attitude toward death as an evil robber of life; death would now be viewed as giving new life.

This picture, considered with the event that led to its creation, compels one to recognize the image's power to spur the transcendent function. Recall that the original drawing, destroyed because it upset him so much, was produced two days previously. At that time, his ego could not integrate the truth revealed by the fading plant and its dead, fallen leaf. However, after sleeping on the incident for a couple of nights, this image of death had time to be resubmitted to his ego and assimilated; his *unconscious* mind prepared his *conscious* mind to accept a new perspective. I am sure it would be enlightening to know what Dennis dreamed those two nights.

In two days' time, Dennis had become aware that his destroyed drawing revealed an important message – one that he had since integrated. Now he wanted to reiterate the message, and in doing so he expressed his reconciliation with what the message meant. Thus, Dennis transcended the limited outlook that led to his destroying the first drawing. It contained Dennis's projection of his unconscious fear and rage related to dying.

The British art therapist Joy Schaverien (1992) speaks of patients' work in art therapy as a form of transference; the picture reflects a new orientation's striving to penetrate the conscious level. Thus, the patient becomes emotionally absorbed by the picture's image or motif, which then becomes the object of transference. Schaverien (1992) also talks about how such a picture may evoke some kind of attack such as having paint thrown on it or having it ripped apart. She says it is possible for the embodied image to sustain the impact of such an assault so that it can be rescued. Dennis held the image of the dead leaf in his memory, and after two days was enthusiastic about redeeming it, not as originally conceived, but in a transformed version.

Dennis's experience with these two pictures supported him in separating himself from a state of panic and rage so that he could relate to what would survive. Drawing the second picture also released Dennis from being fused with the image of death that stood out in the first picture. With the graphite pencil, Dennis printed, "Denny," his last name, and the date on the back of the new picture. This is directly behind the area where the dark green plant sprouts (left of the rose) on the front of the page. Therefore, as he signs his name, claiming this to be *his* picture, he relates to a forthcoming new life.

Dennis's drawings reflecting nature and regeneration came from the soul. His relationship to the archetypal soul produced images that awakened his spirit to embrace life with all the energy he could muster. (Further discussion of spirit and soul energy will appear in Chapters 10-12.)

Although Dennis reverted occasionally to the old fear and dread that his life was being swept away unwillingly (as portrayed in his dream of riding in a hot air balloon), his general attitude changed. He invinced a calm acceptance that life was moving toward closure and a zeal for living to the fullest as long as he could. "Feminine" soul and "masculine" spirit were concurring; opposites were equalizing. The next drawing I got from him reiterates this new perspective.

Three weeks after Dennis's reproduction of the budding rose, his doctor decided to discharge him and follow him as an outpatient. Although his health was not significantly improved, he was stabilized sufficiently to leave the hospital. Not long after the release order was written, I visited his room to bid him goodbye and wish him well. We talked about seeing each other again soon in the outpatient clinic.

Suddenly Dennis remembered that he had made a spontaneous drawing the day before and he wanted to give it to me. Like his drawing of a barn made three weeks earlier, this one was made entirely with graphite pencil. He had filled the page with a drawing of a double-hung window (Fig. 19). As he handed me the picture, he commented, "This is an old, rundown house." When I said to him that a potted plant in the picture appeared to be wilting and quite neglected, he responded in a matter-of-fact way, "Oh, the plant's already dead." With that information, I saw his picture as an abandoned house. The plant was dead because no one lived here anymore. There was no one to maintain this house. I could not help seeing it as a depressing scene.

As though he read my mind, Dennis hastened to explain that I should not get the wrong idea. This was "not a sad or depressing picture because looking out of the window there is a beautiful scene. There is lush green grass, it's a beautiful sunshiny day and a little stream is trickling down the hill." Then, Dennis referred defensively to the circular, noose-looking object that hangs down into the center of the page. "In case you're wondering what that is, it's just one of those things you use to pull down the window shade."

Susan Bach taught that objects in the center of a drawing often relate to what is of central significance in the person's life. Was Dennis focusing upon the possibility of his life's being choked-off by CF – of having the shade pulled down on his life, closing him off from the side that is lush with life? This is one way Dennis might interpret the imaginary view outside, based on his remarks about it. Another way to consider his window shade is to think of the viewer's perspective. If we pull the shade down, we cannot see the beautiful view that Dennis describes. If the view he imagines is the one he glimpsed during his NDE, it emphasizes that we cannot see that scene.

A tiny flower pot on the left side of the windowledge contains the drooping, withered plant that Dennis said was already dead. Two leaves, fallen from the plant, lie on either side of the pot. A knothole disfigures the right side of the window's ledge. There is an ugly crack in the window glass in the left corner of the bottom pane. Dennis had not included in his drawing the beautiful scene he claimed could be seen by looking out the window. Despite his reassurance that this was "not a sad or depressing picture," I felt a sense of doom.

Nevertheless, Dennis went on talking cheerfully about his picture. After all, he was going home in a few hours; why shouldn't he be happy? "I'm going to call this picture 'Imagine' because I want everyone who sees it to imagine what the scene would be, looking out the window." He turned the drawing over and printed his title on the back side of the picture's corner that is opposite the dead plant. To the right of his title he added his name, "Denny," his last name, and the date. He thus claimed the drawing as "his picture" regardless that he drew it with the erasable pencil. Perhaps his drawing medium reflects the fact that his deteriorating body will not last forever.

Suddenly, I realized that Dennis's description of the view he had imagined matched a drawing he had made almost two months before! I told Dennis I had a surprise for him and would be right back. From my office, a few doors down the hall, I retrieved his drawing, "Life Begins" (Fig. 15), and returned to his room. Placing "Life Begins" underneath his latest drawing, I walked over to the window in his room and held the layered drawings up to the light. "Is this the view you imagine seeing from the window?" I asked.

Dennis was astonished. It was exactly what he imagined, and he was excited and delighted by the perfect way they fit. What really surprised him was that he had forgotten doing "Life Begins" until I brought it in. He kept exclaiming to me about how everything in the two pictures fell into place just perfectly. "It's as if I had this earlier drawing with me when I drew this one, and made this one purposefully to fit over the other one!" The image of the previously made drawing *had* been with him, unconsciously.

Dennis held the layered drawings to the light repeatedly, reliving with elated chuckles the joy of discovery. "I honestly forgot I had made this drawing, but now that I see it, I do remember making it – it all comes back to me!"

I was particularly struck by one of the congruencies this combination creates. The new life sprouting in the lower right corner compensates for the dead plant directly opposite it in the left corner.

About a year later (two months after Dennis died), I showed these two drawings to Susan Bach and told her of this incident with Dennis. Susan's response was that Dennis had seen the Garden of Eden – Paradise. The scene that Dennis described seeing outside – the bright, sunny view depicted in "Life Begins" – really was *his* paradise; he possibly glimpsed it briefly during his NDE two years earlier. How could he be certain that everyone else would enter death by way of this landscape? It made sense to name his window picture "Imagine" so that others peering out from the deteriorating house could imagine for themselves what was beyond. Nonetheless, I have always preferred to think of this picture as "Room With A View!"

This drawing shares an intriguing similarity with the dream a clergyman reported to John Sanford (1968) shortly before death. He dreamed of seeing a mantlepiece clock and observed that its hands suddenly stopped. Just then, behind the clock, a window opened through which a bright light shone. The dreamer proceeded to walk out onto the path of light and disappeared.

I used this picture, "Imagine" (Dennis's room with a view), to mirror for Dennis the attitude he was expressing about himself and his illness. The drawing and the imagined outside view could be taken as a portrait of Dennis. The "rundown" house with the dead plant represented somatic reality; Dennis's physical deterioration was quite evident. The knothole on the windowledge suggested the crater-like scars of destroyed tissue that remain on the lungs and like the ulcerated tissue in his stomach. But if the house represented Dennis's diseased body, the beautiful view beyond with its bright sun reflected Dennis's cheerful outlook. In spite of his critical physical condition, Dennis remained remarkably optimistic.

Dennis agreed that he always looked on the bright side; this characteristic was an inspiration to all who knew him. Was this attitude a form of denial that allowed him to cope with CF? This attitude quite possibly expresses the transition he was experiencing. His NDE could be sustaining him – giving him hope and cheer for a new life that he glimpsed briefly during those critical few minutes in surgery. The run-down house with its dead plant and cracked window pane represents Dennis's deintegration, a *nigredo* stage imposed by his realization that death was imminent.

The "beautiful, bright, sunshiny day" is a *rubedo* image representing the alchemical transformation of the dark, heavy lead to gold. This alchemical phase corresponds to viewing dying and death as a final reintegration – birth of a new life. The powerful sun matches Dennis's strong spirit that is emerging to help Dennis reintegrate and see that it is not a depressing picture when he looks beyond.

It was late afternoon and I had commuter car-poolers to meet. I thanked Dennis for his drawing and reminded him that anytime he wished to review his file of drawings he had only to ask. He said something about being grateful that it was I who kept them, that he was afraid he might lose them if he tried to keep track of them.

In the therapeutic process, it is important for the therapist to be able to contain consciously what the patient's unconscious or preconscious presents. This does not mean the therapist must understand the meaning of everything the patient says and does; simply receiving what a patient brings will help integration greatly. Although I did not function as a primary psychotherapist for Dennis, I believe our relationship was a therapeutic one and that my guardianship and study of his drawings honored and nurtured the growth and health of his psyche.

After filing Dennis's folder of drawings and preparing to leave my office, Dennis's cracked windowpane kept nagging at me. On the drive home, I kept mulling it over. I was convinced there was more to this drawing than I had acknowledged. My intuition prompted me to view the cracked pane as an indication of some somatic problem, but what?

It was easy to see the psychological implications of Dennis's cracked window because he had revealed so much in his conversation with me. The window represented his outlook. He could look beyond the physical defects imposed by CF to imagine a better life. His conscious ego still hoped that life would grow brighter for him, but I believe he knew unconsciously that a better life would have to come in another time in another place. I still yearned to know what somatic condition the cracked window pane reflected.

Recalling his drawing, I looked for parallels between a house and a body – perhaps windows representing the eyes. Some kind of fissure in the eye, however, did not make sense to me, especially in light of what I knew about Dennis's physical condition. For fifty miles, I contemplated the drawing while my car-poolers slept.

This was a Friday and I would not return to work until Monday. Our CF treatment team would have its weekly patient conference then and I planned to present Dennis's window drawing and have the whole team pore over it. I needed to focus on my own world and renew my energy during this weekend. A therapist must not become overinvolved or obsessed with a patient's experience. We are called upon to witness and support a patient's situation, not to embody or be possessed by it.

The following Monday, as I arrived for work on the adolescent patient floor where my office was located, I had only taken a few steps from the elevator when a faint, familiar voice called my name. It sounded for the world like Dennis; I wondered how this could be since he had been discharged just three days before. As I stood there, looking up and down the hallway, the call came again; this time it directed me to a room number near the elevators. I was surprised to see Dennis, propped up in bed with oxygen, and I said to him, "I thought you went home last Friday evening."

Dennis explained that he had gone home, but didn't feel well. He reported that on Saturday he felt worse – hardly able to get his breath. By Sunday, he was so uncomfortable with chest pain and labored breathing, even with oxygen, that his parents brought him directly to the emergency room. "We found out I had a pneumothorax," he finished. Instantly, I recalled his crack in the window pane and finally remembered that windows provide ventilation for a house just as lungs ventilate oxygen for the body!

At our CF team conference later that day, I presented Dennis's window picture (without first revealing which patient had drawn it) and asked, "What would you do if you had a crack like this in one of your windows?" With this question, I led my colleagues to deduct what I had missed at first.

Studying the cracked pane, their consensus was that it should be replaced. When I asked why, they explained that a window with such a crack would be vulnerable to breaking or leaking. One speculated that a strong storm might cause the window to break open; wind and rain could blow into the house. I then asked whether the potential situation they described reminded anyone of a pneumothorax. (Although the crack in the window pane is not a perfect metaphor for a pneumothorax, there is a certain similarity; a weakened window that could collapse and allow water damage suggests the potential for Dennis's weak lungs to fail and to be threatened by congestion and fluid retention.)

The pulmonary specialist and everyone else in the room clamored to know who had made this drawing. When I told them it was Dennis, the physician wanted to know precisely when he drew it — had I collected it that morning? I explained that Dennis had drawn it before he was last discharged, three days before his emergency admission.

The physician then mused over two facts: (1) Dennis's declining health, weakened pulmonary condition, and history of previous pneumothoraces not only made him a likely candidate for developing another pneumothorax, but (2) his condition warranted the possibility that such a process might have already started when this drawing was made. Neither he (Dennis's physician) nor any of the medical residents attending Dennis last week could detect that such a crisis was on its way.

Let us reflect on this evidence. Dennis chose to draw a crack in a window pane at a time when his lungs were especially vulnerable to a pneumothorax. Can we not regard the cracked window glass, the run-down house, the dead plant, the window shade pull, and the knothole as remarkably outstanding coincidences with Dennis's impending pneumothorax, his physical deterioration, approaching death, and scarring in his lungs from destroyed tissue? This drawing did not cause Dennis's somatic condition, but we might say that the condition "caused" this drawing. Why else did he choose to draw these particular features at this time? This incident is a synchronicity that illustrates the psyche-soma relationship.

This drawing came 5 months after Dennis's drawing of the redbud tree with its 5 mushrooms. That earlier drawing raised the question whether in 5 units of time Dennis might experience rapid physical deterioration or of psychic maturing. We could clearly observe the rapid decline of his physical condition, and during these past 5 months, Dennis had also made tremendous gains in psychic maturity. Symbolically, five represents the union of the numbers two and three. (Even numbers are considered feminine, odd ones masculine.) Thus, five represents union and wholeness − the integration of "feminine" soul and "masculine" spirit. During the past 5 months, Dennis had come a long way from his fear of being carried away by CF (Fig. 14, hot air balloon). Now, he looks beyond his rundown condition to the bright side − paradise.

Dennis remained in the hospital barely two weeks until he was well enough to return home. Two weeks after the hospital discharge, he came back to the CF clinic for a follow-up examination. The doctor detected a heart mummer and an elevated temperature; unfortunately, these required further hospitalization. While sitting in the clinic, waiting for arrangements for his hospital room, Dennis elected to draw another picture. He said he made it in a cartoon style used by some terminally ill children whose drawings he saw recently in *Readers' Digest.*

His drawing (Fig. 20) was made almost entirely with black coloring pencil. In the lower center, Dennis drew himself as a patient in a hospital bed. His head and lower back are shown propped up on a pillow. He drew his face bearing a scowl and no sign of a nose with which to breathe! The left arm is attached to an intravenous line from the medicine pack hung on a pole that stands behind the bed (on the right side of the picture). Beyond the pole, to the far right, a dark blue candle sits on what is probably a hospital bedside table. The candle burns with a red-orange flame. The table and candle holder are golden yellow, outlined with black.

The medicine in the IV pack is pale yellow. The only other color in the lower part of the picture is a dingy gray made with the black pencil; it is shaded lightly over the sheet and pillow. The table, IV pole, and bed (outlined with black) sit on an uneven, wavy floor line made with the black pencil. The right leg of the table does not quite touch the floor.

The most impressive detail of the picture is the enormous weight, labeled "1,000 lbs.," shaded pale, steel blue. It is just above the center of the page, suspended over "Dennis" as he lies in his hospital bed. Attached to the suspension cables (paper-chopped at the top edge of the paper), Dennis has drawn (again with black) what apparently is a pulley rope, pulled taut; it extends diagonally from the weight's cable to the lower right edge of the page. (A pulley wheel is not visible.) The rope passes above and barely touches the top of the candle flame.

At first glance, this cartoon style picture gives the idea that the flame will burn the rope that holds the suspended weight. That would result in a sudden release of the weight and crush the life out of the bedridden patient. The drawing is gallows humor that expresses Dennis's reaction to the findings at his clinic examination and to the news that he must go back into the hospital. This is probably the most overt expression of Dennis's anger, frustration, and feeling of being a helpless victim of CF that he ever expressed.

The suspenseful, life-and-death element in this picture should be examined. The candle flame barely reaches the pulley's rope. What is the rope made of and how much time would be required for it to be severed by a candle flame? As the candle continues to burn, it will shorten and eventually the flame will no longer reach the rope. Will the rope be severed by the flame before the candle is too low to burn it? Time is the critical factor.

The candle might represent the elevated temperature – a cause for admitting Dennis to the hospital that day. If the temperature rises more, or remains elevated, it poses a serious threat to Dennis's health. Possibly it occurred to him that this might be his terminal hospitalization and that he would never see home again. Contemplating this possibility would feel like being under a heavy, suspended weight. That would be a typical response from his ego self. But if the fever can be brought down quickly (that is, if the candle burns down quickly), the threat to life diminishes. The burden of facing CF is then less menacing; the spirit is not crushed.

Could the IV medicine give the patient strength to get out of bed before the flame severs the rope and crushes life from him? Does Dennis believe there is a contest between the time medicine can revive him and the time the burden of CF might overcome him? We recall that his earlier drawings suggested contests of time – either time to outlive the disease and reach manhood, or time until a CF cure could be found.

While Dennis's ego might now feel threatened fearfully by his relapse with burning fever, his unconscious psyche seems to see the situation from another side. Dennis presents evidence of this in the way he signs his drawing. He leaves the picture untitled, but he signs it on the back in the lower right quadrant. By viewing the back of the drawing with the paper up to the light we can see the picture showing through. Dennis's name appears between the life threatening scene with the candle flame, and the life-sustaining IV medicine pole; it extends underneath the base of the pole. We might conclude that Dennis recognizes he is caught between a life-threatening force (his present relapse) and recovery, however temporary that might be. The position of his name suggests that he is moving closer to recovery. If so, will living longer with the burden of CF be a psychologically crushing blow for him? His last two drawings answer that question.

In a little over a week, Dennis was well enough to return home again. In just one more month he would celebrate his twenty-first birthday. This important milestone had been one of Dennis's goals; to insure that he reached it, he lost no time in seeking some alternative medical treatment – not to replace his CF treatment, but to supplement it in hopes of enhancing his health. This was the time (related earlier) when he consulted the herbal specialist and subsequently made remarkable improvement. After a little more than two weeks of his alternative medicine regime, Dennis came to the clinic again for a checkup. It was just five months and nineteen days before his death.

I described in Chapter 8 Dennis's remarkable physical improvements noted at this latest clinic visit. (The improvements were short-lived; he remained in reasonably good health for about two months, with the exception that he suffered from severe sinusitis.) During this visit, Dennis drew a picture with the coloring pencils and titled it simply "The Sun" (Fig. 21). He later elaborated on the extemporaneous drawing by telling me, "The sun is coming up." The completed picture does not reveal the astounding way that he originally made the drawing of the sun and the brown-green earthen horizon.

Dennis began this picture (Fig. 21) by shading layers of golden yellow, orange, and red to form the top half of his sun. Paper-chopped at the bottom edge of the paper, it reached just above the center of the page. The sun covered almost the full width of the paper. After finishing the sun, Dennis added a green horizon/ground line that extended about one and a half mm from the bottom of the paper and filled the area just from the edges of the sun to the edges of the paper. It appeared that the viewer was behind the sun, with the earth's horizon coming into view below! (This is not the finished view in Fig. 21; Dennis eventually changed it.) I had never seen a drawing of the sun from this perspective. The observer appeared to be separated from the earth and elevated to a magnificent solar position.

The sun often represents God; it is also a symbol of death and rebirth. We might regard this perspective in Dennis's sun picture as his conviction that after separating from his earthly life, Dennis will rise again with God.

In the sky area around the sun, Dennis scrawled some pale blue, cloud-like figures. Whether these represent blue-filled clouds[1] or the blue sky showing through white clouds, I did not learn. Using a regular pencil Dennis made 5 black birds flying in the upper left corner. Their number equals the months remaining before Dennis's death; five also is a number for wholeness or completion (it was also 5 weeks until Dennis's twenty-first birthday). The masculine nature of five (an uneven number) calls to mind Dennis's great dream to reach manhood. (I have already commented on five as a union of the "masculine" three and "feminine" two, thus forming a wholeness, perhaps an integration of "masculine" spirit and "feminine" soul.)

Viewing his completed picture, Dennis suddenly realized the "mistake" conveyed by his unusual rendering of the sun in relation to the ground. "Oh, no – I did something wrong! I made this backwards!" He quickly grabbed the green pencil and shaded heavily all across the bottom of the paper, covering the lower edge of the sun. Then he blended some earth brown and more of the dark green until one could not tell that this horizon had started as if behind the sun. It was as though Dennis had come back to earth and given us the usual view of the sun rising on the earth's horizon.

Dennis turned his picture over and used the graphite pencil to print "Denny," his last name, and the date in the lower left corner. To the right of his name, a little higher on the paper, he printed his title, "The Sun." Thus Dennis put a claim to this expression that appeared to have originated from a preconscious part of his psyche, his greater Self – but only after he altered it to credit the perspective from his ego self.

About a week after his twenty-first birthday, Dennis came back to the clinic and six weeks later, in early January, he came for his next scheduled clinic appointment. It was sad to see that his improved health was rapidly diminishing. For Valentine's Day I received a personal note from Dennis. Among other things, he thanked me for some things that he appreciated and he acknowledged my work as helpful support for him and other patients in our CF center. He believed my work to be instructional to the hospital staff. It meant a great deal to Dennis that our CF treatment team gave attention and honor to the patients' drawings and their potential for conveying meaning. He urged me to "keep up the good work," and said he would see me "on the twenty-sixth" (of February), the date of his next scheduled clinic appointment.

The appointed February clinical examination revealed severe sinus congestion and the doctor decided to hospitalize Dennis for surgical opening and draining of his sinus passages (a common procedure then). While waiting for his hospital admission to be processed, Dennis drew the final picture I received from him (Fig. 22); it was untitled and unsigned. I call the drawing, "Life Ending." This extemporaneous drawing is almost a mirror image of his glorious July drawing, "Life Begins" (Fig. 15). (The July drawing was the one he came to recognize as the paradise scene he imagined outside the window in his "rundown house.")

Dennis started this final drawing (Fig. 22) in the upper right corner and moved downward to the left corner – a movement that Bach (1969) has observed repeatedly in drawings made at times when patients' health has declined critically. He described his picture as "a rocky mountain with a stream running down it [and] turning into a waterfall over some rocks." He identified the two plants in the lower right quadrant as "desert plants." Deserts and mountains have appeared before in Dennis's drawings, and we recognize that they are typical sites for contemplative retreat, spiritual renewal, and transformation.

The portion of yellow and orange sun (faintly shaded), paper-chopped in the upper left corner, lacks rays. If we transfer the suns from this drawing and from "Life Begins" to larger sheets of paper we can complete the circumference of each sun. In so doing we will find that the sun in the final drawing is much larger than the one in "Life Begins." Considered as circles, the larger sun has about two and a half times the area of the smaller one. (If these suns were three dimensional, the larger one would have roughly three and two-thirds the volume of the smaller one.)

I recall how moved I was watching Dennis draw the stream flowing from upper right to lower left, wondering whether his stream of life was running out for him. In "Life Begins," a stream flows with life colors, coming forth to water a new life. In Dennis's final drawing, a faint, pale blue stream spills onto two lifeless stones – one black, the other gray. The earlier picture seems to suggest being revitalized, but in the final one, the stream's flowing down a sparsely-colored mountain, right to left, suggests the flow of life coming to its natural end.

Missing from the picture are the birds we see in "Life Begins" and in so many other drawings by Dennis. The sun in the final picture is much fainter and it emits no rays; this is in contrast to the sun in "Life Begins." Paradoxically, in Dennis's final drawing of the sun, he shows it to be threefold the size of his sun in "Life Begins." Could there be some connection between this fact and the exceptional way that Dennis originally positioned the enormous, rising sun in his final drawing? Is Dennis now identifying more with things of a cosmic, spiritual nature instead of earthly life? Is he coming closer to the light? This barren picture seems to reflect that Dennis's grip on life is weakening.

On the other hand, since Dennis did not identify this as the sun, could it possibly be the pale light of the rising moon? The image of the moon would suggest an *albedo* stage – the second stage of alchemy in which separated elements are washed and purified to begin the process of coagulation and transformation. In this stage, one does not yet see the full light of day; new consciousness is only beginning to dawn.

Is it not possible that this pale yellow image in the upper right corner could represent simultaneously for Dennis both sun and moon? Was he not moving toward integration, wholeness, closure?

During this critical transitional time for Dennis, he was blending elements of spirit-soul, masculine-feminine, and death-rebirth. It was too late for a CF cure to be found in time to free him. The only freedom from CF at this point was through death. This sensitive, gentle young man, who cherished the beauties of nature, who related so warmly to others, had courageously endured many difficulties that had assailed his life. He had asserted himself to seek alternative treatment to supplement his traditional medical care trying to sustain his life. He had lived to "become a man." With courage, he faced the final part of his journey, where a fuller consciousness would lead him ultimately to the golden light of a new day.

The "desert plants" give both somatic and psychological clues concerning Dennis's condition and prognosis. Desert plants are succulents

—plants that store water in their tissue. CF results in peripheral and pulmonary tissue edema and sinusitis; the latter already affected Dennis severely and required his hospitalization. There is, thus, a somatic match between the desert plants and Dennis's congestion. (Later in this hospitalization, Dennis experienced both pulmonary and peripheral tissue edema.)

Psychologically, the storage of water in desert plants could refer to withheld tears. Dennis did not openly grieve his situation, but his profound regret that he could not fulfill his dreams for a college degree, for achieving the full independence and joy of manhood, and for a discovery of a cure for CF in time to free him from the disease, must have been losses he felt deeply.

Except for the 2 rows of narrow green growth bordering the sides of the mountain stream, and the 2 desert plants, the mountain is barren of life. Psychologically, this could signify a feeling of isolation – a typical feeling for one terminally ill with CF.

However, there is an archetypal aspect about the desert plants that may amplify a message carried by this final drawing. There is a similarity in the appearance of Dennis's plants and the lotus. The latter is not succulent; it lives in water. A contradiction such as a lotus becoming a desert plant is typical of images in dreams and drawings that are harbingers of transformation. The contrasting elements of the image are not to be taken as one or the other; the two characteristics or constituents mysteriously become one – a third thing emerges.

The lotus bears buds, flowers, and seeds simultaneously – thus representing the past, present, and future. It can also represent perfection and spiritual unfolding (Cooper, 1978). Hindu culture describes the lotus as the flower with a thousand golden petals from which spring the mountains and the flowing waters (Leach & Fried, 1972). One of the oldest texts of Greco-Egyptian alchemy (dating from the first century) describes the resurrection of life metaphorically as plants awakened back to life by the infusion of the water of life (von Franz, 1987).

Dennis's 2 plants are alike, yet different. Both suggest the lotus, but one plant is much larger than the other. They each have green receptacles, but the one belonging to the larger plant is yellow-green, whereas the smaller plant's receptacle is dark green. The larger plant is colored with dark, earth brown mixed with the same dark green of the smaller plant's receptacle; the smaller one is bright, golden-yellow. The tops of each plant have tips of a color different from the plant itself; these suggest seed pods. The larger plant has bright red tips; the smaller one's tips are the yellow-green color used for the larger plant's receptacle.

Could these 2 plants possibly depict rebirth? Might a succulent desert plant combined with the lotus, a plant that grows in water, be a transformation that symbolizes the transcendent function? I believe it can. This is an excellent example of the *coniunctio* for those who might wish to pursue this Jungian concept. (See Samuels [1986], pp. 35-36.)

Starting with Dennis's drawing, "Life Begins," and progressing to this final one, we see repeatedly the motif of rebirth and the image of the sun. The latter suggests God, the Father. A new orientation toward death as a spiritual passage might be emerging in Dennis's life.

We must not forget the 2 stones in the drawing. In Greco-Roman mythology the black stone is the symbol for Cybele, a nature goddess of mountains, forests, the earth, and reproduction (Leach & Fried, 1972); in Islamic symbolism the black stone is sacred – a central point of connection and communication between God and man (Cooper, 1978). Many primitive cultures regarded stones as having power to give birth to people, animals, and plants. Thus, we have in the stones and in the lotus-like plants strong associations with the rebirth of life and all that is of divine nature. The number of the plants and the stones is repeated in the 2 humps of the mountain and in the 2 dark green strips of turf flanking each side of the stream. As always when a number is repeated, we look for its possible association with a significant unit of time. Could it be that a notable change would occur in 2 periods of time? Possibly.

The stream's downward flow contrasted with life rising in the plants makes the onset of death an obviously suggested change. We recall that images in dreams come in twos when something is striving to reach consciousness. Therefore, in my charting about this picture in Dennis's medical record, I invited the treatment team to question whether these numerical features in Dennis's drawing might express a preconscious awareness of life ending in 2 units of time – the most likely unit being months.

The CF specialist had recently added a psychiatrist to the treatment team. His duty was to use hypnotherapy in helping to relieve Dennis's stress and physical discomfort. The psychiatrist objected to my charting (that Dennis's drawing possibly predicted a timespan before death), and he expressed his disapproval to the CF specialist. He charged that my note was not only inappropriate, but lacked any valid evidence to support its consideration. Unfortunately, this psychiatrist was unfamiliar with the work of Susan Bach and that of her associate researchers; neither had he participated with our CF treatment team for the past four years in the constant monitoring of drawings by our CF patients that had taught us so much. Nonetheless, Dennis's doctor and the rest of the CF treatment team continued to give me full support.

Dennis made this final drawing on February 26, 1981, and died forty-eight days later, on April 15, just short of 2 months after making it. Incredible as it seems, empirical studies document that unconscious expressions in dreams and in drawings might relate to important units of time in one's life. This is especially so at critical times and when the dreams or drawings contain the same number of repetitions of several different items (a phenomenon already discussed in Chapter 1). Nevertheless, our scientific, technological society is extremely skeptical; it discredits such an irrational idea as this one.

Earlier, we questioned whether the 3s in Dennis's plants and birds (Fig. 15) and its title, "Life Begins," were related to the resurgence of a much healthier life (which did occur in three months). We also considered whether the 3s in this July drawing might mark a period of time until his afterlife would begin. The 9 months from July to April (3 seasons) equal the period of human gestation; we have seen that it is 9 months after this drawing that a new life did begin for Dennis – birth of the life he had yet to live. Three seasons after his summer drawing, "Life Begins," he faced death – in the spring of the following year.

A few days before Dennis died, I visited him as he lay in his hospital bed; I stood at his bedside and held his hand. Through the transparent green mask supplying his oxygen, I could see him taking short, panting breaths. I could hear the characteristic sound in his respiration that my clinical experience had taught me precedes death. I explained that I just wanted to stop in to be with him for a while and that it was not necessary for him to use his energy to talk. He nodded and gave my hand a faint squeeze.

After a few moments of silence, I said, "It's going to be OK, Denny." His eyes met mine; again he nodded affirmatively and panted, "I know – I know." He knew I was not saying that he was going to recover and go home. He was affirming to me that dying would be OK and that he had nothing to fear.

Dennis had faced life and lived it with his soul and spirit. I squeezed his hand and remained with him a while longer. How frail and pallid he looked, his body a mere bundle of bones under the bed sheet. Exhausted, his eyes began to close as sleep came to him. The time was here for his soul to dream while his spirit carried him onward.

Dennis did not go into a coma before his death, but I never saw him awake again after that brief conversation. Life was tiring him such that he was always asleep when I entered his room each day; I did not risk waking him from dreams that might prepare him for death. He died within the week.

Chapter 9 Notes

1. Recall from Chapter 2 that we found blue-shaded clouds could signify simultaneously held-back tears (an expression from the psyche) and fluid retention or congestion (a reflection from the soma).

Part 2

HOW WE DIE

In this section, we examine the influence spirit and soul archetypes have on our adjustment to dying. C.G. Jung was concerned with *how* one dies — whether a person's attitude is adjusted to dying. We begin with Jung and expand our perspective to post-Jungian concepts to learn how spirit and soul carry a person into closer relationship with the (higher) Self. This task begs the attention of a person who faces death. A caregiver's thoughtful mirroring of a patient's attitude, and the use of drawings as described in this book, supports the psyche's spiritual process of transcending life by means of death.

Two case studies illustrate soul and spirit modes of dying. Dying and death are presented as important, final individuation tasks of which the psyche must not be deprived. Because death is part of a continuum with life, it deserves the honor accorded to life. We see such honor in the ancient Japanese death poems that show an aesthetic, creative way of living beyond our death.

Chapter 10

THE SPIRIT AND SOUL OF DYING

To find death is to find life, for they are part of a continuum. Each person's journey of life and death is unique. At death, spirit and soul unite in releasing the psyche from the body. Lest these thoughts sound like a string of platitudes, I will review some background significant to this discussion.

According to C. G. Jung (1960), "It seems that the unconscious is ... interested in *how* [his italics] one dies; that is, whether the attitude of consciousness is adjusted to dying or not" (p. 411). This statement provides the nucleus for this chapter. What I offer are my own ideas about how people experience their dying and death. I formed them over a period of twenty years through studies in psychology and thanatology and by visiting the bedsides of many dying patients of varying ages. Dying patients lead me to believe that different archetypal energies contend to establish the attitude of one's consciousness and they influence how one will adjust to death. I am reminded of the fable in which the sun and wind compete to see which one can most influence a man to remove his coat.

The two powers of influence or archetypal energies on which I wish to concentrate are spirit and soul. I believe that spirit and soul are fundamental ingredients in our creation and development. There is as much controversy over what constitutes soul as there is over spirit.

To use both these terms invites confrontation and dissension from all sides; at the outset, I must say that I do not limit spirit and soul to theological definitions. I cannot say that I use these terms in a strictly psychological sense either, although my ideas about them are drawn from the teachings of several Jungian analysts.

I prefer the concepts of spirit and soul presented by L. Corbett and C. Rives (1992). They define spirit and soul following C. G. Jung's definitions of animus as spirit, and anima as soul, and they stress that Jung's use of these terms involves relationship to the unconscious.

> Both men and women experience intrapsychic soul figures which bridge to the unconscious and spirit figures which order and provide discrimination and meaning. But gender does not need to enter into these processes, and when these figures are in fact gendered, for instance, in a dream, this simply indicates the way they operate within human personality concerned – not necessarily generally . . . . It is important to emphasize that the function of relation to the unconscious is a genderless, archetypal potential, but the way we experience it is shaped by our contact with gendered beings. (p. 254.)
>   Clearly, soul and spirit are found within both men and women; within our usage, each sex possesses both anima and animus. (p. 255.)

As Corbett and Rives (1992) point out, the number of different ways Jung used the terms anima and animus has caused considerable confusion. Part of this confusion is probably related to translation problems with the words *Geist* and *Seele*; within the same volume, Jung sometimes used these words to denote something altogether different from what he plainly intended them to mean in other places.

Before plunging into my own ideas about spirit and soul, I offer a quick summary of some meanings that former societies gave to these terms, followed by discussion of some modern analyses of spirit and soul. This anthropological backdrop will help explain how my ideas evolved. Examination of spirit and soul inevitably leads to consideration of body, life, and death. A third-grader once told me, "A soul is what you have when you live, but when you die, your soul turns into a spirit." Historically, theories have evolved on this subject that, lamentably, lack the child's simplicity and succinctness.

In Latin, soul (anima) and spirit (animus) are two parts of one life principle (Simpson, 1960). From this cultural stance, soul and spirit reflect an ancient belief about life; the anima part is the vital principle associated with the physical body in life, the breathing soul, the blood of life, the pulse or heartbeat of life. Holding to this view implies that the anima ends at death, when the body ceases to function.

The animus part is the vital principle that involves the "rational soul." It includes rationality, energy, animation, courage, intention, consciously and actively living. The animus aspect of intention or will is expressed by St. Paul, who writes of being present in spirit if absent in body and declares that his spirit will preside with the Corinthians as they bring judgment to one who has committed incest (I Cor. 5:3-4,

[R.S.V.]). Animus is also associated with meaning, as in carrying out the "spirit of the law" rather than missing the real meaning by merely carrying out the "letter of the law" (Simpson, 1960).

This ancient philosophy suggests spirit/animus as the life of the mind, which presumably transcends death, and soul/anima as the life of the body. Therefore, the soul would cease to be when the body expires, (or it might survive until decomposition is complete.) Although anima and animus are defined as two parts of one life principle, this notion suggests that a definite split between the two is imposed by death.

In modern times, we find that animus/spirit and anima/soul are now regarded as vital life principles that are practically interchangeable. For example, *Webster's Third International Dictionary of the English Language Unabridged* (Gove, ed., 1993) defines soul as:

> The immortal essence or substance, animating principle, or actuating cause of life or the individual life. . . . The psychical or spiritual principle in general shared by or embodied in individual human beings. . . . The immortal part of man having permanent individual existence – contrasted with body . . . A person's total self in its living unity and wholeness. (p. 2176).

The same dictionary defines spirit as:

> The animating or vital principle giving life to physical organisms . . . the active essence of the Deity serving as an invisible and life-giving or inspiring power in motion . . . . One manifestation of the divine nature. . . . The vital principle in man coming as a gift from God and providing one's personality with its inward structure, dynamic drive, and creative response to the demands it encounters in the process of becoming. . . . Life or consciousness having an independent type of existence (p. 2198).

There are, of course, other definitions given for spirit in which spirit is equated with the supernatural as a ghost, goblin, fairy, or sprite, and can further represent the essence of something, or one's mood or disposition. There is also the Holy Spirit as the third person of the Trinity. It is important to recognize how soul and spirit are similar and to see how they contrast.

The various meanings that have been attributed to spirit and soul make it even more confusing when one starts to speak of these in any particular context. Workshop students tell me they have never understood the difference between the soul and spirit. Or, they say they always heard that spirit (or soul) meant something quite different. This is not surprising when we consider that the language has employed these two words in so many different ways. In our summary of the historical meanings of spirit and soul, we must acknowledge the enigma they presented to our ancestors with respect to the brain, the thinking mind, and the body. A popular question raised was: which organ contains spirit and soul?

Hippocrates, the fifth century B.C. Greek physician, expressed new ideas concerning physical and emotional feelings, sensory experiences, and humanity's ability to discriminate and clarify values. He refuted the then popular notion that the heart was the organ of thought, and taught that it takes place in the brain. He conjectured that the brain is the messenger to and the interpreter of our consciousness (Penfield, 1975).

However, by the second century, A.D., Hippocrates' teachings about the mind were completely forgotten, and it was commonly believed that consciousness, or the soul, was in the heart. Galen (131-201 A.D.) advanced the idea that the brain functioned in a mysterious way, as a whole unit, in which "spirit messengers" were both received and discharged (Penfield, 1975, p. 9).

Years later, Rene Descartes (1596-1650) conceived of the body as a machine controlled by the brain, and of a rational, thinking soul that is immortal. He held that this spiritual soul could exist outside the non-thinking body. Descartes claimed that the body was divisible into its various parts, but that the various functions of the soul could not be divided into parts – that they constituted a wholeness operating collaboratively (Drennen, 1969). This stance concerning the soul discarded earlier ideas presented by Plato, Galen, and the early Catholic Church (Durant, 1933.)

Picking up where Descartes left off, Spinoza (excommunicated from Judaism because of his radical ideas) advanced the notion that mind and body are one; whatever is felt in the body is also experienced by the mind, either consciously or unconsciously, and vice versa. Spinoza's thesis does not relate directly to our consideration of spirit and soul, but I throw his contribution into the pot because it asserts the interrelatedness of psyche and soma. Ultimately, my goal is to encourage the reader to consider how spirit and soul interact with soma to bring about closure to one's life; I consider spirit and soul to be an eternal aspect of the psyche.

The twentieth century neurosurgeon Wilder Penfield (1975) presents some intriguing ideas about mind, brain, and body. He concedes that mind and brain sustain their operations ordinarily as an element of the material body; but he comments further, "it seems more and more reasonable to suggest . . . that the mind may be a distinct and *different essence*" (p. 62). Elsewhere in the same work he states, "[the mind] is not to be accounted for by any neuronal mechanism that I can discover" (p. 54). Penfield thought that "mind has energy. The form of that energy is different from that of neuronal potentials that travel the axone pathways" (p. 48).

It occurs to me that the mind's energy is related to the complementarity of spirit and soul. Might the mind use this energy to merge spirit and soul, lead consciousness to self-reflection, and mediate between conscious and unconscious thought? Might this fuel a process in which soul accepts the experience of spirit and gives image to spirit's archetypal potentials such that the ego can absorb them?

Holding on to that thought, let us move on to acknowledge the problem society has in accepting the notion of any kind of afterlife for the deceased – the idea of an immortal or eternal soul. Von Franz (1987) attributes this difficulty to the historical tradition of connecting our feelings of ego-identity to the body. This attitude leads one to view death as unconditional; life could not exist in any form after death.

In the first chapter of von Franz's book, *On Dreams and Death* (1987), she informs us that an ethnological survey of beliefs and practices concerned with death includes earlier cultures that fostered a "motif of the 'living corpse'" (p. 1). She writes that among these people the corpse was either kept in the house or was buried temporarily in a shallow grave until it decomposed. In some areas there was a practice of feeding the dead with liquid nourishment through a tube in the grave, and sometimes a hole was left in the grave to allow the corpse to breathe.

Ancient Chinese believed that if the dead person's needs were drawn on paper and burned, the smoke would carry the items to The Beyond. In other places, a designated person would wear the dead person's clothes to represent the deceased at the funeral. These rituals depict a move away from believing that the corpse was in fact the person of the deceased (von Franz, 1987).

Eventually, ideas arose about The Beyond's having multiple sections to receive different parts of the soul of one person. The Chinese believed there were Yin and Yang aspects of the soul.[1] Yin settled on the earth and wandered toward the West; Yang ascended and wandered to the East. Eventually, there was a reunion of the two and a sacred marriage (von Franz 1987). Comparable beliefs can be found in Egyptian and Hindu cultures.

In early Christianity, there was debate whether resurrection was of the old, material body, or of a new, spiritual body. For a more complete discussion of the evolution of beliefs and practices concerning the dead consult Chapter 1, "The Mystery of the Corpse and the Grave of Osiris" in Marie-Louise von Franz's, *On Dreams and Death*, (1987).

Von Franz (1987) describes the view of death taken by the Catholic theologian, Ladislaus Boros, who claims that death has a profound effect on the seat of the soul. It is not merely a separation of soul from body; at the time of death a mysterious transformation occurs in which the unified, inner soul unites with the world soul. Within this harmonious relationship, the human soul, moved to self-confrontation, decides whether to choose or reject God – a decision that will hold for eternity. Von Franz (1987) concludes:

> Some die with . . . a struggle, whereas others die calmly and with inner peace. In my opinion, these reactions to approaching death represent two aspects of the same process: some are still in agony, in the struggle of the opposites, whereas others seem already to have had a presentment of the end-result of this fight, the pacification and union of the opposites. The more a person has already been engaged in the struggle of the inner opposites before the approach of death, the more he can perhaps hope for a peaceful end (p. 23).

C. G. Jung associated soul with one's mysterious, inner life. He believed this inner life was revealed to us through the "opposite other" of our psyche – in a man, his inner feminine; in a woman, her inner masculine. He gave the names anima to man's "inner woman" and animus to woman's "inner man."

In his view, anima and animus function in either positive or negative ways that depend largely on the relationship between ego and Self. Anima could be experienced positively as creativity and negatively as moodiness. A positive manifestation of animus could be motivation and initiative, whereas animus could be negatively revealed in a stubborn, opinionated attitude.

I consider spirit/animus and soul/anima to be two distinct parts of a single, personal life expression that is eternal. It appears that spirit and soul, personalized by the conscious self, interact with the soma and the personal psyche in profound ways. It is within the context of this hypothesis that I will discuss spirit and soul.

Spirit and soul have a significant relationship with conscious self and the various levels of the unconscious. The complementarity of spirit and soul appears in both the personal psyche (through complexes) and in the objective psyche (through dreams and experiences that are archetypal and numinous). The psyche also contains inflations and projections of spirit and soul (discussed later).

To view spirit as logos and soul as eros is too limiting; spirit and soul represent archetypal energies in addition to personal experiences and associations. We cannot define archetypes because we can never become completely conscious of an archetype. We can only describe the contents that form the archetypal image we perceive. This eternalness of archetypes further defies definition; archetypes have no beginning or end.

We deal with a field of energy that is not confined to an individual's body, life experience, time, or space of any kind. We draw from a universal well, or as Margenau (1987) states it, a Universal Mind. The physician Larry Dossey (1989) refers to this concept as nonlocal mind and nonlocal experiences; he finds much support for this viewpoint from prominent scientists, among others, John Stewart Bell, David Bohm, Erwin Schrödinger, Kurt Gödel, Rupert Sheldrake, as well as from Carl Jung. Jung's theory of the collective unconscious, or objective psyche, is an example of nonlocal mind. It exceeds personal expression and contains the thoughts and experiences of all past, present, and future individuals.

There is something about the archetypal, complementary energies of soul/spirit that seems to influence one's attitude towards life and death. These complementary energies lead one person to fight death and another to gaze into Death's face with acceptance. Susan Bach (1960) says that the latter almost dance out of life (p. 61).

In the Introduction, I said that tension between life and death compels the bonded psyche and soma to follow a soul-searching journey. However, for some individuals, it is spirit, the complementary aspect of soul, that is needed to lead one on the journey to embrace soul. Those who are already soul-focused ultimately need a spark of spirit to carry the soul through the final part of the journey — the life-death-rebirth process. As psyche and soma separate, spirit and soul unite.

Spirit is the energy that is manifested by, or projected onto the masculine and feminine figures of warriors, leaders, teachers, rescuers, adventurers, builders, etc. Soul is the energy that is manifested by or projected onto the masculine and feminine traits of containment, patience, receiving, nurture, steadfastness, anticipation, etc.

Life's path weaves between unconscious, inner reality and the conscious, outer reality of ego and persona. Spirit and soul provide people with two pairs of shoes for traveling this path. Dying persons will favor one pair of shoes over the other, depending upon which type of energy – spirit or soul – most attracts and supports their ego as the psyche prepares for death. Although we may be more conscious of, feel more comfortable with, one energy than the other, we are never without the capacity to slip into the other. The other energy is never totally absent from our behavior, even though our ego may not identify with certain (unconscious) behavior.

I prefer the terms soul and spirit to anima and animus because the latter terms are less familiar and more confusing to those outside the milieu of analytical psychology. Further, those who are familiar with the teachings of Jung tend to associate anima and animus with gender characteristics.

A POST-JUNGIAN PERSPECTIVE

To understand how one dies, I recommend putting aside the traditional Jungian model of anima and animus bound to masculine and feminine associations and substituting a post-Jungian concept of spirit and soul not limited by gender orientation. The earlier model originated in European culture during an era much more limited by the negative shadow of patriarchy. Society is in ferment today; it will not be bound by the old patriarchal wineskin of masculine/feminine stereotyping. We are daring to discover ourselves, our world, and our values in a new, more holistic way.

Although I use a Jungian framework as a therapist, I must confess that I have difficulty accepting some of Jung's ideas. He implies a negative quality about the spirit (animus), as though it might be man's negative, shadow side. However, Jung's wife Emma, like the twelfth fairy who softened the curse of the thirteenth fairy in "Sleeping Beauty," advances the definition of animus as spirit to encompass word, power[2], meaning, and deed (Jung, E., 1978, pp. 2-5).

C. G. Jung believed there was a biological predisposition for men to develop attributes of the spirit and to exhibit spirit characteristics in the ego; he believed attributes of the soul to be virtually unconscious and underdeveloped in men. Conversely, he believed that women, by their feminine nature, excelled in soul attributes and displayed soul-conscious egos; he believed women were mostly unconscious of, and inferior in, attributes of the spirit.

C. G. Jung's writings about the anima and animus imply that soul, as anima, is confined to man, or at least to the "masculine principle," and spirit, as animus, is confined to woman, or the "feminine principle." Jung's pupils have perpetuated this idea. It is a great relief for me to find Edward Whitmont's (1969) description of the anima-possessed, moody *woman*, or the animus-possessed, opinionated *man*. (We will return later to the idea of being possessed by an archetype.)

I have no quarrel with Jung that anima (soul) and animus (spirit) have important roles to play in bringing to consciousness a lost part of the individual's personality. This awakening negates the myth that we are "lost souls" floating around "out there" separated from God. We awaken to find that we are one with God. As Jung (1978) put it, "The soul is . . . the radiant Godhead itself" (p. 69). One might ask, however, "What is the spirit's relationship to the Godhead?" Before addressing that question, I wish to explore further the ideas about genetic realizations of spirit and soul.

There are genetic differences that cannot be ignored – specifically, the contrasting ways that the brain forms in males and females. Could differences that have been found in the male and female hypothalamus predetermine females to develop feeling and relating more naturally than thinking and rational analyzation? Would the opposite occur in males? How much influence do hormonal differences bring to bear on personality? What effect have fetal enzymes on the shape a personality will take? We must recognize that differences between male and female personalities arise from both genetics and an environment influenced by thousands of years of patriarchal cultures.

Post-Jungians such as P. Shellenbaum (1992), L. Zinkin (1992), L. Corbett and C. Rives (1992), subscribe to an integrative theory of anima/animus. This theory acknowledges that, at least in Western society, the "feminine" soul (anima) is commonly underdeveloped in men, and the "masculine" spirit (animus) is often underdeveloped in women. This integrative theory contends that individuation involves efforts to integrate traits of spirit and soul (which reside in both men and women) with those of ego and shadow.

When the day comes that masculine and feminine are commonly understood to be two poles of the life principle and are not limited to gender, we can more freely speak of the feminine in a man and the masculine in a woman without arousing conflict imposed by one's culture. These expressions merely amplify that spirit will be revealed by a woman in her feminine way, and a man will employ a masculine manner in his unveiling of soul. For now, to speak of spirit (animus) as "woman's inner man," or of "soul (anima) as "man's inner woman," is risky and invites misunderstanding.

I like Haddon's (1993) idea that male and female are composed of both Yang and Yin sides[3] (not quite the same as C. G. Jung's complementarity) in which man and woman's psyche each contain masculine and feminine aspects. The idea is to free anima and animus from associations imposed by the old patriarchal culture. Haddon (1993) informs us that in Taoist thought:

> Yang is associated with the bright side of both the mountain and the river, Yin with the shaded side of both. . . . [When] the south side of the mountain receives sunlight, it is the north bank of the river that is illuminated and warmed (p.20).

The mountain and the river each carry expressions of Yin and Yang that appear differently in each of these landmarks. Haddon goes on to speak of the penetrating penis as Yang-masculine, the sperm-containing testes as Yin-masculine, the gestating womb as Yin-feminine, and the exertive, birth-pushing womb as Yang-feminine (Haddon, 1993).

As Corbett and Rives (1992) explain, both men and women have spirit and soul within; each sex contains both animus and anima. Consequently, they point out, one can now assert demeanor previously regarded as the province of the opposite sex. Thus, there is no reason we should "label a man's capacity to nurture as his 'inner feminine,'" nor call "a woman's assertiveness . . . her 'masculinity'" (pp. 254-255). Furthermore, we should acknowledge that neither a female fighter pilot nor a male nurse is necessarily engaging in work contrary to her or his nature. We should recognize the influence of archetypes in the lives of both men and women and abandon our gender stereotypes.

According to Corbett and Rives (1992), we can now accept (at least intellectually) the existence and authenticity of masculine nurturing and feminine assertiveness. Soul and spirit (anima and animus) energy enables the ego to relate to the unconscious in a genderless way. The writers remind us, however, that the way we experience their energy is conditioned by our history of mingling with male and female figures. Our relationship to the unconscious is further influenced by cultural biases rooted in the objective psyche.

While we can imagine the spirit and soul archetypes functioning in the psyche ideally in a genderless way, in reality we cannot completely escape the impulse to associate masculine qualities with spirit (animus) and feminine qualities with soul (anima). Our culture and previous ones have associated qualities of spirit and soul in this manner. Consequently, the objective psyche is culturally imprinted to inspire gender identity in a developing child via the characteristics of these two archetypes.

We observe that young boys in Western society commonly display behavior more dominant in spirit characteristics than those of the soul, and young girls typically reveal just the reverse. These tendencies are probably a reflection of the gender complex (involving personal associations stimulated by anima and animus).

When anima and animus evoke psychic responses that relate to universal human experiences and feelings, they are archetypal in nature. It is an impossible task to draw a line between what is personal and what is shared by the collective unconscious in personality characteristics that resonate with the ego. (As C. G. Jung described the psychological complex, it can be both personal and archetypal.) In all likelihood, there is a conglomerate of archetypal and personal, complex-related content available to the ego.

Occasionally, the social environment, family situations, or other factors may free a boy to experience Yin masculinity and a girl may similarly experience Yang femininity. As our society becomes more soul conscious, each generation is less dominated by the shadow of the patriarchy. However, expressions of spirit and soul will always be manifested by males and females in a gender-distinctive manner.

We might deny that spirit (animus) and soul (anima) are contrasexual archetypes, but this does not make the existence of "masculine psychology" and "feminine psychology" any less real. Males and females differ in body, brain, hormonal structure, and in the way they understand what is masculine and what is feminine.

Schwartz-Salant (1992) avoids the gender jungle by using the terms "dissolve" and "coagulate" to describe functions usually considered as belonging to a particular gender (p. 17). He sees these functions as linked and that each gender can coagulate or dissolve. He recognizes, further, that each gender has its own way to dissolve and coagulate structures. The man may dissolve a structure by separating it into its parts; the woman may dissolve a structure when she "moisten[s] it with a sense of wholeness and unseen linkages to a truth" (p. 17) Schwartz-Salant continues:

> "Man" might represent the coagulation that results from the fixative property of clear thought and a conceptual grasp of psyche, while coagulation may come from "woman" in the form of an inward pull toward a sense of contained space, "ovular" in distinction to "open." (p. 17.)

Haddon (1993) gives two illustrations of the same concept of inter-linkage. The first is a man's testicular capacity to "hang in there" while ripening takes place in a "feminine," self-generating way and the man's staying power, steadiness, and steadfastness supports the process. The second is a woman's "masculine," exertive womb energy pushing and birthing a new project, idea, method, or whatever else might need birthing.

One might consider spirit as having some Yin (feminine) content and soul as having, similarly, some Yang (masculine) content. The various possibilities and meaning of this idea should be explored. Yang spirit might refer to spirit expressed through a man's ego, whereas Yin spirit might refer to a woman's unique way of expressing spirit. (The converse would necessarily be true for Yin soul and Yang soul.) For now, I prefer to speak of spirit and soul in the general way that Corbett and Rives have referred to them.

HONORING PICTORIAL EXPRESSIONS OF DYING

Sullivan's (1989) advice should be followed in caring for dying patients: "Instead of trying to act on the patient . . . attempt . . . to receive from him what his psyche is trying to produce" (p. 81). The psyche's striving with spirit and with soul influences the way the psyche crosses over into death. By receiving, validating, and reflecting back a patient's inner reality, we aid the reintegration process and support the patient's growing sense of wholeness and completion.

One very effective way for patients to express their inner reality is through drawing. We need to remind ourselves that it is not up to us to judge the attitude toward living or dying revealed in these drawings. We should honor these expressions and accept them as authentic representations of the psyche and soma. This task is easier said than done. It is very tempting to begin interpreting patients' drawings. Instead of amplifying what is there and honoring the myriad possibilities of the patient's inner world, we begin to project our own intuitions, values, desires, fears, and objectives.

In Bach's *Life Paints Its Own Span*, (1990) she contrasts the pictorial expressions of Peter and Priska, a boy and a girl both diagnosed with brain tumor at the age of 8. Bach appears to suggest that the boy's presumed need of help, from feeling so "alone and forlorn" (p. 146) in his dying, was not recognized in time. She implies that his dying was likely a "bad" experience of torture and agony (p. 25) that might have been made better.

In contrast, Bach (1969) describes (in a previous publication) the dying experience for the girl as one in which the child appears to "almost dance out of life, lovingly related to . . . flowers . . . birds," and "newly hatched" chicks (p. 61). Bach concludes that it was as though from Priska's very first picture she knew her destiny and voluntarily, with virtually excited expectation, went on her way, displaying an "unforgettable . . . undoubting readiness to 'go home'" (p. 61). Bach (1990) goes on to invite her readers to speculate that Priska died contentedly.

Peter's drawings depicted figures fighting threatening situations or attackers. He drew a sow that did not want to be slaughtered. One of his rebellious characters made a hole in St. Nicholas's sack to claim its contents instead of waiting for a delivery; this character dared to cry repeatedly to a saint for help. Bach interpreted his drawings as suggesting Peter believed his illness to be punishment from God.

Bach (1990) suggests that we might view a person as consisting of two energies: (1) psychic energy, and (2) body or somatic energy, and that an expression of one's life situation is the sum of opposing or complementary powers in one's life at any given time. These powers could be male and female, Yin and Yang, body and mind, life and death, or any powers that represent one's relationship with God. I would add spirit and soul to her list of complementary powers.

Bach postulates that, depending upon which of the powers is in the lead, one may die "in harmony related to God or in the grip of fear experiencing the power of darkness often called the Devil" (p. 188). Bach (1990) claims with regret that Peter "died a tortured person" (p. 25), feeling "alone . . . forlorn" (p. 146), forsaken by the very saint who is supposed to protect children, suffering "the anguish of sin and guilt," and mourning for a paradise he could never gain (Bach, 1969, p. 62).

On the other hand, Bach evaluates Priska's drawings as expressing her passage toward death with remarkable receptiveness. According to Bach (1969; 1990), it appears that Priska was preconscious of her dying and at some level had accepted it. She revealed this, nine months before her death, in her drawing of newly hatched chicks; it contained a sign that instructed: "*Nicht futtern*" (Do not feed) (1990, p. 123).

Such a sign is posted on cages or fences enclosing animals at zoos. The warning is often followed by an explanation that the animal's particular nutritional needs are maintained by a special diet, and that extra feedings pose a health risk for the animal. Sensing her destiny, Priska may have felt that the hospital's medicine was not needed and only interfered with nature and her soul's path. The fact that this drawing occurred nine months before her death reflects Priska's gestation for rebirth through death.

Bach (1969) describes Priska as steadily pursuing her path, secure in her identity, at home with nature, and with a good, trusting relationship with St. Nicholas; Priska reveals this through a drawing in which she steals (gleefully, it appears) a tangerine from the sack of the saint's helper, explaining that she is not afraid of the saint.

Hans Peter Weber was the clinical artist at the University Neurosurgical Clinic in Zurich where both Peter and Priska were patients. He came to know Peter and Priska well and he often invited them to draw and paint. He collected ninety-four pictures from Priska and over two hundred from Peter, who did some of them at home and mailed them to Weber.

Weber submitted all these children's drawings, along with a careful account of the children's case histories, to Susan Bach for a second evaluation. (I do not know whether Bach met either of these children in person.) She reported on them in her two publications previously referenced. In addition to the way Bach viewed these histories and pictures, I suggest there is yet another way to view them that we may consider.

We can acknowledge that Peter's drawings contain images compatible, for the most part, with the spirit archetype – cars, tanks, airplanes, an Indian shooting an arrow, a parachutist, a skier, a train, a man wearing double holsters with pistols. In two of his drawings he paints himself fighting a fire, revealing to us his fighting spirit that wants to overcome the burning tumor he had.

Peter's spirited assertiveness is also expressed in the two drawings of St. Nicholas mentioned earlier. In one of these drawings, the bag (containing what Peter said was all the good things) has the characteristics of a mandala, a symbol depicting a movement toward recovering the Self, or reintegration (Bach, 1990, picture supplement, Fig. 34).[4] This drawing came a year and a half before Peter's death.

The good times were unquestionably running out for him (symbolized by the good things running out of the saint's sack), and Peter was striving for psychic recovery even if he could not achieve a physical one. But he does not give up the somatic struggle willingly. As projected in his drawing, he is "a disobedient one" (Bach, 1990) fighting against the cancer that would seize him and carry him away (p. 31).

On the other hand, Priska drew pictures of a tortoise, a mushroom house, lilies-of-the-valley, May bells, tulips, forget-me-nots, her special, "magic flower," baby chicks, various birds, an apple tree, a mountain range, and gnomes (folklore figures who inhabit the interior of the Earth and guard Her treasures). These are all typical features of *Anima Mundi*, the World-Soul.

Must we presume that the dying process evoked either positive or negative feelings in these children? I am not sure we can judge their experience as "good" or "bad." The contrasting ways these children responded to their dying process concurred with a particular archetypal energy; for Peter it was spirit, for Priska it was soul (at times for her, counterbalanced with spirit).

It is unfortunate that some die with unnecessary anguish as the result of malevolent remarks, misinformation, or physical abuse. We must be cautious and avoid hasty conclusions in making assessments about the way persons experience their deaths. Receptiveness to differentiating spirit and soul characteristics in one who is dying can broaden our understanding of the person's life and shed light on their transition from life into death.

Peter needed to die as a warrior, and thus the spirit archetype directed him to fight the good fight. Priska came from an unstable, discor-
dant family, Bach's (1969) readers are told, and apparently needed to
make friends with the world and be in harmony with it. Lacking ade-
quate nurture from her physical parents, Priska turned (at least unconsciously) to the Great Mother, symbolized by Mother Earth. Priska's
death released her to a condition in which she possibly received the
love and care she always longed for but never experienced fully in her
earthly life.

One seems to know, at least unconsciously, when death is near.
Facing death with a soul perspective involves a state of receptiveness
and anticipation tempered with patient waiting, imagining, and taking
one day at a time. Although there is an underlying acceptance of one's
fate, life becomes especially real and cherished. One wants to celebrate every moment as though it may be the last conscious time one
has. There is no dwelling on the past; the prevailing mood is an acute
awareness and acceptance of today – living in the moment. Robert
Sardello (1992) says that soul is also future oriented. Soul dreams
about and longs for a time that is to come. A woman about two-thirds
through a pregnancy can especially relate to this paradoxical feeling of
patient containment coupled with a longing for her infant's birth.

Those who die with a soul perspective wish to complete unfinished
business; this includes taking in new knowledge and experience. This
characteristic, while anchored in the soul's curiosity and receptiveness,
relies on the spirit for initiation. The soul stance allows one to be content through relatedness to reality in spite of circumstances, while
simultaneously intuiting possibilities for change. What appears to be a
passive, contented surrender to death is really an animated embrace of
what is left of one's life and wishful reaching out to encompass a new
life.

A soul-directed approach to dying is compatible with the philosophy of the hospice movement. We recall Woodman's (1985) words:
"death is birth of the life we have yet to live" (p.14). Dreams and fantasy both sustain and prepare one in completing life and preparing to
journey beyond. A soul-directed perspective of death is grounded in
spiritual contemplation (not necessarily synonymous with religious
contemplation).

With conscious or preconscious knowledge that one is nearing the
end of life, a spirit-oriented adaptation to this truth employs an attitude

of perseverance and tenacity. The spirit does not give up striving for a healthy condition. One fights like a soldier to support the healing force. A disease process is viewed as an enemy that must be opposed to the end. It is a campaign to actively resist the disease as much as possible until (one hopes) the willpower, faith, or some other power will lead to overcoming and transcending the illness. Spirit is reluctant to acknowledge the certitude of death. Emphasis is upon meeting the challenges life presents and upon accomplishing as much as one can.

The spirit's way seeks information assiduously and pursues untried methods of treatment. The spirit is intolerant of limitations and it stubbornly pushes against physical deterioration while obstinately identifying with a healthy state. A dragon-slaying style prompts one to defy losing consciousness and to withstand the pain of battle with courage and undying faith in the Self.

An example of employing a spirit method in dealing with a life-threatening illness comes from The Wellness Community of Central Indiana – a support program for cancer patients. Part of their stated purpose claims that "the program is not a place to learn to die or adapt one's life to the illness. It is a program where cancer patients learn whatever they need to know to participate in their fight for recovery along with their physicians and other health care professionals rather than acting as hopeless, helpless, passive victims" (Excerpt from *Fight Cancer Together*, printed brochure, The Wellness Community of Central Indiana, Indianapolis).

It is possible, of course, to face one's death by integrating[5] spirit and soul attitudes. This could be seen in Dennis's last year of life (reviewed in Chapter 9). Dennis did not achieve this integration by merely differentiating spirit and soul, but by appreciating, honoring, and consciously personifying their differences. However, I believe that young children do not usually make this integration until much closer to the moment of death. An important task for young children is to establish gender identity. As pointed out earlier, the objective psyche associates soul with the feminine, and spirit with the masculine, and mistakenly classifies these according to gender. Never mind that not all men possess every aspect of the spirit archetype, nor all women embody every expression of the soul archetype.

It will take several generations yet for the objective psyche to evolve and to adopt images for spirit and soul archetypes apart from those for male and female archetypes. For now, little boys will most often identify with behavioral patterns associated with spirit energy, and little girls will usually present themselves in a manner synonymous with soul. This identification will exist as projections until sufficient mirroring supports the ego to embody what has been projected as part of one's Self.

But let us examine how the spirit and soul principles provide a profoundly transforming reintegration as a young child's life nears closure. To begin, consider spirit and soul as vital archetypes that provide patterns of being that reside within the young child. My observations lead me to believe that a little boy who knows (consciously or unconsciously) that death is near, will experience a strong urge to establish firmly his identity (mythologically speaking) as the "royal prince," symbolic of the Divine Self. Similarly, a little girl in the same position feels that she must establish her identity as the "royal princess." (These goals reflect the theme in C. G. Jung's work that the purpose of human existence is to individuate.)

The urges to realize the "prince" or "princess" are connected to the central archetype – the regulating Self. These psychic urges may be related to the natural inflation that occurs in early childhood when ego identifies with Self.

There is also an inner wisdom that advises a child of potential not yet realized or recognized. At the ego level, the boy will usually identify with figures that manifest spirit characteristics, and the girl will identify most likely with those that are linked to soul. Through various forms of transference and fantasy, "prince" and "princess" will experience spontaneously the spirit and soul archetypes.

These archetypes will invigorate those experiences stored in one's memory that will enable Self affirmation and nurture ego growth. Thus, a sense of wholeness occurs via expanded consciousness. The succession of these reintegrative actions paves the way for integrating the less dominant or yet unembodied archetype; ultimately, spirit and soul unite. Life and death are reconciled; like the Uroborus (mythical snake that bites its tail), the end is the beginning.

As I have already suggested, one does not die without soul or lacking spirit; the two are complementary poles of a vital principle of life. It is simply that children will usually excel in developing the pole that most corresponds to the gender to which they most relate.

Next, I present two of my own cases that represent the spirit-soul dichotomy in the individual's dying process. A few drawings from each patient will illustrate how differently one can experience death from spirit and soul perspectives. The case illustrating soul perspective comes from a young girl and the one illustrating spirit perspective comes from a little boy. This is the way we usually see this dichotomy manifested in children (for reasons previously discussed); it is conceivable that a male subject could approach death from a soul stance, and a female subject could employ the spirit mode.

Chapter 10 Notes

1. In ancient Chinese philosophy and religion, Yin (feminine) and Yang (masculine) were two principles thought to influence the destiny of life and matter.

2. The German word, *kraft*, can also be translated as strength, vigor, or might.

3. In ancient Chinese philosophy, all of creation was classified as having either Yang energy or Yin energy. Mountains, lightning, the sun, or a bull, e.g., were Yang; caves, clouds, the moon, or a cow were Yin. (See note 1., above.)

4. Bach did not comment on the mandalic feature of the bag of good things.

5. Complete integration of any archetypal energy is humanly impossible.

Chapter 11

A TREASURE SEEKER AND A WARRIOR MEET DEATH

Ronda McGraw's CF was diagnosed when she was two years old; she had previously been treated elsewhere for what appeared to be asthma and bronchitis. She was one of the first to join my study, which began in 1976, about the time of her sixth birthday; she died at home at the age of ten. Ronda contributed 17 drawings to the study; we will consider 5 that were produced during the last three months of her life.

Ronda was in a very advanced stage of her disease. Her symptoms included increased coughing and frequent vomiting caused by the violent paroxysms. Her congested sinuses produced frequent headaches, her cardiopulmonary functioning had worsened, her respirations were quite labored. She had a severe bronchial infection (pseudomonas), and needed nightly oxygen to counter cyanosis (blueness under fingernails and toenails).

Ronda drew two pictures the same day at a visit to the outpatient clinic. While Mrs. McGraw was taking care of checkout forms at the desk, Ronda sat down and said to me, "Let me draw a quick one here." I gave her the pencils and paper and she drew a shamrock (Fig. 23) in anticipation of St. Patrick's day. The shamrock is the emblem for Ireland, St. Patrick, and the Trinity in Christianity. (Ronda had Scotch-Irish ancestors.)

Her shamrock does not grow in the ground; it appears to float in the air. First, she outlined the shamrock with dark green, then using the lighter shade of green, she colored a border on each of the three petals; the top petal bows slightly toward the left. It looked as though she were going to continue this light green down the length of the stem, but she stopped just below the petals and changed to the dark green for filling in the stem. Although she had outlined the bottom of the stem in a straight, horizontal green line, she went below this line with the dark green pencil. This made a very ragged look – almost as if the plant had been torn from the ground. She applied the same dark green to the inside of the petals. The top petal bows slightly toward the left.

Some novices at amplifying pictures are tempted to "see" additional images in drawings in much the way one sees images in puffy clouds, or discovers the image of the Virgin Mary reflected in the glass wall of an office building. One might "see," within the outline of the shamrock, for example, a parallel with some divine figure such as Jesus on the cross, or an angel. However, seeing images that are not depicted goes beyond amplification; novices must guard against projecting what the drawing evokes in themselves – images related to their *own* psycho-spiritual and somatic experiences. We must stress that Ronda has drawn *only a shamrock.*

One of the basic steps in understanding the language of drawings is to notice what is absent that seems likely to be included in such a drawing. The ground is notably missing from Ronda's drawing; we might expect at least a flower pot or vase of water to hold and help sustain the life of the shamrock. Is Ronda's means of sustaining her own life fading away? Does she need help in "containing" her dying process? If so, where might she find a container that seems satisfactory? Might the container be life at home?

We might recognize some similarity between Ronda's shamrock that appears destined to wilt and die and Priska's newly hatched chicks that are not to be fed (discussed in Chapter 9). Ronda's picture shows a shamrock that has been plucked from the mother plant. Its isolation illustrates Ronda's experience having a life-threatening disease that sets her apart from others; possibly, she has a sense of being "picked" to face death soon. Bertoia (1993) comments that the floating quality in patients' drawings (such as we see in Ronda's shamrock) suggests "distancing from this world" and "floating free of earthly attachments" (p. 84).

Earlier, I mentioned Bach's (1974/75) comment that two shades of green on the same object might signal a chemical imbalance. In CF, the electrolytes are often out of the normal range of values. CF cells take in too much sodium and cannot emit enough chloride. When Ronda's lab tests were completed that day, her sodium level was within normal range, but her potassium was low (3.3; normal range 3.4-4.7), her carbon dioxide was high (41; 28 is considered high), and her chloride was low (89; high-low range is 98-106). Could these values relate in any way to the two shades of green on her shamrock? On the other hand, could the weaker, yellowish green that encapsulates the petals of the shamrock indicate gradually diminishing healthy growth and physical weakening?

When Ronda finished this drawing, her mother approached and announced they must go upstairs to the X-ray department. I asked if I might accompany them there, and Ronda proceeded to explain to her mother, "That's so if I get any inspirations to draw, she'll be there to get it." Mrs. McGraw welcomed me to join them and we didn't have long to wait before Ronda went to the X-ray room.

During Ronda's absence, Mrs. McGraw began to voice her concerns about her husband, whom she claimed denied that Ronda was dying. The mother wanted to prepare for having Ronda die at home; she said she believed that was what Ronda wanted also. Apparently, her husband did not want to admit that Ronda was about to die and he did not want to discuss these plans.

Mrs. McGraw was relieved to have someone to talk with about this matter. She said she had learned from the clinical social worker that dying at home would be possible for Ronda if she had a "heparin lock." (This is a device for eliminating repeated needle insertions for IV medicine; it requires inserting a hypodermic needle in the vein and anchoring it for repeated use. It must be flushed with an anticoagulant after each IV infusion, and capped until time for the next infusion.)

Ronda's dying at home had been a point of discussion with Ronda's doctor that day in the clinic. Ronda didn't want the heparin lock inserted that day, so the doctor decided to try a different oral antibiotic for a week. Mrs. McGraw explained that if the new antibiotic did not work, their plan was to admit Ronda to the hospital and begin intravenous treatment. Then, a heparin lock would be introduced and Ronda's mother would be instructed how to manage it before they sent Ronda home. Throughout this conversation, I continued to reflect back to Mrs. McGraw what I was hearing and what it seemed she was feeling. She looked more relaxed now and became even more talkative.

"She's smart; she knows *everything* that goes on! The other day it was so nice out that we sat outside for a while. I said, 'Just think, Ronda, in a few weeks it'll be like this all the time.' And she said, 'But I may be dead in a few weeks.'" Mrs. McGraw's eyes met mine. "That's what I mean; she knows!"

"Yes," I agreed. "She certainly seems to know just what's happening, all right. And we need to respect that, don't we?"

"People say I should talk with her about her dying – that she might have questions to ask about it. But I just can't . . . ."

Our conversation was interrupted by Ronda's return from the X-ray room and her announcement that she would like to draw another picture while waiting for her X-ray to be developed. "What are those men called that go after the pot of gold? I'm going to draw one's hat!"

"You mean a leprechaun?" I asked.

"Yeah, that's it, a leprechaun. I never drew one of those for you. I'm going to draw one's hat."

The hat appears in the upper left quadrant of her paper (Fig. 24) near the center of the page where quadrant boundary lines would meet. The right edge of the hat and part of the hat's brim cross over into the upper, right quadrant. The hat's proximity to the center may signify that something about this hat is related to a central issue in Ronda's life. In sandplay analysis, according to Ammann (1991), objects in the center pertain to the relationship of the ego to the Self; they symbolize the centering of the personality. Ammann considers that objects or motifs in the upper left pertain to one's inner world – their spiritual impulses. Could it be that Ronda has entered a significantly contemplative phase of her life? This is a question to hold onto as we study other features of the drawing.

Ronda shaded the hat heavily with dark green and put a yellow-green band just above its brim. She drew the petals of a shamrock, colored the same yellow-green, rising from the middle of the band, but she shaded over it with the dark green. (The shamrock is difficult to see against the dark green of the hat.) Why did she draw just the hat? She could, and often did, draw people. Why is a human figure missing now? This is yet another question to keep in mind as we examine more of her drawing.

In about the middle of the lower right quadrant, Ronda drew a large pot of gold. The cauldron is thickly shaded in a rich-looking earth brown and it is filled to the top with gold. She spent a lot of time coloring this pot of gold. She completed the picture by adding her first and last name in bright red and underlining it. (See lower, left quad-

rant – I have blocked out her last name to preserve confidentiality.)
When children put their names on their pictures, I take this as a sign
that they feel satisfaction about their picture; it is something they feel
related to and claim as coming from them.

I responded to Ronda's "inspiration" with gratitude and deep interest by commenting, "I see the leprechaun's hat, but the leprechaun
seems to be gone. And what is this over here – a big pot of gold?"
Ronda cheerfully confirmed this. Then I asked, "Well, now that the
leprechaun is gone, I wonder who is going to find this pot of gold?"

Ronda flashed me a big grin and blurted out, "I am!"

Why is a human figure absent and why is attention given to a hat?
Might the hat's position on the paper suggest centering on something
that is of main concern now? Ronda never promised me a leprechaun,
a human figure; she announced from the beginning that she would
draw the leprechaun's *hat.* The circular hat and its brim form a circle
within a circle, one form of the mandala, a symbol of wholeness. (This
could be detected from a bird's-eye view better than from the sideways
rendition Ronda has given. Possibly this side view shows her inability
to grasp a full view of the wholeness and completion of her life.) A
hat's relationship to the head suggests thinking, ideas, personality, and
ultimately, the individuation process.

If Ronda feels a need to move toward the wholeness of Self identity, she is on a path from deintegration to reintegration. She has not yet
discovered the treasure of her Self (and may not until the moment of
her death), so it is fitting for the human figure to be absent. If there is
any doubt that this child is moving toward a redemptive, reintegrative
phase (possibly the final one of her life), note that she took much time
and care drawing a large pot of gold (the container for her treasure).

I note that this treasure is in the quadrant where Bach (1990) has
found images related to one's immediate past or their potential future.
Gold is a common symbol of the Self as a treasure. We could say that
Ronda is "becoming" the pot of gold, the treasure of the Self. She confirmed this not only by stating her intent to get the gold, but by sign-
ing the picture in red – the color of the transforming fire and the blood
of life, and by pouring so much time and energy into drawing the pot
of gold.

The hat is positioned just off center in the upper left side of the
paper. We can make the following associations about that, based on
various theories of analytical psychology: left symbolizes one's inner

world and that which is not yet conscious; center symbolizes a central issue or what is of chief concern. We might consider the hat's location to reflect Ronda's yearning for some forgotten, repressed, or undiscovered part of her psyche that needs to be brought into consciousness – some potential that needs to come to light in her mandalic, soul-spinning effort to reunify her Self.

What else is missing from this drawing besides the human figure? According to myth, the pot of gold is usually buried at the end of the rainbow (Leach & Fried, 1972). The rainbow is a bridge between heaven and earth, according to the mythologies of several cultures (Leach & Fried, 1972). Native Americans recognize the rainbow as the road of the dead, whereas some Australian aborigines see the rainbow as a serpent, and it is through this rainbow serpent that ritual initiates are believed to be reborn after being swallowed (Leach & Fried, 1972).

Perhaps the rainbow is omitted from Ronda's drawing because she is not yet ready to travel the bridge from earth to heaven; it is too early for her initiation into the life after death. Had Ronda drawn the leprechaun, we might see the drawing as conveying spirit quality, but the mandalic hat and the container of gold are representations of soul.

About a month later, Ronda's condition required hospitalization. Although her right (dominant) hand was attached to an IV board when I visited her bedside, she insisted she could draw a picture for me (Fig. 25). She began in the upper left quadrant and outlined a large egg with the orange drawing pencil. (It was the Easter season.) She filled in the top part with the same orange, then used the pale green to cover the bottom part of the egg. She used this green to overlay a few, sketchy lines to the upper, orange area of the egg. This produced a two-toned egg that reminded me of plastic "eggs" that come apart in two sections to allow the insertion of little candies or prizes.

Alongside the egg, she drew 2 flowers in the upper right quadrant. Each plant has a pale green stem and 2 leaves – one on each side. She outlined the leaves with the pale green pencil, but left them otherwise colorless. Using red, she then outlined a blossom with eight petals for the left flower, and in the center of the blossom she outlined, again with red, seven more petals; she left these colorless except for their red outlines. For the flower on the right she made a blossom outlined in red and having a circular center edged with eight petals. She identified these flowers as roses. Like the first flower, these petals have no color.

In the lower, central area of the paper, Ronda drew an Easter basket. She outlined the handle and upper part with pale blue and drew
two blue lines to form the top two rows of the basket. Then she added
succeeding lines in pairs, showing further rows of the basket weave.
From top to bottom, the first pair is blue, the next pair is yellow, the
third pair is red, and the last is purple.

In the top of the basket, to the far left, Ronda outlined a purple
object and put a purple chevron design on it; she said it was "candy."
To the right of this, she outlined a similar candy with the yellow pencil and then outlined a pink candy. Then she went to the bottom of the
page, and under the basket, to the left, made a pink, upper case letter
E. She moved back to the top of the basket, and with the brown pencil, drew to the right of the pink candy what she identified as a "choco-
late bunny," with a zigzag, *M* design in the ears. To the right of the
bunny, next to the basket's handle, she outlined a pale blue object that
is probably another candy.

At this point, she returned to the bottom of the picture and continued with her lettering to misspell the word, Easter. Next to the previously made pink *E,* she made a pale blue *S,* followed by an orange *T,*
a pale green *E,* and a red *R.* She completed this with a red exclama-
tion point. (The face to the left of the basket was not yet a part of the
picture.)

She signaled that the drawing was finished and I remarked that it
looked as though this picture had a story to go with it. I invited Ronda
to tell the story. She responded, "No, I'm too tired; *You* tell it!" She
gave me a grin with a look of expectation.

I began a story: "One fine Easter morning the Easter bunny came
and left a magic egg, made two roses bloom, and left an Easter basket
filled with all kinds of goodies." I leaned a little closer and looked
Ronda right in the eye, "And who do you think came along and found
them all?"

Ronda tilted her head, wrinkled her forehead as though in deep
concentration, and feigned mental strain while mulling the question
over. After milking her performance of bafflement, this dramatic little
ham turned directly toward me and blurted out, "Ronda!" As though
her answer had triggered some memory, she quickly added, "Oh, I
ain't finished; I forgot something." She grabbed the red coloring pencil with her left hand, carefully positioned it in her right hand that was
awkwardly restrained by the IV board, and drew a head to the left of

the basket handle. The image had red hair just like Ronda, a red smile, red cheeks, and red eyebrows. She then outlined the eyes with black and filled in the irises with dark green, the color of her own eyes.

I remarked that this drawing reminded me of another one she drew earlier of a pot of gold. "That's right!" She reacted, knowingly, to my remark.

She had been quick to tell me that she would be the one to claim the pot of gold in her previous drawing; today she let me know that all the good things in her picture (and the potential they represented) would be hers as well.

We have already discussed the significance of repeated objects and their correspondence with important units of time, especially in drawings made at critical times in one's life. Ronda has 2 flowers with 2 leaves, 8 petals on each flower, and 8 horizontal lines (in four pairs) detailing the weave of her Easter basket. Ronda died two months later in approximately eight weeks.

There are other features of this drawing that I find more remarkable than forecasting her death. (It was already obvious to the hospital staff that Ronda was in the terminal stage of her illness.) I am particularly interested in the item she drew first – the egg. It is so large it would fill her Easter basket and it is bigger than the two flowers combined.

The egg is an ancient symbol for regeneration and rebirth. Before Christianity, eggs represented rebirth or re-creation in vernal equinox celebrations. The Easter egg is a Christianization of the pagan symbol for the rite of spring. Gimbutas (1989) informs us that there are several categories of egg symbolism. One of these links the egg with water and with the bull and his horns as life generators. (Recall the bull's skull and the floral design on its forehead in one of Dennis's drawings in Chapter 5).

Ancient European pottery dating from 4600 B.C. to 4500 B.C. has been found decorated with eggs alternating with horns (Gimbutas, 1989). We learn from Gimbutas (1989) about egg-shaped burial chambers where the bones of the deceased were laid after the flesh had decomposed; the bones were supposed to incubate and regenerate. She mentions also the cosmic egg from whence all of creation supposedly began. The egg is a notable image in our objective psyche. It corresponds to the feminine and to soul.

Earlier I remarked that the color pattern on Ronda's egg reminded me of the plastic eggs used to contain Easter candies or favors. The egg as a container of a prize suggests the idea of searching for the prize of the true Self. As both adults and children come closer to their deaths the journey to find and affirm the Self becomes a vital task. This task prompts one to live life as completely as possible. Ronda validated this idea when she fantasized gaining the pot of gold, the magic egg, the Easter basket of goodies, and the roses.

We explored the symbolism of the rose as it relates to death and rebirth when we studied Dennis's rose drawing in Chapter 9. The Grimm's fairy tale "Little Briar Rose" (also known as "Sleeping Beauty") is a story with the theme of death and rebirth. When the time is right, Briar Rose awakens; when the time is right, Ronda will end her journey and awaken to a new life beyond ego consciousness.

The chevron design on her purple candy (further suggested in the basket's handle) meant nothing to me until years later when I was studying a curious detail in a drawing she did ten days later. We will return to this feature shortly, when I describe that incident.

Ronda was growing homesick at this time (ten days after drawing the Easter picture), regardless that her mother came in daily. Ronda was thoroughly bored with the hospital and she made many complaints in contrasting it with her home; she missed her mom's cooking and the opportunity to play with her siblings and the cousins who lived in her neighborhood.

She began drawing a picture for me that appeared to be a self portrait – a girl with red hair and green eyes (Fig. 26). A purple turtleneck top covers the long, thin neck. Ronda added a necklace with an orange, heart-shaped, transparent medallion that has a V shape suspended in the middle.

Why such a long neck? Freudian interpretation would consider a long, thin neck to suggest splitting off from socialization and life-related sources – a schizoid characteristic. A long neck also exaggerates separation between head (rational thought) and body (impulse). An unusually long neck might, in Jungian dream analysis, represent compensation needed for the absence of a neck. What would having no neck mean? It suggests having no backbone. Sticking your neck out means you dare to speak up or take a risk. This behavior is opposite of "having no backbone." Is there an issue that Ronda needs to speak up about more boldly? We should keep this in mind as we continue to examine her drawing.

Her mouth is a big, open smile. With a graphite pencil, Ronda added teeth, then erased them; they had made the girl look angry. (Did Ronda not wish to admit her anger over being kept in a hospital that could not make her get better?)

The portrait ended just below the shoulders. A halo of pale blue sky filled the top edge of the page. Her final touch was to add bright yellow wings to each shoulder. At the bottom of the page she wrote in script with the dark green pencil, "Ronda an angel!"

Earlier during this hospital admission for Ronda, I had talked with her about another child with CF who had been in my study. She and Ronda had been close friends and the little girl had died about a year ago. Ronda and I talked about what happens when we die. Ronda had it all figured out – "God turns you into an angel."

The chain or cord holding Ronda's medallion does not reach completely around the left side of the angel's neck. We might take this as a reminder that Ronda is not yet included as one of God's angelic flock; she waits faithfully for the transformation she is sure will bring her into that fold.

I thanked Ronda for her touching picture but was so overcome by it that I was almost speechless. I told her I had to hurry down to the CF clinic to see someone and left quickly. The CF specialist was finishing the last outpatient examinations for the day and would later make evening rounds to see his inpatients. Certain that he would want to see Ronda's drawing, and believing it important for him to see it before making evening rounds, I rushed to the outpatient clinic.

Ronda's doctor viewed the drawing carefully. He seemed hesitant to state the obvious message the picture conveyed; he turned to me, instead, and asked what I made of it. I told him I thought she was telling us very clearly that she would not be on earth much longer; she not only drew this message, she had even spelled it out in words.

I reported Ronda's various complaints about hospital life and how much she missed being at home. As he listened, I commented that she had convinced me that she wanted desperately to go home to die and that she wanted us to know this. I inquired whether it might be possible with a heparin lock and he affirmed that it would.

For him, the problem was in knowing whether more could be done to improve her medical condition if we kept her hospitalized. It was not an easy decision for him to make because of his responsibility to the pediatric residents. As he put it, "She's an excellent teaching case."

As director of pediatric medical education, he was clearly torn by an unavoidable conflict of interest. I had car-poolers to meet; I told him I had to leave and added, "I know you'll decide what's best."

The following morning, the CF specialist was the first person I saw when I entered the hospital and approached the elevators. I was eager to know what had happened. "What did you decide about Ronda when you made rounds last evening?"

A sly smile crept over his face. "If you hurry upstairs, you'll have a chance to tell her goodbye before they leave. She's all packed to go."

I was so happy for Ronda that I blurted out, "I knew you'd make the right decision!"

He replied, "It wasn't really a matter of my making a decision; it was a matter of listening to what the patient is telling us and respecting that." Put that way, sending Ronda home to die was a valuable lesson for the residents to learn. He knew how to juggle his hats to be fair to his patients and not cheat his students.

For quite some time, I was puzzled by the *V* on the medallion of Ronda's angel portrait (the chevron designs on her basket meant nothing to me). I began looking for influences from her personal unconscious. I could not discover any family member or close relative whose name began with the letter *V*. Colleagues suggested that it could be *V* for victory," but that old Churchillian expression came out of World War II and it was probably unknown to Ronda. The peace sign with spread fingers would be a more likely association.

Was the figure actually a letter *V*? Could it be, instead, a bird in flight? Sometime later I came across Marija Gimbutas's book, *The Language of the Goddess* (1989); she discusses pictorial motifs of the pre-Adam Goddess-Creator mythology. She revealed that the *V* and chevron designs are hieroglyphs (corresponding to the female pubic triangle) of the Bird Goddess, the Goddess of Death and Regeneration. Other symbols of this Goddess include the skull of the bull (see Chapter 6, Fig. 8) and the egg, which had appeared in Ronda's previous drawing.

As Gimbutas (1989) reminds us, the prehistoric Goddess period and its symbols lasted for thousands of years – longer than the period that produced the Indo-European myths and longer than the Christian period. It is not surprising that the ancient goddess symbols would leave a lasting impression on the collective psyche. What more can we learn about the symbols of the Bird Goddess that might amplify Ronda's picture?

In the Neolithic and Copper Age, artifacts of the bird goddess were frequently embellished with *V*, *X*, and *M* designs. (Notice the details in the Easter basket in Fig. 25.) These signs linked the goddess with the cosmic waters, which were her element (Gimbutas, 1989). The goddess was a water bird, linking heaven and earth; Gimbutas (1989) tells us that she was the "Source and Dispenser of life-giving moisture, an early and enduring preoccupation" (p. 29). It is ironic to consider the somatic contrast between this ancient, life-giving moisture and life-threatening CF in which a cellular disorder causes the lungs and the tissue around the joints to retain too much moisture.

Gimbutas (1989) tells of a universal myth in which a sacred water-fowl lays the cosmic egg; this myth is illustrated on Grecian, Bronze Age vases. In the same text, she comments on the egg-shaped tombs found in the central Mediterranean area, where there are amazing underground burial chambers cut into rock, in three different levels, as much as thirty feet below the surface.

The Bird Goddess is merely one aspect of the Great Goddess. Gimbutas (1989) informs us that "the Life Giver and the Death Wielder are one deity . . . she may be a waterfowl or a bird of prey, a harmless or a poisonous snake, but ultimately she is one indivisible Goddess" (p. 316).

In the second half of the fifth to early fourth millennium B.C., a new goddess icon appeared in Sardinia, Sicily, southern Italy, and Greece. She was flatter and not so round as the previous figurines. She was *T*-shaped; her upper arms and torso formed a rectangle, the lower body tapered into a cone, and she often had a long neck and a *V* sign engraved above the breasts (Gimbutas, 1989).

Influence of this Great Goddess, including aspects of the Birth Giver, Earth Mother, and Death Wielder, prevailed until the rise of Christianity. We learn from Gimbutas (1989) that Christian thought eventually integrated the Birth Giver and Earth Mother with the cult of the Virgin Mary.

Consider the leap Ronda made using the collective unconscious and her experience. By using the long neck with *V*-embellished medallion of the Bird Goddess in her angel picture and suggestions of the cosmic egg in her Easter picture, she blended her Christian beliefs with archetypal remnants from ages long past.

After Ronda's hospital discharge, I saw her once more before she died. She came to the CF clinic for her posthospitalization physical exam. She was still able to walk by using the portable oxygen her mother pushed along beside her. Ronda told me it was much better being at home than in the hospital. She eagerly drew a picture for me – one quite different from any I had seen her do before (Fig. 27).

She began with an orange sun, paper-chopped in the upper left corner; it has nine rays. If Ronda could live until September, the ninth month, she would realize her eleventh birthday. I also thought of nine as the number of months for human gestation. Was a rebirth on Ronda's horizon?

Next, she added a narrow band of blue sky across the top of the paper and then concentrated on three figures suspended in the lower middle of the paper. She drew these left to right, but described them – center, to left, to right – as "a cat and a dog and a mysterious boy flying a kite." Then she added, "Nobody knows who he [the boy] is." These figures have a striking, ghostly quality. Their heads bear enough detail to distinguish dog from cat, and animals from boy, but the animals have no real body; they look more like snakes or other crawling creatures headed to the left – westward. One might also imagine that each animal is stuffed into a huge stocking, pillow case, or bag of some kind, with just its head sticking out; their mobility is greatly restricted.

The boy has no ears and his eyes are blank and without pupils. His arms are rendered crudely and he has no hands to grip the string of the kite. The string is attached to the bottom of the boy's shirt sleeve, or possibly his hand grips it inside his sleeve. The expression "having something up one's sleeve" comes to mind. Does Ronda know some trick or surprise that others do not know?

The rising kite string has two, possibly three, loops (maybe one is a knot). The diamond-shaped kite flies near the paper's right edge about halfway up the page. The kite has a black outline and a crosshatched design of black, orange, and dark green.

Except for the sun, the drawing has very little color and it looks lifeless. She outlined the dog with dark brown and shaded just its ears – using the same brown. She outlined the cat in black and left it colorless. The boy's head and facial features are outlined in black; she added dark brown hair. He has no neck, but she outlined shoulders, arms, and a torso with dark green; they are not shaded in. His body appears to be severed just above the genitals.

The disabled appearance of the boy is remarkable. He can neither see, hear, nor clearly grasp anything, and he has nothing to stand on.

He has no capacity for eliminating waste from his body; it is in a paralyzed state. Paradoxically, he is somehow connected to a kite in flight. The "mysterious boy," separated from his most masculine feature, still has "something up his sleeve."

Bach observed that the motif of the bird can represent the soul, and that children sometimes extend the bird motif to airplanes. Is it possible that other flying objects in children's drawings, such as a kite, might also be unconsciously associated with soul energy?

I have already mentioned that Bertoia (1993) finds a "floating" quality in drawings made by terminally-ill children. She also refers to the fading away of detail and color in such drawings. The unknown, mysterious quality about the boy might signify some unintegrated facet of Ronda's psyche.

There is no plant life of any kind. The picture conveys an overall feeling that life and connectedness to the reality of this world are diminishing. This sort of picture would likely bring from Susan Bach the remark that the sun is setting for this child.

The sun *was* setting for Ronda; we all knew she could not live much longer. But along with distancing and detaching from her life on earth, as shown in her drawing, she has another process in motion. The dog and the cat have eyes with which to see, ears with which to hear, and noses to "sniff out" the good from the bad. These features reveal Ronda's natural, instinctual and intuitive Self. The dog often represents a watchful guardian and the cat is best known for its independence. Female cats are very maternal; they often take in other species to nurse. This nurturing, self-reliant, watchful waiting expresses soul energy. We might even view Ronda's three figures as waiting for three units of time; she died three months before her birthday.

Ronda died in June, five weeks after making a picture that contains five prominent items: a cat, a dog, a mysterious boy flying a kite, and a setting sun. She died quietly at home, with no apparent pain, in the loving circle of her family. She did not want to die away from what she most treasured. I am sure her belief in life after death as an angel helped sustain her as she waited soulfully for that special moment of leaving consciousness and life. With no need to fight death and struggle to hold on to life, Ronda died with confidence and peace.

JASON, IN FINAL BATTLE

Susan and Noah Tansey rejoiced over Jason's birth and continued to feel blessed, regardless that Jason was forever coming down with respiratory infections. Then, after nursing Jason through an unusually long period of illness, a diagnosis came that hits a parent's heart like a heavy death sentence: cystic fibrosis.

Jason's parents knew of no history of this disease in their respective families. They read diligently everything they could find about the disease and talked with other parents of children with CF. The diagnosis changed their plans to have more children.

Although they were not prepared for the emotional and financial burden of parenting a child with CF, they faced reality with enduring courage, strength, faith, and love. The combination of courage and love in this family was remarkable.

I first met Jason when he was five years old, although he and his family were already known to others on the CF treatment team. Both his parents participated in his medical care and there was never lack of tender support and patience in their parenting. Susan spent the most time with Jason while he was hospitalized only because of Noah's demanding work schedule. The Tanseys never misdirected onto our health care team their anger and frustration concerning Jason's diagnosis, or the burden the illness imposed on them. It seemed that the Tansey's love and patience extended equally to us.

It was obvious also that these parents reflected to Jason his experiences and accomplishments in a way that affirmed and validated for him a positive sense of identity. I noticed how skillfully they showed him empathy without promoting overdependency.

A shy but spunky youngster, Jason had a definite mind of his own. With a wisdom and maturity beyond their years, the Tanseys respected this quality in Jason without relaxing the boundaries he needed.

Heroes were very important to Jason. He had many, many comic books about human heroes and superheroes. Like his father, Jason had a talent for drawing, and he drew many pictures of heroic adventures. Noah painted a large picture of Spider Man (one of Jason's favorite characters), which they hung at the head of Jason's bed at home (where other parents might have preferred to hang a crucifix). Spider Man watched over Jason like a guardian angel and gave him the courage both to fight the infections that CF made him harbor, and to live out his life.

Ultimately, it was Spider Man and all of Jason's other heroes who gave him the courage to die. After projecting heroism onto his fantasy figures, onto his parents, and onto the medical personnel who cared for him clinically, Jason internalized the hero archetype for himself. He died as a hero at the age of seven.

It was our practice to have a meeting of family and CF staff a few weeks after the death of any CF patient; its purpose was to promote closure both for parents and staff. We shared our memories of the departed person and expressed the loss we felt. It was a time for us to affirm for the parents their devoted and enduring care, and it also gave the parents an opportunity to say things to us they had not already voiced.

About a month after Jason's funeral, his parents accepted our invitation to meet with us. When it was my time to meet individually with the parents, we sat in my office and went through Jason's folder of drawings. Suddenly, Jason's father said, "I've always wondered if I said the right thing when Jason asked whether he was going to die." I asked when it was, approximately, that such talk began. Noah replied, "It was around Christmas before last." I pulled two pictures from Jason's folder; the first one was painted on December 7, 1979 (Fig. 28), at the time when Jason began to question whether he was dying. He painted this picture while hospitalized for a relapse of CF. He drew the second picture (Fig. 29) in the CF clinic one month later – two weeks after his hospital discharge.

Jason had started to sign his name across the top of the first picture (Fig. 28). A spelling mistake inspired him to turn his misspelled name into what he called "a flying car." Then he added his name, spelled correctly, above the flying car.

A flying car is a departure from reality. Fantasy in a drawing often corresponds with a tendency to deny something in one's reality. I was certain Jason fantasized being a healthy boy, free of CF, just as Dennis wished to be released from CF and be "free as a bird." Jason tried to deny in various ways that he was "a cystic"; one of these was his attempt to hide spells of paroxysmal coughing. Perhaps he fantasized that with a flying car he could magically transcend his physical limitations.

We recall that spontaneous drawings, like dreams, are expressions of unconscious thought. Do flying birds in Jason's picture conspire with his flying car to express his soul's longing to flee what one must face on earth? On the other hand, could the birds reflect a precognition that such an escape will become real?

Shoreline, water, birds, and other flying figures are motifs rich in symbolism. We could fill pages amplifying these images in Jason's painting. Instead, I wish to discuss the boy with outstretched arms at the edge of the shore. Having collected from Jason several drawings of human figures depicting various body positions, I knew that this was not the only way possible for him to draw humans. I believed he drew the boy's stance purposefully and that it was significant.

The boy in the drawing might be reaching for help to get to the opposite side. Somatically considered, the opposite side for Jason would be the healthy one. But from his psyche's perspective, the boy could be beckoning to the side opposite earthly life, the other life, or afterlife. C. G. Jung (1976c) observed that "standing on the bank" is a common motif that appears in dreams when one is rising from the unconscious "to see with one's eyes what is happening . . . aware of individual fate and the relation to the deity" (p. 111).

The archetype of transition reveals itself often in our dreams through myriad symbols. Water and birds are common symbols of transition; Jason's parents and I needed to consider whether Jason had come to the great transition of life to death when he made this painting.

With the advancement of COPD, was Jason losing the battle to restore somatic order? Comparing the picture in Figure 28 with the one (Fig. 29) done a month later, we find green grass in both. Grass is a symbol of life and growth; it might suggest the amount of Jason's lifetime already spent. In Figure 28, grass covers barely one-third the distance across the paper, as contrasted with grass spreading a little more than two-thirds the way across in Figure 29. Could this reveal that Jason's lifetime was running out? Did he, within one month, come to grips (at least unconsciously) with the reality of losing ground in his struggle with CF? If so, what did this mean to his psyche? We must examine other features of Jason's pictorial expression to find out.

The human figure we saw in Figure 28 is gone from the shore in Figure 29. The birds and the flying car are also absent. Instead, Jason has superhuman hero figures. Superman holds a large black object high as though it requires little or no effort. Could Superman's posture represent a triumphant, heroic bearing of the burden of CF?

Jason's parents recalled what a prominent role superheroes played in Jason's life during his last year. Identifying with hero figures gave energy to Jason's hero archetype within. This projected fantasy stimulated Jason to constellate for himself certain heroic characteristics. After repeatedly identifying with heroes in fantasy play, Jason displayed an inner strength and peace that undoubtedly helped him to carry the burden of CF.

By noting the similarities and contrasts in these two pictures, Jason's parents could see that in one month's time, their son had compensated for the outrage of CF and for his inner knowledge that he was dying, by calling upon the hero side of his personality. Jason made Figure 29 in the clinic, January 23, 1980; he died January 22, the following year.

Jason's last hospitalization was short. He was admitted through the emergency room, in critical distress from a sudden relapse. Soon stabilized, he seemed to be rapidly improving. Then his health and energy failed just as rapidly and he died quickly. The last week of his life he spontaneously drew several cartoons of warriors in battle. None of the drawings were dated and we do not know their proper sequence. Before his last hours, he must have stashed the drawings in the shallow drawer of his over-the-bed table that he used as a drawing desk. After Jason died, the nurse who cleared his room discovered the drawings. Figures 30 and 31, from this series, inform us that Jason faced the completion of his life by calling upon his hero within.

The meaning of death and how one chooses to encounter it varies among individuals. Jason placed value on fighting his disease and upon enduring the pain of battle like a brave soldier. Recognizing his final battle, and sharing Ronda's belief in a new life after death, Jason could die in peace, knowing that he had fought a good fight. As for Ronda, celebrating her homecoming allowed her to slip out of consciousness and life with confidence and peace.

Chapter 12

CAREGIVING AND THE SPIRITUAL ASPECT
OF THE PSYCHE

Those who minister medically or on a psychospiritual level to dying patients tend to evaluate and label their deaths as "good" or "bad." Patients judged to be candidates for a "good" death tend to do the following things: they seem not to fear death; they openly express feelings about dying; they do not complain about their condition; they sort methodically through and tie up their affairs in anticipation of death; they wait patiently – almost long for that event and receptively take one day at a time. These patients are described as "prepared" and are thus considered to experience death as a peaceful event.

Patients judged to be candidates for a "bad" death tend to complain, to fight death in every way, to maintain persistently that recovery *is possible*, and to identify with and enthusiastically validate life by making plans for the future. These patients are usually judged unprepared because of their denial; their attitude supposedly makes death a difficult, violent event.

I am reminded of an English friend whose husband died after a drawn-out battle with cancer. This woman and her husband were devoted to one another; they had been through many hardships together, including escaping from the Nazis in Germany. They ran a small, intimate bed-and-breakfast and enjoyed the many interesting people they met this way, several of whom remained their friends throughout the years. Whenever they could, they enjoyed closing temporarily and traveling together to explore new places and meet new people.

This couple refused to dwell on negative consequences when the husband's cancer was diagnosed. They preferred to concentrate on the goodness of life and to continue to enjoy it to its fullest. They went

162

about their activities as usual and looked past the advancement of the creeping illness. The husband cooperated with treatment, but neither he nor his wife allowed the disease to dominate their life together; instead, they related to all they could find that was healthy and good.

After the man died, a social worker, a well-meaning friend of the couple, chided the wife for not discussing openly with her husband her feelings about his dying. This social worker told my friend that she had done her husband disservice by not getting things out in the open, and that she had denied him the opportunity to put closure to his life. The social worker claimed that the man died with "unfinished business."

My friend confided to me that she knew her husband well enough to know that had she broached the subject of his dying, he would have quickly changed the subject. She knew he needed her to remain undaunted and cheerful; I recognized that she also needed that attitude for herself.

The social worker labeled this couple's behavior denial, and viewed it as unhealthy and leading to a "bad" death. But denial is not always unhealthy; more often than not it is employed to protect the ego until the individual has the strength to integrate reality. Shneidman (1978) says that "denial is not a stage of dying . . . [but] rather a ubiquitous aspect of the dying process" that emerges now and then throughout one's time of dying (p. 212).

The social worker was concerned with feelings that involve soul work. My friend and her husband did not need soul energy for him to die; their lives had been filled with the quality of soul. This man's capacity to anticipate and reflect (via soul) upon the potential of life, dying, and death triggered spirit to challenge his perspective and ultimately show him how to die.

This couple related to each other with compassion, receptiveness, and gentleness. Their attitude allowed them to present spirit outwardly — their corresponding energy that was needed to give support in dying and death. It was spirit energy that gave them the determination to continue with their style of life. Spirit calls forth heroic actions, analytical problem-solving, and penetration into the meaning of experience. Spirit complemented the souls of this couple; it gave the man the boldness to face his death by living life to the last breath; it helped his wife endure his dying and it fortified her to continue with their business.

I have come to believe that death is neither "good" nor "bad"; it is simply the closure of this life. We do the things we need, behave the way we need, and endure the challenges we need to aid that closure. For some, this involves fighting; for others, it may involve withdrawing from the fight. Psyche (which includes, but does not possess or retain, spirit and soul) and soma come to an agreement about the path to take. As we prepare for our death, we crystallize our thoughts and attitude about life and about who we are. I believe this new attitude is the final reintegration of the total Self.

In instances of sudden, unexpected death, I believe that one's life stance is unconsciously reviewed in a "split second" in a holistic, non-linear way; one establishes by that final reintegration an acceptable balance and resolution for psyche and soma. "Acceptable" does not mean perfect, or ideal, or imply that one achieves unlimited insight; such a state is neither necessary nor a possibility of human experience. Most everyone dies with some unfinished business.

The same clinicians who judge deaths to be "good" or "bad" often assert that we caregivers are, at least to some extent, responsible for helping our patients toward having a peaceful, "good" death. They imply that if we can help a patient die peacefully, without either denying or fighting death, it will be a "good" death.

Formerly, I supported the idea that professional caregivers were empowered to influence the quality of a patient's death. I still believe we can affect the quality of a patient's dying. However, I no longer believe we have any influence or control over one's experience with the moment of death except by manipulating life support systems in a persistent attempt to delay the patient's personal somato-psychical resolution.

By exception, we might exert some influence if the patient struggles to hold on to life in the attempt to carry responsibility for another person's well-being. Many caretakers can tell stories of patients who died almost immediately after some remark was made that served as permission to die.

When the body can no longer be sustained, the thinking, feeling, intuiting, sensing, conscious and unconscious psyche (including spirit and soul), which was temporarily bonded to soma by the act of birth, is now released from soma by death. This release represents a final "letting go" – a cessation of all physical and mental functions.

Situations, events, and conditions leading to this separation may work in concert with one's particular mode of dying. This mode will depend on and be related to whichever aspect of psyche – spirit or soul – has the most influence on the individual. Two individuals of the same age may be at quite different stages of their life's journey; one may need to relate to archetypal images associated with soul, and another may need to relate to those images associated with spirit. This necessity dictates the particular attitude and behavior that will be manifested as a prelude to death. (Some persons might refer to this phenomenon as karma.)

The professional caregiver's greatest contribution to this process is to recognize and validate whichever mode of dying is chosen; it will further encourage the individual to draw upon the archetypal resources needed to guide the separation of psyche from soma when the time is right. This calls for complete faith in what C. G. Jung called the self-regulating principle. One must trust that everything needed by a patient is within the patient's own psyche. Only if psychosis, a mental dysfunction, or profound neurosis is present will a patient resist a caregiver's observations that, in time, can inspire the particular compensation the psyche needs.

Regardless that dying is an inherent part of life, it might not feel natural or come easily. We bring into our dying process all the biases, weaknesses, fears, and complexes that we have carried through life. Our dying process offers opportunity for personal inventory, evaluation, and reckoning. With proper support, we can be sustained through this period so that it becomes a spiritually productive, transformative time.

One hardly operates entirely from the field of either soul or spirit, but it is possible for the predominant archetype to become exaggerated or inflated. C. G. Jung described this as being possessed by an archetype. The dominant archetype governs the conscious self; the less powerful archetype is withdrawn from consciousness and cannot be actively embodied. As a result, the shadow aspects of the dominant archetype become exposed; spirit and soul both fall from grace.

When soul energy possesses the ego instead of being related to it, we find such characteristics as smothering, overprotecting, and devouring instead of nurturing, receiving, enduring, or becoming. Where spirit energy rules, we find haste, stubbornness, rudeness, negative avoidance, merciless criticism of self and others; these replace motivation, courage, constructive movement, penetration.

It is possible to exaggerate spirit or soul energy by projecting it through some other person's spirit or soul attributes. Spirit or soul becomes hooked by qualities in another personality; one then lives vicariously through the other person's experience and has no authentic adventure, sensation, insight, or growth to claim as one's own.

Such persons fail to recognize their own potential, but like Narcissus, they are enamored with that potential when it is reflected back by another. When the reflector is absent, however, they feel forsaken and lifeless. In a sense, they are lifeless – narcissistic personalities forsake who they really are or can become. Fear makes it difficult for them to let go of their projection and to reclaim and integrate what is rightly their own image of spirit, soul, or other aspect of themselves they have projected.

When archetypal possession or projection takes the spotlight, conscious attitude is blinded to the psyche's spirit/soul life principle. When we deny the inclinations of the instinctual Self, ego or persona identification obstructs our developmental process. This situation arrests spiritual development. (Persona relates self to the outer world; spirit and soul relate self to one's inner world.)

Individuals who either project or inflate archetypal energy are those who most need to have their attitudes mirrored to them. Mirroring does not exacerbate an attitude that is a stumbling block in the path toward wholeness. It calls attention to the ego's position in a way that stimulates closer scrutiny and that leads to confrontation with reality, which enables reintegration.

Mirroring also includes acknowledging the archetype that is secondary, e.g., "This is the way it is for you now. . . . It is not like – [such and such]. . . ." Or, "At one time your idea may have been . . . [and here the therapist/caregiver describes a viewpoint from the inactive, or less active, secondary archetype]. And someday you may feel a little like that again, but for now, you are thinking that . . . " [and the therapist/caregiver then mirrors how the activated archetype is manifested].

When one mirrors a dying patient's life, one trusts the patient's inner wisdom, however deeply buried it may be, to choose the way that feels right to live and die. Mirroring illuminates relationship – relationship to Self, to God, to others, to spirit, to soul, to life and death. It also articulates positions between polarities, such as human and divine, masculine and feminine, spirit and soul, psyche and soma, life and death. Tibetan Buddhists speak of death as a mirror in which the entire meaning of life is reflected (Rinpoche, 1992).

We use a mirror to discover whether our image is acceptable for a significant occasion and to help us make changes. When we mirror the way one is dying, we augment the person's conscious view of how he or she lives. Mirroring is a valuable gift we can give to the dying. A caregiver's frank, compassionate mirroring will either confirm that the path a dying person follows is efficacious, or it will urge that individual to change paths.

Those who attend the dying, whether physicians, nurses, chaplains, hospice personnel, mental health professionals, or other clinicians, are sometimes convinced that their role is to *do* something to the dying individual to make dying easier to bear. (I do not refer to giving pain relievers or trying to make the patient physically comfortable.) Professionals are often convinced they have a responsibility to *intervene* so they can help the patient die *peacefully*. They assume that the professional caregiver knows exactly what the patient's psyche needs. I make a distinction between dying and death; one may have a peaceful death precisely because dying was made an active venture to embrace and honor life to the last breath. It seldom occurs to caregivers that dying peacefully may not be what a psyche requires!

In the early 1990s, Bill Moyers presented a PBS television series titled, "Healing and the Mind." He concentrated on Commonweal in one segment; Commonweal is a retreat center where cancer patients come to honor and celebrate life, living, and positive thinking. At Commonweal, the patients fortify themselves to live life; their total focus and expectation are on living rather than preparing for death. The fact of human mortality is not denied, but the presence of one's life is given maximum focus and preferential recognition.

The Commonweal approach contrasts the attitude of accepting one's death and taking a purposeful role in preparing to die – an approach commonly associated with the hospice movement. Actually, the hospice philosophy promotes the uniqueness of each individual's way of facing death. For some, this is to let go; for others, it is to hold on as long as possible. Some hospice patients do face dying with a sense of reconciliation to death; others never lose hope in healing.

A nurse at Commonweal reported that all of the patients who died while still conscious fought to live to the end. This mode of dying represents a spirit approach; it cannot be considered universally appropriate for all humankind. Nor can a quiet dying at home with a submissive attitude of acceptance of death be universally correct.

Everyone has his or her own way of attaining that final reintegration of life that becomes death/rebirth.

Earlier, I referred to von Franz's (1987) notion that the more experience one has in the struggle between the "inner opposites," the more peaceful one's ending of life might be. I wish to qualify her statement.

I believe we all have comparable experience in dealing with "inner opposites." How we respond to and use that experience will make a difference in the quality of our living and dying. Peaceful dying is related to the way we interpret life. This interpretation will be based on the degree of inner maturity gained through specific encounters with spirit and soul.

Children who wrestle for years with life-threatening illness develop a profound respect for life. This respect gives them a profoundly mature attitude toward dying and death. They regard death as an event to anticipate and for which they want to be prepared.

These children differ from many I saw in counseling practice, who seemed to take life for granted. The latter group sought happiness in material things; their biggest concern was whether they could get the newest high-tech toy, the latest fad in clothing or whatever else was "in" with their friends. They had to compensate somehow for the void created by failed relationships in family life. They neither thought about death, nor could handle it if it came.

This latter type of "child" comes in all ages. In inner maturity, such persons are worlds apart from the patients in my study and from Peter and Priska whom we met in Chapter 10. Does this mean that we must suffer or be terminally-ill before we can develop a satisfactory adaptation toward the certainty of dying? Surely not, but I am equally sure that life-threatening adversities, our own and those we witness in others, develop our reverence for living and dying. This reverence is most pronounced when the ego resonates with spirit and soul.

Individuation and Spirituality

The terms spirit and soul are often used interchangeably. We hear of spirit that lives on, of the soul's leaving the body, of dead spirits, and departed souls. I regard soul and spirit as two facets of one life. Spirit and soul function together to bring one into a closer relationship with the authentic Self. This reintegrative process is repeated throughout life until one comes full circle to find death as the ultimate reality of the Self: "birth of the life we have yet to live" (Woodman, 1985, p. 14).

Whether spirit or soul leads the way to die depends upon the individual's present psychic attitude, but the complementary energy eventually becomes an equal partner. The result is more than the combination of spirit and soul; a third, transformative phenomenon now leads. Jung refers to this phenomenon as the transcendent function (discussed in Chapter 1). Applied to the dying process, the balancing act of spirit and soul allows the deintegrative experience of dying to be followed by the final, reintegrative experience of life: death-rebirth.

The complementarity between spirit and soul forms a spiritual component of the Self. Spirit and soul are elements of eternal life given by grace to every mortal; they are divine gifts to humankind. I subscribe to the idea of a nonlocal, universal soul, a Christ-within, or Divine Self, in which spirit is an integral part. Paradoxically, this Divine Self is within us, but a part is also outside our being. It contains all parts of the psyche.

Some might think of Self as The Eternal that lives within humankind, relating men and women to the natural world and various deities. For others, Self might be what connects one with whatever is held to be most sacred and everlasting. Still others might conceive of Self as a transcendent aspect of humankind that relates to the cosmos.

The Self is the regulator of all parts of our human psyche, which includes spirit and soul. In my view, the Self is God incarnate within us, not that we are gods, but that God is forever, potentially accessible to live and move within us. This explains to me how spirit and soul relate to the Godhead.

Jesus' exhortation, "I am the way, and the truth, and the life; no one comes to the Father but by me" (John 14:6, [R.S.V.]), was a call to transcend our subservience to the ego and to become aligned with the greater Self, the God-within. He did not define what he meant by the Kingdom; the Kingdom of God might well represent the individuation process that achieves transcendence, a following of the Tao, a "born again" experience, and a profound rebirth that is experienced through death − the loss of significant things or persons along with our own lives. When one prays the Lord's Prayer ("Thy kingdom come, thy will be done") is one not asking for a better relationship between ego and Self, where God-within lights one's way?

Psychotherapy has often ignored or denied the spiritual dimension of the psyche. I believe we commit a grave error when we separate psychology from spirituality. However, I do not sympathize with the spiritual-minded purists who say that because only God can make a soul it is blasphemous to speak of men and women as "soul-makers"; it is not sacrilegious to describe an activity as "soul-making" or "creating soul." I insist that when we engage in activities that honor soul and allow for soul to be revealed, we can be called soul-makers. The more revelation of soul we bring about, the closer we are related to the "Divine-within," the "Christ-within," the "God-within"—all are terms for our relationship with the Godhead. When we care for our psyche, we also care for our soul.

> In the words of Thomas Moore (1992): Ultimately, care of the soul results in an individual "I" I never would have planned for or maybe even wanted. By caring for the soul faithfully, every day, we step out of the way and let our full genius emerge (p. 305).

Spirit and soul reside with the psyche throughout life, but they transcend it at death. While spirit and soul archetypes are eternally present, one may not be conscious of them. The task of individuation – *the journey* – calls one to acknowledge and embody these archetypes so that they help us become who we are. This requires a collaborative effort between archetypal energy and the ego complex; the ego relates to archetypal energy but should not identify with it completely nor be determined by it. In this way, the archetype is used to advance individuation. At death, spirit and soul energies withdraw from our mortal life; I believe they carry to eternity the imprint of who we have become and rejoin a collective repository.

Ryce-Menuhin (1988) proposes that our reintegrative experiences are made possible by con-integrates (discussed in Chapter 6) that develop during the first two or three years of life. Con-integrates are psychic preservations of experiential content that help the ego, when ego recognizes them, to differentiate from the Self. Ryce-Menuhin has identified at least seven con-integrates and acknowledges that there may be many more. One of these, the ego-ideal, is especially relevant to our discussion of the archetypes of spirit and soul.

According to Ryce-Menuhin (1988), the ego-ideal con-integrate[1], although theoretically related to Freud's superego, is different from Freud's concept of ego-ideal. According to Ryce-Menuhin, primary narcissism is displaced early in infancy by the emergence of the ego-ideal, which is stimulated by nutritive acts coming from the parents – especially the mother.

Actually, both maternal and paternal influences are felt by the child very early; this introjection of parental influence fosters and builds the ego-ideal independently from the Oedipal development that also begins in infancy. Thus, ego-ideals are not the outcome of Oedipal or Electra complexes, but they develop simultaneously with these complexes. (Ryce-Menuhin reports that the Oedipus complex continues to affect adult psychology at different stages and ages.)

The idea that ego-ideals develop in early infancy (an outgrowth of bonding, relating, and Eros energy's shaping the child's ego in the first year) represents a possibility unrecognized by Freud. Ryce-Menuhin (1988) suggests that the ego-ideal con-integrate is grounded in the discipline and expectations of one's parents or caretakers, is also imprinted by siblings, relatives, and friends of one's household, and continues to function, with revisions, throughout life.

I submit that the archetypes of spirit and soul present vital patterns as potential for attitude and behavior to be evoked by the ego-ideal con-integrate. A child's early experience with the opposite sex parent stimulates unconsciously the images of soul in boys and images of spirit in girls. At the child's conscious, ego level, we observe that a reverse correspondence typically occurs. Boys identify with their fathers or male caretakers and thus manifest spirit attributes; girls identify with their mothers or female caretakers and consequently display soul attributes. The contents of these two archetypes help to build the ego-ideal.

While we have acknowledged that Jung's ideas concerning the anima and animus (soul and spirit) may be problematic for contemporary cultures, his premise that these archetypes compose a syzygy may yield a more receptive response (Jung, 1968). A syzygy, in Jungian terms, involves a relationship between two initially polar forces that can be transformed to form a union, as illustrated in the alchemical procedure.

Examining spirit and soul in the light of the syzygy concept of differentiation and reunification, we find that when one relates to images of the spirit, it reconnects one to soul, and vice versa. The result of this, let me reiterate, is much more than a combination of spirit and soul; it introduces an experience of wholeness – reconciliation with the central archetype, the Self. This wholeness is far greater than the sum of its parts.

Chapter 12 Notes

1. I recognize that the con-integrates of play and persona also coordinate with soul/spirit content to support the ego's deintegrative-reintegrative process. For a further explanation of the model involving ego-conglomerates and how they lend vital support to the ego processes, the reader is referred to *The Self in Early Childhood*, by Joel Ryce-Menuhin, listed in the References.

Chapter 13

CLOSURE

We began our exploration into the art of dying by asking (1) what the drawings by patients with life-threatening illness can teach us; (2) whether we can "read" the images in these drawings as a map of psyche and soma; and (3) what psychodynamic impact (if any) the images in these pictures might have on the patient. We have observed that images reveal meaning for both the psychic and somatic situations. Images evolve simultaneously from psyche's conscious and unconscious content and are expressed via archetypal patterns.

Several motifs and corresponding archetypes were common in the drawings of my study. Birds and other objects flying or floating in the air symbolized the soul's transcending life on earth. The journey to redeem the treasure was another motif we identified; it represents finding the treasure of the Self – a process involving introspection, reintegration or individuation, and representing soul energy.

The regenerative greening or blooming of plant life found in many drawings reflects the ritual of death and rebirth. A river or stream suggests the flow of life, the passage of time, the division between this life and the afterlife, or crossing from one part of life to another phase of life, and in that sense represents transition.

Suns relate to the father archetype or the father complex and to one's life span. Warriors, superhuman heroes, and athletes playing to win impart spirit energy.

To take a more particular look at what has been presented here, let us review some remarkable images and motifs that correspond to the process of dying and rebirth; we begin with the examples examined in the case studies.

Dennis's images that recurred most were green foliage or other plant growth, suns, blackbirds, and rays of light. One or more of these features appeared in 17 of the 20 drawings he rendered in the advanced stages of his illness during the last three years of his life.

Dennis's physical deterioration was in stark contrast to the abundant greening and signs of new life that his drawings displayed. He made these drawings at various times after his NDE at the age of 18. These pictures of thriving life suggest an interesting polarity. Consciously, he hoped that a cure for his disease would come in time to save him. I speculate that Dennis recalled unconsciously an abundant life, of a different kind, experienced at his near-death episode; his unconscious psyche must have realized this new life could come only through death. In almost all of his drawings, we find a motif of new life or the dawning of a new day.

Life themes appear in Dennis's drawings approximately twice as often as death themes. Life is especially emphasized by Dennis's baby birds in a nest (Fig. 6). He also suggests life by the ear of corn or flower design on the dead animal's skull, and the "birth rock" in "Bad Lands" (Fig. 8). He reiterates the life theme through a redbud tree in spring bloom (Fig. 13); lush vegetative growth, including a sprouting plant (Fig. 15); a "sapling just beginning to bud" (Fig. 10); green growth that thrives on a dead tree stump along with mushrooms and green grass (Fig. 13); a healthy-looking green cactus that grows in a desert where a mountain covered with green growth on one side rises in the background (Fig. 12); and a sprouting bulb bathed by rays of sunlight (Fig. 17).

"Energy," the title Dennis gave to Figure 17, also emphasizes the life theme. Other titles he chose for his drawings also amplify life themes. These include "In the Beginning" – the picture he described to be the time God created the earth (Fig. 3). "Beginning" (Fig. 10) has a rainbow of hope and a budding sapling; "The red Bud" (Fig. 13) has spring buds. "Life Begins" (Fig. 15), "Energy" (Fig. 17), and "Budding Rose" (Fig. 18) all depict new growth.

Death is suggested by Dennis's sunken ship (Fig. 11), a dead plant on a window ledge (Fig. 19), a 1,000-lb. weight threatening to crush a bedridden patient (Fig. 20), a single volcano that emits a large cloud of smoke (Fig. 9), the active volcano in a mountain range (Fig. 3), a dead animal's skull (Fig. 8), a dead tree stump (Fig. 13), and a dead, fallen leaf (Fig. 18).

These last four pictures (Figures 3, 8, 13, and 18) also depict the polarity of life and death. The active volcano (Fig. 3) appears in

Dennis's drawing of the beginning of creation; the dead animal's skull is in the picture with the birth rock and the corn or flower design (Fig. 8); and the dead tree stump is countered by the green growth on its side, and by the mushrooms, green bush, and grass (Fig. 13); the dead leaf is in contrast with the new leaf, the budding rose, and the two new plants (Fig. 18). This polarity of life and death corresponds with Dennis's conscious hope for survival and his unconscious acceptance of death (the latter likely aided by his near brush with death).

The greening of new life in many of Dennis's pictures can be associated with his ambivalence about life and death. Dennis could relate to the transformation and regeneration that occur in the spring greening of deciduous trees and perennial plants. Quite possibly he felt a harmony with the nature of creation. He came to terms with the physical decline of his body and portrayed it symbolically by the fallen rose leaf and his dead potted plant on the window ledge (absence of green).

There is a striking similarity between Dennis's motif of the greening of new life, present in many drawings after his NDE, and the dream motifs of Edward Edinger's analysand who also had a near brush with death. Edinger (1972) reported on a series of dreams by a man in his fifth decade, who survived an NDE after attempting suicide. Comatose for nearly two days, he died two years later from a different cause. During those two years, the man began consulting with Edinger on a series of metaphysical dreams.

Edinger had the impression that the dreams were trying to teach the man some meaning about his close brush with death or to prepare him for death soon to come. Some dreams were presented from an ego standpoint; they were devastating and left the man depressed. These dreams correspond to Dennis's drawing of being carried away by a hot air balloon (Fig. 14) and to his original drawing of a budding rose – the picture with a dead, separated leaf that distressed him so much he destroyed the picture.

Other dreams by Edinger's analysand brought him a sense of "peace, joy, and security" (p. 200). These can be compared to Dennis's corrected drawing of the budding rose (Fig. 18), especially to "Beginning" (Fig. 10), "Life Begins" (Fig. 15), "Energy" (Fig. 17), and even "Imagine" (Fig. 19) given Dennis's positive comments about the latter.

The older man reported a dream in which he saw an elegant formal garden where a green man composed of herbs and grass emerged and performed a beautiful dance. The dreamer claimed this dream gave him a sense of peace, regardless that he did not understand what he had seen in the garden. Edinger (1972) equates the green man to the vegetative spirit that brings forth birth from death. Edinger has given us an archetypal view of the dream; he refers to C. G. Jung's comment (in *Mysterium Coniunctionis, C.W., 14*, par. 623) that green is associated with the creative principle.

Writing in the *Mysterium*, Jung interpreted an alchemical text about a psychic transformation in one's wandering among images: Wandering finally brings one to a "secret happiness," a reintegration with Self that is "like a hidden springtime when the green seed sprouts from the barren earth, holding out the promise of future harvests" (quoted in Edinger, 1972, p. 214).

This quotation can easily be applied to several of Dennis's drawings. Edinger (1972) writes that for his analysand who is soon to die, the unconscious presents "a vivid and beautiful image of the eternal nature of life, whose particular manifestations are continually passing away, but which is being continually reborn in new forms" (p. 214). Considering how his dreamer was affected by the dreams, Edinger concludes:

> All of the dreams . . . had an intense emotional impact on the dreamer . . . *but only when recounting [them] in the analytic session, not beforehand. Somehow the presence of the analyst was needed to release the numinosity of the dream images* [italics mine]. Taken as a whole, the dreams conveyed a series of small religious experiences that caused a gradual and definite change in the dreamer's life attitude (p. 224).

Reading this recalled Dennis's hot air balloon dream, his urgency to tell me about it, his eagerness to illustrate the dream, and his resolution of the tension the dream initially created. Remember his picture of a budding rose that upset him so much he destroyed it, and that after revealing this incident to me, how much better the disclosure made him feel. He went on to "reproduce" the drawing for me; he described significant changes in the drawing and they corresponded to changes in his attitude towards dying. The above quote from Edinger makes me question whether Dennis would have transcended his old attitudes without our relationship.

We can read in Dennis's pictures the symptoms of his physical dying even while his spiritual life was being strengthened. We recall that from the window of his "old, rundown house" he envisioned a sunny side of life – like the garden of paradise (Fig. 19). Dennis drew a dead rose leaf (Fig. 18) that he equated with his own dying; he did this during hospitalization in an advanced state of CF eight months before he died. He included in that drawing a resurrected, new rose leaf and two additional plants.

Jason also drew green objects in the 54 pictures I collected from him. Several of his warrior drawings featured a popular superhero. Jason called him "The Great Green Hulk." Besides several drawings depicting green grass, Jason drew threatening green creatures such as dragons or dinosaurs. In alchemy, the green dragon symbolizes a solvent used to change metal into gold, thus transformation (Biedermann, 1992).

However, Jason's use of green does not usually suggest the regenerative, reintegrative, or transformative qualities we see in Dennis's use of this color, or in the dreams of Edinger's analysand who survived an NDE. In Jason's drawings, the motif of overcoming evil and courageously persevering to the end is much more significant.

Most often, Ronda used motifs of human figures and home-life settings in her 19 drawings (we examine just 5). Many of these showed celebratory times such as Christmas, birthdays, and other parties. Human love and relationship represent soul energy and they were obviously important to Ronda (see Chapter 11). Her green shamrock and partially green egg are closer to the idea of the greening or birthing of a new life conveyed by Dennis's pictures.

Ronda included suns in 2 of 6 drawings that were unquestionably outdoor scenes; one of these was her final drawing, Figure 27. Suns are common in drawings of outdoor scenes, especially those made by children. I found this to be true of the drawings in both my U.S. study and my British study. Most of Dennis's outdoor scenes include the sun or rays of light beaming down. Jason, however, put a sun in just 3 of his 54 drawings; Figures 28 and 29 are two examples.

We discussed previously the psychological symbolism of the sun as representing the human father, the Great Father archetype (Wise, Old Man), or the Heavenly Father. The sun might also be associated with spirit energy (defined in Chapter 10). Bach (1990) observed that the sun relates to a person's age, the span of one's life, or important events in one's life. For example, a setting sun (in the west, to the left) might suggest life's ending or the ending of some phase of one's life.

Von Franz (1987) tells us that ancient Egyptian culture compared the sun's path to the mystery of life and death. For them, the sun symbolized new life after death. Von Franz points out that "psychologically . . . the sun is a symbol of the source of *awareness*" (p. 66).

Somatically, the sun might represent a burning process such as high fever. The sun's rays might symbolize radiation therapy for oncology patients.

The bird motif often corresponds to the soul, according to Bach (1990). (We must keep in mind our hypothesis, from Chapter 10, that spirit and soul are two aspects of one entity – the eternal nature of psyche.) Bach invites us to look at the bird symbolically as "the messenger between man and his god, as a symbol of the soul" (p. 84); she says that "we can understand the bird as flying towards a realm which surpasses the here and now" (p. 85). This latter comment recalls Dennis's drawing, "Free," (Fig. 7) and his comment that he would be free as a bird if a cure could be found for CF.

Other flying objects might take on the same symbolic significance as birds; we might look at balloons, airplanes, kites, and even Jason's flying car as significant when they appear in the drawings of those holding on to life tenuously. A major cultural icon throughout the ages, birds are motifs worthy of examination in dreams and drawings because they offer useful opportunities for amplification.

Children who use the sandtray in therapy are often attracted to the treasure chest, "jewels" or other valuables, the infant Christ Child or another holy figure; they unconsciously associate the miniature object with the treasure of the Self – a sense of the Divine Self. Similarly, young children in early stages of their ego development are fascinated by games of "Hide the Object" or "Hide and Seek." A child's urge to find or to be found corresponds with both (1) the childhood narcissism that is necessary to encourage ego development and (2) the innate desire to reintegrate, to become more conscious of one's initial wholeness present before and after ego formation.

When one senses the nearness of death the reintegrative urge becomes heightened. It is not surprising, therefore, to see images that represent the treasure of the Self in patients' drawings. We can regard Dennis's underwater treasure and even the precious coral beside it, as representing important aspects of Self that he was striving to bring into consciousness.

In anticipation of a time when she "may be dead," Ronda expressed the reintegrative drive towards life's closure using the pot of gold,

Easter basket full of goodies, giant-sized green and orange egg, 2 roses, and later, by her transformation into an angel.

The flower appears prominently in drawings and dreams of those approaching death. Recall Dennis's imposing rose (Fig. 18) that was just beginning to open. Besides the shamrock (Fig. 23), Ronda drew 2 roses in her Easter picture (Fig. 25). A border of flowers appeared in the 30-year-old woman's drawing (Fig. 1); flowers were a conspicuous detail in several other drawings by the CF group from the U.S. and from those in England. Bach, too, found flowers to be a significant detail in drawings by patients with a life-threatening illness.

A single, prominent flower conveys especially the feeling of soul's being embraced by Self. This is different from inflation; ego is forgotten or replaced by a spiritual bonding with a central creative force (God). Von Franz (1987) comments that flowers are a prevailing archetypal image for postmortal existence – the soul freed from the body.

Bach (1969) identifies the image of a single flower as the "magic flower" in a drawing Priska made nine months before her death. Bach (1990) also calls attention to this "magic flower," life-sized, in the drawing of an 8-year-old a few months before she died. Priska even said of her drawing, "This is the magic flower" (Bach, 1969, p. 42); this flower has prominent mandalic features. (Recall the comment in Chapter 11 about the leprechaun's hat and the mandala's affiliation with wholeness.)

Further evidence of the flower as symbol for a postmortal container for the soul comes from a 54-year-old woman who was an analysand of von Franz (1987). One month before her death, this woman engaged in an "active imagination" (defined by von Franz as "a form of meditation taught by Jung, in which one conducts a conversation with inner fantasy figures" [p. 38]). This woman longed to go into the "wonderful flower"; she explained that she could not "live without this center" because outside it "everything is meaningless." Her imaginary bear companion helps her get to the flower and she goes on to say,

> I am very happy . . . in the center. . . . The flower radiates a wonderful healing light. I am not in the flower yet, but I am near it, in its protection, in its mild warmth. It is inner order, the center. There is no splitting here, no halfness (pp. 38-39).

Water, either as a river, stream, or ocean appeared in pictures of 6 patients from the U.S. group and in 1 from the British group. Flowing water that separates one side from the other is a common image for the archetype of transcendence. It might illustrate transcending some phase of life, completing a rite of passage, or fulfilling transition from life to death. One patient made a bridge across her river, another included passengers in a boat – a robber who had robbed the light-house, and the "good guy" who was going to stab the robber. (Did this patient feel that CF had robbed him of life, had deprived him of feel-ing safe, protected, secure?) We have already examined Jason's boy on the shore, his flying car crossing the river, and his superheroes who could fly. All reflect the myth of Charon, the ferryman who bears the souls of the dead across the River Styx to the Other World.

Jason preferred to concentrate on warriors and superhuman heroes and to derive from them the spirit he needed to complete life. We might say that Ronda received a similar spirit power from her image of an angel – the heroine aspect of her soul.

I collected several drawings of houses and animals. The latter often suggested instinctual knowledge of the patient's situation, and some-times also reflected the somatic condition. Similarly, houses (as con-tainers for both psyche and soma) were frequently linked to physical developments and the psychological response to them, also to family dynamics significant to the patient.

What about our question whether drawings can be read as a "map" of psyche and soma? Several drawings had images that, when totaled, the number related to a date, age, event, or time in a person's life. Blue-shaded clouds appeared frequently in the drawings of patients who experienced fluid retention – either sinusitis, pulmonary edema or congestion, or peripheral tissue edema. (Blue-shaded clouds appeared in 15 pictures, representing 13 patients from the U.S. and 1 from Great Britain. Additional drawings contained blue patches in the sky, but they were not clearly intended as clouds; these were not con-sidered.)

Psychologically, blue clouds suggested the held-back tears when many patients seemed to deny or suppress their true feelings of anger and grief over having CF. I suspect the anticipated loss of life's quali-ty, which having an incurable disease predicated, gave patients many negative feelings – often suppressed.

These feelings would include grief and anger (often at their parents, who carried and passed on the CF gene, or at the medical profession, all of whom were helpless to rescue them from CF). Eventually, this anger could provoke guilt as well as depression and despair. Yet, this is what patients typically held back, as though it were a matter of pride to face life with chin up and not feeling sorry for themselves. We might consider this behavior as a way of adapting to the incurable illness; one's refusal to give in to anger and despair could help to detach from CF anxiety.

These psychological responses are identified by Bowlby (1969) in describing attachment and loss reactions of infants and young children. Regardless of patients' psychosocial adaptations to living with CF, my studies have shown that children with CF and advanced COPD suffer a loss of self-esteem (Williams, 1985). Recognition that they will never be like other children causes handicapped children to grieve the loss of whom they could have been and might wish to be (Weininger & Daniel, 1992). The blue-shaded cloud seems to collect and carry that grief.

I have shown somatic features reflecting the growth of infection, metastasis, collapsed lung, gastric ulcer exacerbation, and, among other things, physical weakening. We have observed the mother and father complexes, the struggle to redeem the treasure of the Self, and transcending life on earth, to name the more outstanding reflections of psyche in drawings.

I am convinced that engaging in some kind of art process, such as drawing or painting, has power to sustain one in critical times. I am aware of drawings by children in Nazi concentration camps that appeared to do just that. We cannot possibly articulate or identify all the meanings that a picture's image might convey; that is evidence of the power of an image to reconcile the conscious, verbal self with the unconscious. In no way can our interpretations limit the role of the image in its interaction with the image-maker.

Many patients obviously felt honored by my interest in their drawings and by my request to keep them in an individual folder, labeled with their name, which they could examine at any time. Whenever a patient asked to review the folder's contents, I sensed a feeling of awe as we opened it and turned through the pictures. Often, the children would present their drawings to me with the request, "Keep it in my folder," or "Save this for the collection of my drawings." Sometimes, I wondered whether the drawings in their folders were a poignant reminder to these patients that a legacy would remain after their deaths as a statement of their lives.

Health care professionals are occasionally hesitant to encourage a patient to draw; they fear their study and analysis will not accurately reflect what the patient's psyche and soma express. Readers who first encounter the interpretation of drawings via this book might be especially hesitant. Actually, it is erroneous and even dangerous to attempt fortune telling from drawings – or even to declare what the images "mean." More to the point, our amplification should include meanings that are possible or potential as well as those we might believe are actual. Such amplifications, correct and incorrect, will broaden and deepen our understanding of the patient's experience and bring us into better relationship.

Even if the patient's drawing is interpreted incorrectly, its expression still has intrinsic value. Such amplification broadens the understanding of potential available to the patient. Acknowledgment of this potential helps draw one closer to the patient. By investing effort in the study, one honor's the patient's process. This reverence for the pictorial expression contributes to an alliance between patient and caregiver.

Therapists should not jump to conclusions in their study of patients' drawings – should not believe there can be just one meaning and declare dogmatically what it is. Nonetheless, I dread to see therapists bending over backwards to avoid the accusation of "diagnosing" patients. I hear too often from art therapists, "We never diagnose in art therapy." This statement is what I label "the art therapy myth"; art therapists believe in it wholeheartedly.

In reality, art therapists are all the time diagnosing not only that a person is ill at ease (dis-eased) but often why; what is more, they often deduce prognostic signals from patients' art work. Art therapists can observe, as did the late Edward Adamson (1984), "that paintings which are forebodings of future tragedy often have a . . . colour combination of red and black" (p. 37); or that an impressive, mostly red painting of a couple embracing with golden rays emanating all around them, emphasizes an institutionalized patient's intense "need to give and receive affection . . . during the patient's separation from loved ones" (Adamson, 1984, p. 35).

Adamson (1984) explains further that patients' self portraits are a great help in understanding how they visualize themselves and he gives remarkable case examples. He says, "Doctors and psychotherapists find these illustrations of self-conception particularly helpful in their work" (p. 28).

Is it just physicians and psychotherapists who can understand the symbolic language of these paintings well enough to find diagnostic or prognostic hints in them? I think not!

The British art therapist Joy Schaverien (1992) says that even though the use of art therapy as a diagnostic tool is:

> against the stated aim of most art therapists, *there is none the less an element of diagnosis* [italics mine] .... [Art therapists] may suspect that there is a potential for a psychotic breakdown in the detailed pattern made by a particular patient, but another patient making similar pictures may not arouse such concerns. This is because the art therapist takes account of the picture in relation to the artist. Thus, they assess the whole person in relation to the pictures, and in relation to the art therapist (p. 3).

If therapists withhold observations related to diagnosis or prognosis, they deprive other clinicians of important information about the patient. This information should come out when they participate in team conferences or enter notes in the patient's medical record. Other clinicians could use such information to broaden their understanding of the patient and to enhance the patient's care and treatment.

Some therapists put in the medical record just the raw data about a child's symbolic play, sandtray, or painting without any explanations of what such data might suggest. Their rationale for this practice is that medical personnel have the responsibility to draw conclusions. Unfortunately, medical personnel do not have the training art therapists, play therapists, or psychotherapists have and are unable to translate the motifs and symbols that would suggest psychological or somatic elements.

We should recognize that doctors resist having nonmedical personnel offer judgments or conclusions about conditions the doctors have not already discovered in their patients. There is a professional protocol for art therapists and others to follow. First, give a judicious summary of the patient's activity followed by a statement such as, "These observations raise some questions to consider: .... " Then list two or more possibilities concerning what the patient might be experiencing either presently or in the near future.

Patients' attitudes toward life can influence their immune systems. These attitudes can be discovered quite easily in their drawings. It is important for a treatment team to examine what patients feel emotionally as well as to know how they feel physically. A therapist's thoughtful feedback on patients' drawings can unquestionably help this undertaking.

You and your patient are two human beings seeking to understand the ways of life and death; it is a spiritual quest. Relying on drawing evaluations, you might fail to connect at an analytical level with a patient, but your interest and effort can connect you in an almost mystical way because of the art process.

The art process is of therapeutic value not only to the patient, but also to the caregiver. Benefit comes from being the safekeeper of drawings, living with them, studying them, allowing them to speak, and amplifying their images. We foster a supportive alliance between patient and caregiver when we discuss with patients their experience with the drawing. We should listen to the story they might tell about it, share with the patient impressions that the drawing evokes in each of us, and encourage the patient to elaborate on certain details of the drawing.

Even when patients' drawings are never "analyzed," evidence shows they benefit from the process of making them. I attribute this to the image's power to carry the tension between one's conscious and unconscious life until psychological quickening leads to its resolution. Dennis's drawing of a budding rose (Fig. 18) is an example. No one but Dennis saw the drawing; he promptly destroyed it. Yet the image continued to carry the tension until something mysteriously unfolded. The following day a broadened view of life and death emerged within Dennis as he discussed the original drawing and then began to repeat it (discussed in Chapters 8-9).

Von Franz (1987) has commented on the significance of the dreams of people facing death; she notes that they reflect the way unconscious instincts prepare the conscious self for the important transition from life to death. (This transition is a developmental milestone that Elisabeth Kübler-Ross identifies as the final stage of growth.) What von Franz says about dreams in this stage can also be said about drawings; substituting the word "drawings" for "dreams," I quote von Franz thus:

> All of the [drawings] of people who are facing death indicate that the unconscious, that is, our instinct world, prepares consciousness not for a definite end but a profound transformation and for a kind of continuation of the life process which, however, is unimaginable to everyday consciousness (p. 156).

We do not have to know what a picture means; it is enough to realize that a picture has meaning and to feel moved by its images.

As we study the art of dying patients, we discover that when death comes soul and spirit reside united. Sometimes we can recognize images that helped that union – the transcendence. (Soul and spirit might unite fleetingly other than at death, but this state cannot be maintained.)

In Chapter 5, I mentioned Jung's idea of the child's splitting the image of the mother into a good and bad side. I believe we are sometimes like children when it comes to our image of God. Particularly, when confronted with a crisis such as a life-threatening illness, we may be tempted to split God into a good, healing God, and a bad God that allows suffering and death of good people. In our childish way, do we assume, when we attribute an event to God's will, that we know who God is or what He or She will do? Would that we could learn to acknowledge and revere the sacred mystery of life and death, and to see death as more than an enemy or a mere robber of life.

We are called to live life, and life includes death. The question is, how shall we live unto our death? One must answer that question for oneself. If spirit and soul can mediate between our conscious living and our eternal connection through God (to all who have lived before us, with us, and those who will live after us) we can step into the mysterious valley of the shadow of death, the dark unknown. It is by confronting the unknown, I believe, that we learn how to endure life to the end, when darkness will give way to light.

Dying patients can teach us what this process is like if we allow them. I question the benefit of assisted suicide because it interrupts this important, final stage of growth. Individuals who plan suicide are consciously adjusted to the idea of *death* – being released from this life – but they are not adjusted to the idea of *dying.* A suicide prospect's everyday consciousness (i.e., ego) can anticipate no value in the dying process. The ego, severed from unconscious instinctual needs, desperately strives to remain in control, but it is an inadequate manager for the total psyche.

I understand and sympathize with one's need for release from physical pain. Hospice care allows one to have control over pain, to die free of agonizing pain, and, if chosen, in the comfort of home. Hospice care wisely tolerates and even supports a patient's refusal of food and liquid. When the body begins to shut down, food is neither digested normally nor needed. Dehydration actually benefits the patient by its euphoric and sedative effect.

There are many ways of keeping the body comfortable and free of excruciating pain. Hospice offers an acceptable alternative to depriving life (through assisted suicide) of its most profound stage that is "unimaginable to everyday consciousness" (von Franz, 1987, p. 156).

Dying individuals can give us the gift of living by showing us what is essential as they unburden themselves of the unimportant matters that typically hound us all. In fact, we and they can support each other in the learning process of living and dying. I have shown how that might be done by communicating with drawings and mirroring to patients what their verbal and nonverbal messages seem to be saying about their experience.

Jung (1960) wrote, "We grant goal and purpose to the ascent of life, why not to the descent? The birth of a human being is pregnant with meaning, why not death?" (p. 408). Of course, death is pregnant with meaning as well, but our difficulty in finding meaning in death comes when we forget that life and death are part of a continuum, and give honor to life only.

Giving equal honor to life and death is beautifully illustrated in an ancient Japanese custom of writing one's death poem, a custom no longer kept, unfortunately. I learned of this tradition in a workshop, "Death Poems: Dying in Beauty," led by Kazuhiko Higuchi, from Kyoto, presented at the "Festival of Archetypal Psychology" at Notre Dame University in 1992.

For generations, the Japanese acknowledged that death, like God, had many faces, which made dying for every individual a unique experience. They believed that everyone became a hero through living unto death. Writing one's death poem was a way of "living" beyond death. The truth of one's poem would reach past the ending of one's life; the poem would serve as a kind of mediator between life and death.

The following death poems are my favorites from those presented by Higuchi:

> I thought to live
> two centuries or three –
> yet here comes death
> to me, a child

just eighty-five years old.
(By Hanabusa Ikkei, died 1843)

I wish to die
in spring, beneath
the cherry blossoms,
while the springtime noon
is full.
(By Saigyo, died 1190)

Death poems
are mere delusion –
death is death.
(By Toko, died 1795, age 86)

Bury me when I die
beneath a wine barrel
in a tavern;
with luck
the cask will leak.
(By Moria Annan, died 1838)

I hope this book will help redeem death as a sacred, final part of life. I hope, too, that it will inspire the use of patients' drawings as symbolic expressions about life and death and the use of the Jungian-Bach method displayed here for evaluating drawings made at critical times.

If we can regard death as a redemptive experience, we might in our own way, through grace, seek ways to give this momentous event a deserved, aesthetic quality. Accomplishing that, we can all contribute to the art of dying.

Appendix A

GUIDELINES FOR READING AND EVALUATING SPONTANEOUS PICTURES

By Susan R. Bach
(An Excerpt)

Printed by Department of Pediatrics, University of Zurich and Clinic and Research Center for Jungian Psychology, Zurich, 1977.

(Used with permission from Christopher Donovan, M.D., Executor, Susan R. Bach Estate)

Attitude and Approach to Spontaneous Pictures

What is your immediate impression? What are the feelings that the picture evokes in you? Hold on to these, rather than dismiss them as frightening and irrational, even though to the intellect they may at first seem absurd.

It is the sense of wonder so natural to a child, which leads us later on to systematic observation and investigation of what is not yet known but may be knowable.

How to "Read" Spontaneous Pictures Systematically

a) Before recording observations in detail it is advisable to copy the picture on transparent paper.

b) See what is there.

c) See what is missing.

d) See what is odd.

e) Count colours used. Of those offered note which have not been used. Follow individual colours through a series of pictures, noting where they appear in the right place, and especially where out of place.

f) Be aware of remarkable and striking objects or motifs, and whether filled in or not.

g) Note numbers of any kind of object, especially when recurring.

h) Realise that a child's spontaneous picture is painted "directly" on to the paper: right is right and left is left. His right side is on the right side of the drawing and his left on the left, in contrast to an artist's portrait where the left side represents the right side of the sitter or vice versa.

189

i) Give the picture a name as an aid to memorising and communicating.

j) Finally, compare it with the natural surrounding world.

Aids to Translation and Evaluation of Spontaneous Pictures
Both Somatically and Psychologically

a) Realise that a spontaneous picture may be an expression of the patient himself or herself. He may be identified with any human figure in the drawing as well as any object, be it a house, an animal, a car, an aeroplane, etc.

b) Try to follow the patient INTO his picture. Try to feel what it is like to be a child without feet, a tree without roots – try to become any person or object in the picture, viewing it from inside, as it were. Then use your professional skill to evaluate the clinical condition.

c) Make use of the device of crosswires (see Susan R. Bach, P6-7, quoting Spontaneous Paintings of Severely Ill Patients, a contribution to Psychosomatic Medicine, Acta Psychosomatica Geigy, Vol. 8, 1966; English version 1969; P. 16f.) which indicates, as in microscopy, the centre and the four quadrants. Note the position and direction of any figure and object within this scheme, and also changes of position and direction throughout a series of pictures.

What We May Learn from Reading, Translating and
Evaluating Spontaneous Pictures

We may comprehend that the human being can and does convey through these wordless communications and in his own idiom both his somatic and psychological condition. Somatically, such pictures may point to events in the past (e.g. accident) relevant to the anamnesis, early diagnosis, and prognosis. Psychologically, we may see what goes on and has been going on deep in the mind (for instance past traumas, say the birth of a sibling), and how the drawing can help him to express his hopes, fears, and forebodings. Moreover, these pictures can build a bridge between doctor and patient, the family and surrounding world.

Indeed, their meaning and what it implies could guide the Helping Profession to assist especially the critically ill patient in living as near to his essential being as possible, whether in recovery or before his life's circle closes.

Finally, we may ask how it could be that spontaneous pictures reflect, as dreams do, the total situation of the human person. I have come to see in decades of clinical work that through the imagery of spontaneous pictures and of dreams something "shines through" which I have called "inner knowingness." Thus, a new dimension may be opening before us.

Appendix B

THE STRUCTURE OF THE PSYCHE ACCORDING TO THEORY OF ANALYTICAL PSYCHOLOGY

Imagine a pyramid divided horizontally into three unequal parts. The lower part contains the large area from the base of the pyramid to a little above its middle. The second part extends from the line just above the middle to a line just a little below the top. The third part is the smallest area that comprises the tip of the pyramid. These three areas represent areas of the psyche as follows:

Part I. Collective Unconscious/Objective Psyche

A. This part of the psyche comprises an individual's connection with a universal, psychic reservoir that contains the archetypes.

B. The individual psyche cannot actually contain this psychic reservoir of archetypes itself; it merely has access to this field.

C. The objective psyche communicates symbolically with consciousness via archetypal images.

D. This part of the psyche is not confined to present, personal experience; it functions as a repository of organic and psychic potential common to the past, the present, and to future generations.

E. This part of the psyche relies on universal instincts predisposed to give image to archetypes.

Part II. Personal Unconscious

A. This includes forgotten and repressed memories, complexes, shadow aspects of personality, and latent possibilities.

B. It communicates symbolically with consciousness via dreams, images, fantasies, myth, metaphor, and parapraxes.

Part III. Ego & Persona – Conscious self

A. Ego manages the conscious, rational mind.

B. One's various Personae help ego to connect with the outer environment.

C. Ego has no control over unconscious aspects of the psyche except to decide what will be allowed to pass through to consciousness.

In summary, the (Whole or Greater) Self encompasses *all* of the above. Psyche means: (a) personal psyche (conscious self and personal unconscious self); and (b) influences that come from the objective psyche (collective unconscious).

191

Archetypal content such as spirit, soul, or shadow, connect to both the objective psyche and the personal psyche. The personal psyche has access to archetypes but does not contain them. Archetypes are immortal, numinous, and primal energies with manifold meaning independent of personal experience. Humanity can only realize an archetype through an image, and can integrate only what that image evokes. Full comprehension or integration of an archetype is never possible (see Chapter 1).

REFERENCES

Adamson, E. (1984). *Art as healing.* York Beach, ME: Nicolas-Hays, Inc.

Ammann, R. (1991). *Healing and transformation in sandplay: Creative processes become visible.* (W-D. P. Rainer, Trans.) Peru, IL: Open Court.

Bach, S. (1969). *Spontaneous paintings of severely ill patients.* Basle: Geigy.

_____. (1974/75). Spontaneous pictures of leukemic children in an expression of the total personality, mind and body. *Acta Paedopsychiatry. 41,* 86-104.

_____. (1977). *Guidelines for reading and evaluating spontaneous pictures.* Zurich: Department of Pediatrics, University of Zurich and Clinic and Research Center for Jungian Psychology.

_____. (1980a). On the archetypal motif of the bird. In A. Hicklin, (Ed.), *Spontaneous images: Relationship between psyche and soma.* New York: Interbook, Inc.

_____. (1980b). Why do we do this work? In A. Hicklin, (Ed.), *Spontaneous images: Relationship between psyche and soma.* New York: Interbook, Inc.

_____. (1990). *Life paints its own span.* Wilmette, IL: Chiron (U.S.A. distributor for Daimon Verlag).

Bertoia, J. (1993). *Drawings from a dying child.* London and New York: Routledge.

Bettleheim, B. (1977). *The uses of enchantment.* New York: Alfred A. Knopf.

Biedermann, H. (1992). *Dictionary of symbolism: Cultural icons and the meanings behind them.* (J. Hulbert, Trans.) New York: Facts on File.

Boa, Fraser. (1987). *The way of the dream.* [Film]. (available from Windrose Films, Ltd., P. O. Box 265, Station Q, Toronto, Ontario, M4T2M1.)

Bomholt, U. (1990). *The archetype of disobedience: Birth of new life.* Unpublished dissertation, C. G. Jung Institut, Zurich-Kusnacht, Switzerland.

Bowlby, J. (1969). *Attachment and loss.* London: Hogarth Press.

Burns, R. C. and Kaufman, S. H. (1972). *Actions, styles and symbols in kinetic family drawings* (k-f-d). New York: Brunner/Mazel.

Cooper, J. C. (1978). *An illustrated encyclopaedia of traditional symbols.* London: Thames & Hudson.

Corbett, L. and Rives, C. (1992). Anima, animus and selfobject theory. In N. Schwartz-Salant & M. Stein, (Eds.), *Gender and soul in psychotherapy.* Chiron Clinical Series. Wilmette, IL: Chiron Publications.

Dossey, L. (1989). *Recovering the soul.* New York: Bantam Books.

Dougherty, M. (1996). The creative process in individuation. *Transformation.* 26(3), 1-2;4-5.

Drennen, D. A. (1969). *Baron's simplified approach to the methodical philosophy of Rene Descartes.* Woodbury, NY: Barron's Educational Series, Inc.

Durant, W. (1962). *The story of philosophy.* New York: Time Incorporated.

Edinger, E. (1973). *Ego and archetype.* New York: Penguin Books.

Fordham, M. (1944). *The life of childhood.* London: Routledge & Kegan Paul.

Fredrick, J. F. (1976-1977). Grief as a disease process. *Omega 7*(4), 297-305.

Freud, S. (1913-1914). The psychological interest of psychoanalysis. *The complete psychological works of Sigmund Freud. Vol. 13.* Standard edition. (J. Strachey, Trans.). London: Hogarth.

Furth, G. (1973). *Impromptu paintings by terminally ill, hospitalized and healthy children: What can we learn from them?* [C-D ROM]. Abstract from: ProQuest File: Dissertation Abstracts Item: 7403170.

_____. (1988). *The secret world of drawings.* Boston: Sigo.

Gimbutas, M. (1989). *The language of the goddess.* New York: Harper & Row.

Gove, P. B. (Ed.). (1993). *Webster's third new international dictionary unabridged.* Springfield, MA: Merriam-Webster Inc.

Haddon, G. P. (1993). *Uniting sex, self, and spirit.* Scotland, CT: PLUS Publications.

Helsing, K. J., Szklo, M., & Comstock, G.W. (1981). Factors associated with mortality after widowhood. *American Journal of Public Health, 71*(8), 802-809.

Higuchi, Kazuhiko. (1992). Death poems: Dying in beauty. *Festival of Archetypal Psychology.* Conference in honor of James Hillman, University of Notre Dame, Notre Dame, Indiana.

Hillman, J. (1973). The great mother, her son, her hero, and the puer. In P. Berry (Ed.), *Fathers and Mothers.* Dallas: Spring.

_____. (1983). *Archetypal psychology: A brief account.* Dallas: Spring.

Jacobi, J. (1959). *Complex, archetype, symbol.* Bollingen Series LVII. (R. Manheim, Trans.) Princeton, NJ: Princeton University Press.

Jung, C. G. (1960). *Collected works,* vol. 8. H. Read, M. Fordham, G. Adler, and W. McGuire (Eds.), & (R. F. C. Hull, Trans.) Princeton: Princeton University Press.

_____. (1965). *Memories, dreams, reflections.* Aniela Jaffe, (Ed.), (Richard and Clara Winston, Trans.). New York: Vintage Books.

_____. (1968). *Analytical psychology: Its theory and practice.* New York: Vintage Books, Random House.

_____. (1970). On the significance of number dreams. In *Freud and psychoanalysis, collected works,* vol. 4. H. Read, M. Fordham, G. Adler, & W. McGuire, (Eds.) (R. F. C. Hull, Trans.) Princeton, NJ: Princeton University Press.

_____. (1971). *Psychological types. Collected works,* vol.6. (R. F. C. Hull, Trans., revision of H. G. Baynes, Trans.). Princeton, NJ: Princeton.

_____. (1976a). *Symbols of transformation. Collected works,* vol. 5 Bollingen Series XX. (R. F. C. Hull, Trans.). Princeton, NJ: Princeton.

_____. (1976b). *The symbolic life. Collected works,* vol. 18. Bollingen Series XX. H. Read, M. Fordham, G. Adler, & W. McGuire, (Eds.), (R. F. C. Hull, Trans.). Princeton, NJ: Princeton.

_____. (1976c). *The visions seminars. Book two.* Zurich: Spring Publications.

_____. (1978). *Psychology and the east.* (R. F. C. Hull, Trans.) Princeton, NJ: Princeton.

_____, von Franz, M-L., Henderson, J. Jacobi, J. & Jaffe, A. (1964) *Man and his symbols.* Garden City, NY: Doubleday & Co., Inc.

Jung, E. (1978). *Animus and anima.* Dallas: Spring

Justice, B. (1987). *Who gets sick: Thinking and health.* Houston: Peak Press.

Kellogg, J. (1984). *Mandala: Path of beauty.* Private printing, second printing.

Kellogg, R. (1969-70). *Analyzing children's art.* Palo Alto, CA: Mayfield Publishing Co.

Kiepenheuer, K. (1990). *Crossing the bridge.* LaSalle, IL: Open Court.

Leach, M., & Fried, J. (Eds.) (1972). *Funk & Wagnalls standard dictionary of folklore, mythology, and legend.* San Francisco: Harper & Row.

Leonhart, M., Rothberg, R. & Seiden, D. (1984). Art work of cystic fibrosis patients. *Art Therapy,* May, 68-74.

Mattoon, M. A. (1978). *Applied dream analysis: A Jungian approach.* New York: John Wiley & Sons.

Moody, R., Jr. (1975). *Life after life.* Atlanta: Mockingbird Books.

_____. (1977). *Reflections on life after life.* Atlanta: Mockingbird Books.

Moore, R. and Gillette, D. (1990). *King, warrior, magician, lover.* San Francisco: Harper Collins.

Moore, T. (1992). *Care of the soul.* New York: Harper Collins.

Morse, M. L., Conner, D., & Tyler, D. (1985). Near-death experiences in a pediatric population. *AJDC 139,* 595-600.

_____. (1990). *Closer to the light.* New York: Ballantine Books.

Penfield, W. (1975). *The mystery of the mind.* Princeton, NJ: Princeton.

Professional Education Committee, Cystic Fibrosis Foundation. (1980). *Guidelines for health personnel.* Rockville, MD: Cystic Fibrosis Foundation.

Quintana, S. M. & Kerr, J. (January/February 1993). Rational needs in late adolescent separation-individuation. *Journal of Counseling and Development 71*(3), 349-354.

Rinpoche, S. (1992). *The Tibetan book of living and dying.* P. Gaffney & A. Harvey (Eds.). San Francisco: Harper San Francisco.

Ryce-Menuhin, J. (1988). *The self in early childhood.* London: Free Association Books.

Samuels, A. (1985). *Jung and the post-Jungians.* London & New York: Routledge & Kegan Paul, Ltd.

_____, Shorter, B. & Plaut, F. (1986). *A critical dictionary of Jungian analysis.* London & New York: Routledge.

Sanford, J. A. (1989). *Dreams: God's forgotten language.* Philadelphia/New York: Lippincott.

Sardello, R. (1992). *Sophia: Facing the world with soul.* Workshop presented July 11 at *A Festival of Archetypal Psychology,* Notre Dame, Indiana, July 7-12, 1992.

Schaverien, J. (1992). *The revealing image.* London: Routledge.

Schleifer, S. J., Keller, S. E., Camerino, M., Thornton, J. C., & Stein, M. (1983). Suppression of lymphocyte stimulation following bereavement. *Journal of the American Medical Association 250*(3), 374-377.

Schwartz-Salant, N. (1982). *Narcissism and character transformation: The psychology of narcissistic character disorders.* Toronto: Inner City Books.

_____. (1992). Anima and animus in Jung's alchemical mirror. In N. Schwartz-Salant & M. Stein (Eds.). *Gender and soul In psychotherapy.* Chiron Clinical Series. Wilmette: Chiron Publications.

Shellenbaum, P. (1992). The Role of the anima in analysis. In N. Schwartz-Salant & M. Stein (Eds.). *Gender and soul in psychotherapy.* Chiron Clinical Series. Wilmette: Chiron.

Shneidman, E. S. (1978). Some aspects of psychotherapy with dying persons. In C. A. Garfield (Ed.) *Psychosocial care of the dying patient.* New York: McGraw-Hill.

Simpson, D. P. (Ed.). (1960). *Cassell's new Latin dictionary.* New York: Funk & Wagnalls.

Sullivan, B. S. (1989). *Psychotherapy grounded in the feminine principle.* Wilmette: Chiron Publications, 1989.

von Franz, M-L. (1970a). *An introduction to the interpretation of fairy tales.* Dallas: Spring.

_____. (1970b). *The problem of the puer eternus.* Dallas: Spring,.

_____. (1972). *The feminine in fairy tales.* Dallas: Spring.

_____. (1974). *Shadow and evil in fairy tales.* Dallas: Spring.

_____. (1976). *Individuation in fairy tales.* Dallas: Spring.

_____. (1987). *On dreams and death.* (E. X. Kennedy & V. Brooks, Trans.). Boston & London: Shambhala.

_____. (1997). *Archetypal patterns in fairy tales.* Toronto: Inner City Books.

Weber, G. (1980). Experiences with spontaneous drawings. In A. Hicklin (Ed.). *Spontaneous images: Relationship between psyche and soma.* New York: Interbook, Inc.

Weininger, O. & Daniel, S. (1992). *Playing to learn.* Springfield, IL: Charles C Thomas.

Whitmont, E. (1969). *The symbolic quest.* New York: Putnams.

Williams, Y. B. (1981). The use of patients' drawings as an aid in diagnosis and treatment. *CF Club Symposium Abstracts 22,* 167. Rockville, MD: Cystic Fibrosis Foundation.

_____. (1985). Reactions to stress in cystic fibrosis projected in patients' drawings. *Caregivers' Papers, Medical/Scientific Conference, Anaheim, California, May 16 and 17, 1985.* Rockville, MD: CF Foundation.

Woodman, M. (1985). *The pregnant virgin.* Toronto: Inner City.

Zinkin, Louis. (1992). Anima and animus: an interpersonal view. In N. Schwartz-Salant and M. Stein (Eds.). *Gender and soul in psychotherapy.* Chiron Clinical Series. Wilmette: Chiron.

INDEX